Emotional Abuse of Children

Emotional Abuse of Children draws upon important studies and findings to summarize essential information about this complex and disturbing form of maltreatment that can damage self-esteem, affect adult relationships, and even influence one's health. Although emotional or psychological abuse of children can be difficult to document, Royse describes behaviors and symptoms that identify emotional abuse, points the reader to instruments for assessing the problem, and offers explanations as to why abusers lash out and hurt children. Designed to prepare students for practice in the child welfare field, the book also provides helpful information about the process of intervening and treating emotional abuse.

David Royse is a professor in the College of Social Work, University of Kentucky, and the author of seven previous books for social work students. This book builds upon the stories and accounts contained in *How Do I Know It's Abuse?* (1994) by summarizing the current research on the problem and its effects on children and adolescents.

Emotional Abuse of Children
Essential Information

David Royse

Routledge
Taylor & Francis Group
NEW YORK AND LONDON

First published 2016
by Routledge
711 Third Avenue, New York, NY 10017

and by Routledge
2 Park Square, Milton Park, Abingdon, Oxon OX14 4RN

Routledge is an imprint of the Taylor & Francis Group, an informa business

© 2016 Taylor & Francis

The right of David Royse to be identified as author of this work has been asserted in accordance with sections 77 and 78 of the Copyright, Designs and Patents Act 1988.

All rights reserved. No part of this book may be reprinted or reproduced or utilized in any form or by any electronic, mechanical, or other means, now known or hereafter invented, including photocopying and recording, or in any information storage or retrieval system, without permission in writing from the publishers.

Trademark notice: Product or corporate names may be trademarks or registered trademarks, and are used only for identification and explanation without intent to infringe.

Library of Congress Cataloging in Publication Data
Royse, David D. (David Daniel), author.
Emotional abuse of children / by David Royse.
  pages cm
  Includes bibliographical references and index.
  1. Child abuse. 2. Psychological child abuse. 3. Psychologically abused children–Services for. 4. Child welfare. I. Title.
  HV6626.5.R69 2015
  362.76–dc23   2015026639

ISBN: 978-1-138-83178-0 (hbk)
ISBN: 978-1-138-83179-7 (pbk)
ISBN: 978-1-315-73640-2 (ebk)

Typeset in Adobe Caslon and Copperplate Gothic
by Wearset Ltd, Boldon, Tyne and Wear

Printed and bound in the United States of America by Publishers Graphics, LLC on sustainably sourced paper.

To D.B., L.B., T.B. and children everywhere whose formative years were made so painful and difficult by emotionally abusive and neglectful parents and adult caretakers.

Contents

	Preface	IX
	Acknowledgments	XIII
1	Recognition and Basic Information	1
2	The Underlying Causes of Emotional Abuse	35
3	The Effects of Emotional Abuse	65
4	Assessment of Emotional Abuse	94
5	Intervening and Treating Emotional Abuse Sarah Ascienzo	129
	Appendix A: Additional Instruments for Assessing Abuse/Neglect	174
	Appendix B: Resources	179

APPENDIX C: BIOPSYCHOSOCIAL AND TRAUMA-INFORMED
CLINICAL ASSESSMENT OF CHILDREN   181

BIBLIOGRAPHY   191
INDEX   208

Preface

This book is for those who wish to obtain a good understanding of emotional abuse; however, other types of abuse and neglect will also be discussed along the way. Its goal is to acquaint students in the helping professions with what has also been called psychological abuse and emotional neglect and, specifically, to assist with the preparation of those who are interested in becoming child welfare/child protection workers. *Emotional Abuse and Children* will also provide a useful foundation for those who wish to work as clinicians and therapists for children who have been mistreated and traumatized. No prior knowledge of psychology, social work, or counseling is needed for understanding its content. We have drawn upon and summarized the most current research available on the topic to best inform you, the reader.

Emotional Abuse and Children was envisioned to serve as a supplement for courses on child abuse and neglect, child welfare, and other courses where the focus is on children and adolescents. However, it may also be beneficial for adults who suspect that they were emotionally abused in childhood as well as those unsure of what might constitute "normal parenting" who experienced bleak, hurtful formative years. In that sense, the book may illuminate or confirm that past maltreatment and help those who were emotionally abused or neglected to begin recovering from it. Although its information may be useful for that first step, it is not a self-help guide.

We hope you enjoy the book and find it valuable.

Acknowledgments

Special thanks to the following reviewers:

Austin Griffiths, Western Kentucky University
Ashley Crews, University of Central Florida
Rebecca Bolen, The University of Tennessee, Knoxville
Chelsea Madsen, The University of Utah
Paul Felker, Temple University
Victoria Jackson, Loma Linda University
Jay Miller, University of Kentucky
Shelagh Larkin, Xavier University

1
RECOGNITION AND BASIC INFORMATION

Our children's future and the future of the world are one.
—Dr. C. Henry Kempe

Overview: This chapter will answer several important questions: What is emotional abuse? How does it differ from neglect and other forms of child maltreatment? Nationally, how many children are estimated to be affected by abuse and neglect? Are children who are emotional abused likely to be mistreated in other ways as well?

Introduction

Although it is easy to assume that police and other authorities have been responding to child abuse ever since humankind became "civilized," that would be an erroneous assumption. In fact, in the United States public awareness and professional response weren't really kicked into high gear until the publication of the article "The battered-child syndrome" by physicians Kempe, Silverman, Steele, Droegemueller, and Silver in 1962. That study was the first major medical investigation of child maltreatment and was one that advanced the assessment and diagnosis of abuse by physical examination and radiographic (X-ray) findings (Leventhal & Krugman, 2012). A popular book that followed, the

Battered Child, authored by Kempe and Helfer in 1968, did much to educate the public and nonmedical professionals.

Most of us could probably recognize the results of physical abuse on a child. Indeed, we would be suspicious of injuries that looked like cigarette burns on a child, unusual bruises or lacerations, or a toddler's broken arm. But what about emotional abuse? Is it as easy to identify as physical abuse? What forms might it take? Let's start our discussion of emotional abuse by looking at four different examples that show how emotional abuse can take varied forms in different contexts and settings.

Case Example 1

Ronnie, an overweight 12-year-old, was eating an after-school snack and watching television when his stepfather came into the room, plopped down on the couch beside him and said, "Well, Fatty, what did you do at school today? Play dolls with the girls?"

They have a history: The stepfather played football in high school. He has long resented that Ronnie has shown no interest in sports. On multiple occasions Ronnie has refused to pass the football with him and makes excuses—like needing to practice the piano. Ronnie avoids his stepfather whenever possible and spends Sunday afternoons in his room doing his homework instead of watching football games on the couch with his stepfather. But then he pays the price. After coming to the table for Sunday dinner, his stepfather refers to him as the "Bookworm" or the "Wimp." Ronnie's mother doesn't say anything to defend him but passes the mashed potatoes to Ronnie and changes the subject. Lately, Ronnie has been praying that something bad would happen to the stepfather on the construction site where he works.

Case Example 2

Sheila, a petite redhead starting the ninth grade, is sensitive about the size of her nose. She feels that it is too large and that it makes her unattractive. Her older brother, a junior in high school, has been calling her "Beagle nose" to tease her. Recently she has been growing her hair long so that some of it falls across her face. Her brother, Rob, has responded by calling her "Sheep dog." He bought some plastic fake dog poop from the Internet and secretly placed it in her backpack so that she would be embarrassed when she found it at school. Whenever he is around his friends and sees her, he goes "Woof! Woof!" until she hears and runs away in tears.

RECOGNITION AND BASIC INFORMATION 3

Sheila feels that her parents like Rob better than her. Even though she's complained many times about Rob's hurtful words and actions, they have never given Rob any consequences. She's started stealing some of the prescription drugs from the medicine cabinet to help her deal with the situation.

Case Example 3

Chanita lives with a grandmother who has struggled with drugs and depression most of her life. Twice in the last year, her grandmother has overdosed on prescriptions and Chanita has had to call 911. Now, at age 11, Chanita has to get herself up each morning, prepare her own breakfast and get to school. She dreads going home after school. If her grandmother is awake, she makes Chanita scrub the tub or the kitchen floor on her hands and knees. When it meets her grandmother's approval, then Chanita must go to the grocery, buy food, and then make supper for the two of them. Afterwards, she has to wash the dishes not once but twice, to make sure they are clean. Earlier this year when Chanita refused to do the second washing, her grandmother turned on the gas oven and told Chanita that she was going to kill both of them. Luckily, the grandmother passed out soon afterwards and Chanita could turn the gas off.

Case Example 4

Juan Pablo's dog, Greta, just had three pups. His father, however, never liked Greta and said that he was going to get rid of her. "No, please no," said Juan Pablo. "Please let me keep her."

"Well, OK," said the father, "but you have to give the pups away."

"I'll take care of them," Juan Pablo said. "You'll see. I'll get jobs in the neighborhood to buy their food."

He kept his word and mowed grass and raked leaves and used his money to buy food for the pups and their mother. One day in October when the pups were about 10 weeks old, Juan Pablo came home from school and couldn't find them. The same thing had happened last year when the cat had kittens. One day they were in their box and then the next day they were gone.

That night, after his factory shift was over, his father denied knowing anything about them but Juan Pablo didn't believe him. His Aunt Rosie told Juan Pablo not to ask any more questions—that it would just make his father mad. His father offered 13-year-old Juan Pablo a beer and told him to "Be a man."

> Two days later while looking for his baseball, Juan Pablo found a cloth bag with bloodstains on it in the back of the old truck his father drove to work. Juan knew then his father was a liar and the pups would never be seen again.

Despite being different, in all four scenarios Ronnie, Sheila, Chanita, and Juan Pablo were made to feel unwanted, unloved, worthless, disrespected, or endangered by their close family members. They don't trust these individuals and fear what else they may do. Worse yet, there appears to be little that they can do to improve their situation. They often dread tomorrow, knowing that things won't be any different. Often they feel that their situation is hopeless and that no one can help them.

What is Emotional Abuse?

There is no standardized definition of emotional abuse that applies across all settings, cultures, or families. The lack of a strong societal agreement makes it difficult to clearly define emotional abuse and contributes to the problem of differentiating emotional maltreatment of a child from something that might be viewed as less harmful than physical or sexual abuse—something that might be called "suboptimal parenting" (Hibbard, Barlow, MacMillan, Committee on Child Abuse and Neglect, & American Academy of Child and Adolescent Psychiatry, Child Maltreatment and Violence Committee, 2012). Poor parenting skills may not always result in emotional abuse, but possibly could. A parent who forgets to latch the door before napping and creates an opportunity for a toddler to get out of the house and walk alongside a busy highway will very likely be charged by the police and be investigated by a child protection worker. That is different, however, from severe and usually escalating behaviors that reject, frighten, insult, and demean a child enough to be described as chronic and which could increase the likelihood of psychological harm or developmental disruptions—that is the essence of emotional abuse. (We'll discuss the problem of distinguishing poor parenting from emotional abuse more in Chapter 4.)

As can be seen in Table 1.1, emotional abuse is often known by different terms. A recent tabulation of these terms in the Web of Science's article database found the following number of terms in the titles of published articles between 1900 and October 1, 2014:

Table 1.1 Frequency of Terms Describing Emotional Abuse in Web of Science Database

Term	Number of articles
Emotional abuse	168
Psychological abuse	97
Psychological maltreatment	59
Emotional maltreatment	38
Mental cruelty	3
Psychological battering	1

Because emotional abuse is used more commonly than other terms describing the same hurtful behavior or treatment, it will be the term used most often in this book. Further support for the use of this term is found in a heavily cited journal article by Glaser (2002) entitled "Emotional abuse and neglect (psychological maltreatment): A conceptual framework." Glaser noted that while others (e.g., O'Hagan, 1995) have attempted to distinguish between emotional and psychological abuse, that distinction is not useful. O'Hagan's thinking was that psychological abuse would involve inappropriate behavior that damages the child's developmental potential for healthy mental processes and mental faculties while he defined emotional abuse as inappropriate emotional responses to a child. However, any child emotionally abused would very likely be psychologically abused as well. Thus, spending a lot of time debating the distinction between the two may not be worthwhile.

A letter published in the *British Medical Journal* in November 1979 by W.R. Guirguis ("Physical indicators of emotional abuse in children") shows up as the earliest title on emotional abuse in the Web of Science. Remarkably, the description found in that letter, though written over three decades ago, remains an accurate depiction:

> It is not a single condition, but a whole range of maltreatment.... It describes an abusive environment rather than an abused child. That is why there is no one recognizable or constantly identifiable clinical picture which is diagnostic of emotional abuse.
> (p. 1290)

All of the terms found in Table 1.1 share a common basis in that recipients of emotionally abusive behavior feel wounded—usually by someone they love. Because it is vitally important that we have a solid foundation for understanding emotional abuse, we will next examine more in-depth some of the various ways this form of mistreatment has been defined.

In 1995 the American Professional Society on the Abuse of Children (APSAC) created a set of practice guidelines and defined emotional abuse this way: "Psychological maltreatment means a repeated pattern of caregiver behavior or extreme incident(s) that convey to children that they are worthless, flawed, unloved, unwanted, endangered, or only of value in meeting another's needs" (APSAC, 1995, p. 2).

The definitions of the American Academy of Pediatrics Committee on Child Abuse and Neglect of psychological maltreatment in the two quotations below are informative:

> a repeated pattern of damaging interactions between parent(s) and child that becomes typical of the relationship. In some situations the pattern occurs only when triggered by alcohol or other potentiating factors. Occasionally, a very painful singular incident, such as an unusually contentious divorce, can initiate psychological maltreatment.
> (www.pediatrics.org/cgi/content/full/109/4/e68)

> Psychological maltreatment of children occurs when a person conveys to a child that he or she is worthless, flawed, unloved, unwanted, endangered, or only of value in meeting another's needs. The perpetrator may spurn, terrorize, isolate, or ignore or impair the child's socialization.
> (Kairys, Johnson, and the Committee on Child Abuse and Neglect, 2002, p. 1)

Note that the exact, legal definition applying to acts of abuse or neglect will differ state-by-state. Federal legislation lays the groundwork for state laws on child maltreatment by identifying a set of acts or behaviors that define child abuse and neglect. The Federal Child Abuse Prevention and Treatment Act (CAPTA) (42 U.S.C.A. §5106g), as amended and reauthorized by the CAPTA Reauthorization Act of 2010, defines child abuse and neglect as, at minimum:

> Any recent act or failure to act on the part of a parent or caretaker which results in death, serious physical or emotional harm, sexual abuse or exploitation; or an act or failure to act which presents an imminent risk of serious harm.

Most federal and state child protection laws primarily refer to cases of harm to a child caused by parents or other caregivers; they generally do not include harm caused by other people, such as acquaintances or strangers. Some state laws also include a child's witnessing of domestic violence as a form of abuse or neglect. (www.childwelfare.gov/pubs/factsheets/whatiscan.pdf).

Almost all states and the District of Columbia include emotional maltreatment as part of their definitions of abuse or neglect. Approximately 32 states and the District of Columbia have specific definitions of emotional abuse or mental injury to a child. Typical language used in these definitions is "injury to the psychological capacity or emotional stability of the child as evidenced by an observable or substantial change in behavior, emotional response, or cognition" and injury as evidenced by "anxiety, depression, withdrawal, or aggressive behavior" (www.childwelfare.gov/systemwide/laws_policies/statutes/define.pdf). The vast majority of the legal definitions of psychological maltreatment focus not on the parent or caregiver's acts but on the impact on the child (Baker, 2009).

Within the minimum standards set by CAPTA, each state is responsible for providing its own definitions of child abuse and neglect. Most states recognize the four major types of maltreatment: physical abuse, neglect, sexual abuse, and emotional abuse. (Indications of each type of maltreatment are discussed later.) Additionally, many states identify abandonment and parental substance abuse as abuse or neglect. While these types of maltreatment may be found separately, they often occur in combination. For state-specific laws pertaining to child abuse and neglect, see the Child Welfare Information Gateway's State Statutes search page (www.childwelfare.gov/systemwide/laws_policies/state/).

One of the keys to understanding emotional abuse is the notion that it is *not* a one-time, single, or isolated event. The behavior may not be perceived as or considered as abusive if it occurs occasionally or infrequently and as long as the parent or other significant person is experienced generally as a loving and caring individual. It almost goes without saying that parents do get angry; they can lose their tempers and say things they don't really mean and regret later. However, emotional abuse generally refers to a sustained or repeated pattern of behavior that, more than making the child unhappy, has the potential for affecting the child's self-esteem, development, view of the world, and sense of belonging. The child feels unloved or unimportant at a deep level. This is different, for example, than an occasion when a small child is told to "Shut the hell up!" after being verbally reprimanded by an exasperated parent for something (e.g., throwing Daddy's cell phone onto the concrete sidewalk) and perhaps an hour later has forgotten all about the incident.

The American Academy of Pediatrics Committee on Child Abuse and Neglect in 2002 (see Kairys et al., 2002) identified nine types of psychological maltreatment and these are shown in Box 1.1.

Three items (rejecting, unreliable or inconsistent parenting, and witnessing domestic violence) have not been highlighted in the box. This is because a more recent conceptualizing of psychologically abusive behaviors (Hibbard et al., 2012) did not include these behaviors in its listing. And, if you think about it, rejecting behavior can be subsumed under denying emotional responsiveness. Further, rejecting and inconsistent parenting are carried out by the perpetrators of abuse whereas witnessing intimate partner violence is something that the child or adolescent might observe. Watching one's mother or other loved one get severely beaten constitutes emotional abuse and is traumatic even though the act may not be inflicted directly upon the child. While unreliable and inconsistent parenting may apply to many emotionally abusive parents, it is not a single behavior that can be easily described or detected—thus, the focus on the six behaviors in italics.

BOX 1.1

Psychological Maltreatment Types

1. ***Spurning*** (belittling, degrading, shaming, or ridiculing a child; singling out a child to criticize or punish; and humiliating a child in public).
2. ***Terrorizing*** (committing life-threatening acts; making a child feel unsafe; setting unrealistic expectations with threat of loss, harm, or danger if they are not met; and threatening or perpetrating violence against a child or child's loved ones or objects).
3. ***Exploiting or corrupting*** that encourages a child to develop inappropriate behaviors (modeling, permitting, or encouraging antisocial or developmentally inappropriate behavior; encouraging or coercing abandonment of developmentally appropriate autonomy; restricting or interfering with cognitive development).
4. ***Denying emotional responsiveness*** (ignoring a child or failing to express affection, caring, and love for a child).
5. **Rejecting** (avoiding or pushing away).
6. ***Isolating*** (confining, placing unreasonable limitations on freedom of movement or social interactions).
7. **Unreliable or inconsistent parenting** (contradictory and ambivalent demands).
8. ***Neglecting mental health, medical, and educational needs*** (ignoring, preventing, or failing to provide treatments or services for emotional, behavioral, physical, or educational needs or problems).
9. **Witnessing intimate partner violence** (domestic violence).

Source: Kairys et al. (2002)

A second key to understanding emotional abuse is accepting the fact that it is intangible. That is, there are no bruises or visible indications that show someone has been emotionally abused. It can be invisible to others, or at least, may not get registered on everyone's radar—even if they are in the same vicinity. Consider the following scenario.

Case Example 5

Recently I was walking my dog in a park when a mother let her small, perhaps four- or five-year-old son, out of the car and then proceeded to open the trunk to get out an assortment of fishing gear as I walked past. The boy was a cute, talkative child

> and I could hear just enough to know that he was carrying on just about all of the conversation. He seemed so verbal, so full of things he wanted to talk about. I might have even smiled to myself thinking perhaps he might have a career as a talk radio personality or a politician when he grew up. Suddenly, almost like an explosion, the mother seemed to snap and shouted, "Shut up, you little brat!" She didn't lay a hand on him and since he didn't cry or act injured from her angry words, it immediately occurred to me that this was a term that he knew quite well.

If you had a pair of binoculars and were able to observe this scene from some distance away, you would have had no evidence of abuse. People 100 feet away or more would have observed nothing out of the ordinary to become alarmed about. But up close, hearing the mother's angry tone might have given you plenty of reason to be concerned about the hostility and lack of sensitivity for the son that the mother communicated. But perhaps the mother was simply having a bad day. Would it have been enough to make you concerned?

Let's change the scenario a slight bit: suppose the mother had said in a normal conversational tone, "Shut up, you talk too much." Would that have been emotional abuse? Or just a fatigued mother at the end of her patience? What if the woman was actually his big sister and had said, "Shut up, you little brat" because he was teasing her about something she didn't want to be reminded of? Or what if her remark had been made with a smile on her face?

You can begin to understand why emotional abuse is hard to define. Perhaps being called "Brat" isn't as bad as other names the child might have been called such as "Runt," "Stupid," "Dummy," or "Retard." Even these hurtful words might be tempered by a good relationship or if someone says it in a playful exchange with a smile on his or her face.

A third key thing to remember about emotional abuse is that the context is important. For instance, few individuals make it through high school without being called some unkind nickname or hurtful term. If a young man tried out for the football team but then later decided he really didn't enjoy it, he might be referred to by some of the players or even the coach as the "Quitter." If overweight, one might be teased by classmates with names like "Thunder Thighs" or "Fat Ass." We don't necessarily expect good treatment from all our classmates when we are growing up and so the power of their words might not always be experienced as hurtful as that coming from, say, a family member saying the same thing (although certainly bullying and prolonged bullying by classmates in school can be quite injurious).

What makes emotional abuse so hurtful to the child is that it generally comes from those who ought to love the child. It is one thing to be called names by someone we don't live with and quite another to have our mother or father not protect us—and worse yet, to indicate that we deserve whatever mistreatment we receive. While a physical wound like a bruise or broken bone will eventually heal, the emotional wound of regularly hearing hurtful things and feeling unloved and unwanted as a child may never heal.

> **Case Example 6**
>
> Robert, an 11-year-old described by his mother as a "wild child," is out riding his bike on the sidewalk and accidently runs into his 86-year-old neighbor who is out watering her yard. She falls onto her face breaking her glasses. The paramedics are called and are concerned she might have broken a rib. She is taken to the emergency room for evaluation. Robert's father learns about this accident that night at supper. He looks up from his meal and without thinking calls Robert a "crazy sonofabitch" for being so careless and injuring Mrs. Washington. Robert's father is usually slow to anger and seldom curses but he is worried about having to pay for the ambulance and Mrs. Washington's health. Robert has a good relationship with his dad and feels chastised but not personally attacked by his father's expression of anger. This was the first and only time that Robert's father called him that or any other hurtful name.

Contextual factors mean a lot. Robert, as an 11-year-old, is big for his age. He is not a kindergartener who has to be told when it is safe to cross the street or warned to look out for someone sharing the sidewalk. He bears responsibility for injuring his elderly neighbor. Had he been more cautious, that injury could have been avoided. Also, there is no indication that Robert was irreparably harmed by the name his father called him—and it had never happened before.

Glaser (2002) has noted that "Children can be temperamentally difficult, provocative or, in some cases, have physical or psychological conditions that cause serious stress for the parent and challenge their ability to cope" (p. 698).

This is not to say, by any means, that children should be blamed for their abuse or deserve to be called upsetting or spiteful names. Rather, this case points out that occasionally parents say things while distressed that they might later regret and wish that they hadn't said. These incidents should not be labeled as abusive without considering the contextual factors associated with event. Definitions of emotional abuse always indicate that in some way the child is harmed or likely to be harmed by generally a series of repeated hurtful words or actions.

A major theme running throughout various conceptualizations of emotional abuse is that the child is not recognized, respected, or valued. Although some authors (e.g., O'Hagan, 1995) have proposed that emotional and psychological abuse might be conceptualized as different entities, Glaser (2002) has disagreed. She has written that:

> Psychological abuse is defined as impeding the mental (especially cognitive) and moral faculties. This distinction is not considered to be useful since cognition and emotion are not independent of each other, cognitive appraisal of experiences contributing to the affective experience and vice versa.
>
> (p. 698)

This perspective makes a great deal of sense when we take note of the categories of emotional abuse and neglect as she defines them:

1. Emotional unavailability, unresponsiveness, and neglect. (A parent demonstrating these characteristics is insensitive to the needs of the child.)
2. Negative attributions and misattributions to the child. (Where parents or caregivers show active hostility, denigration, and various forms of rejection of the child.)
3. Developmentally inappropriate or inconsistent interactions with the child. (This refers to having expectations beyond the child's developmental capabilities. It can also include overprotection and severely limiting a child's discovery of the world. Exposure

to domestic violence and traumatic events where others are hurt are also part of this category.)
4. Failure to recognize the child's individuality and psychological boundaries. (This occurs, for example, when the adult uses the child for his or her own purposes or psychological needs.)
5. Failing to promote the child's social adaptation. (Corrupting influences such as participation in illegal activities, poor role model performance, failure to provide cognitive stimulation and opportunities for appropriate experiential learning, as when a child is kept isolated from others, make up this category.)

Thus, the emotional maltreatment of children involves both acts of commission as well as acts of omission. For example, if a parent allows a child to stay home from school because she likes to have the child's company, that's an act of omission. Doing nothing about the teenager who is habitually truant and beginning to get involved with gang behaviors is an act of omission. On the other hand, if the parent refuses to let the child go to school or deliberately doesn't register the child for school, that's an act of commission.

Let's turn our attention to neglect to understand how emotional neglect overlaps with abuse.

How is Child Neglect Defined?

To state it very simply, neglect occurs whenever a caretaker fails to provide for the essential needs of a child. In this society we expect parents and caretakers to meet the physical needs of children that include shelter, food, clothing, along with medical care, and education. Children must also be protected from harmful or predatory influences, be provided with supervision of their activities, and shown how to become productive and useful members of society. The failure to provide for basic physical and emotional needs constitutes neglect (Crosson-Tower, 2009).

The World Health Organization's Consultation on Child Abuse Prevention (1999) identified specific areas of concern with neglect and defined it as follows:

the failure to provide for the development of the child in all spheres: health, education, emotional development, nutrition, shelter, and safe living conditions, in the context of resources reasonably available to the family or caretakers and causes or has a high probability of causing harm to the child's health or physical, mental, spiritual, moral, or social development. This includes the failure to properly supervise and protect children from harm as much as is feasible.

(p. 15)

The Child Abuse Prevention and Treatment Act of 2010 (P.L. 111–320) defines both child abuse and neglect this way:

at a minimum, any recent act or failure to act on the part of a parent or caretaker which results in death, serious physical or emotional harm, sexual abuse or exploitation or an act or failure to act which presents an imminent risk of serious harm.

(p. 6)

While abuse is generally understood in terms of acts of commission, neglect is almost always discussed in terms of acts of *omission*. That is, neglect occurs when the parent or caretaker *fails to take action* which would be in the child's best interest—applying, of course, common sense. For instance, not preparing meals for a two-year-old is a much more serious issue than telling a 15- or 16-year-old to make himself or herself a sandwich or to get a bowl of cereal for breakfast.

Both in the United States and in the United Kingdom, neglect is more commonly reported than abuse for children who come to the attention of the child protection authorities (Sedlak et al., 2010; Appleton, 2012). Like emotional abuse, neglect

rarely comes to light as a result of a specific incident ... and often relies on practitioners making a judgment about the adequacy of ongoing care within a child and family context.... It is the persistent failure to meet a child's needs and provide adequate care ... with cumulative negative effects being detrimental to the child over a considerable period of time.

(p. 77)

Types of Child Neglect

Like emotional abuse, child neglect can take many forms. The Children's Bureau identifies four categories of neglect (physical, medical, educational, and emotional—see the Child Welfare Information Gateway's *What is Child Abuse and Neglect?* (2013) but Hornor (2014) has identified several more specific types that we will discuss below. Many times, it is easy to see the connection between poverty and child neglect. For example, a child could be injured in a traffic accident because the parents didn't have the money to buy a car seat and didn't know about resources in the community where one might have been loaned or obtained free of charge. Failure to place a child in a safe child car seat can be viewed as an act of neglect.

It is important to remember that neglect, like abuse, can be multifaceted and various forms of abuse and/or neglect may co-occur besides the presenting or first identified feature. To continue with the earlier example, parents who can't afford a car seat for an infant may not be able to afford well-baby checkups and vaccinations for the child and could live in a home in a rural area without indoor plumbing and be unable to stop the rats that come into the kitchen. Or, they could be city dwellers who live in a dilapidated apartment with crumbling plaster and peeling lead-based paint that their children could pick up and eat. Medical neglect can include infants who don't gain weight (failure to thrive) as well as children and teens who weigh too much. (A case several years ago in South Carolina appearing in *USA Today* reported that the mother of a 14-year-old boy who weighed 555 pounds was charged with criminal neglect.) Obesity is a concern when caregivers have received medical advice for the child and do not take the problem seriously.

If you try to envision a child in a family where one or more types of neglect are present, you'll immediately see how attempting to list all neglectful behaviors would be almost impossible. For instance, under the category of *Food Inadequacy*, would a parent be neglectful if the only beverage allowed in the house for a seven-year-old to drink was water? What if the water was from an untested well? What if the mother complained that the only thing the child wanted to drink was cola and so

Table 1.2 Types of Child Neglect

Type of child neglect	Examples
Nutrition/food inadequacy	No nutritional food in the house, no formula or milk for infants, not enough food (e.g., too many people sharing too little), inappropriate food for developmental age.
Supervision/safety neglect	Leaving medications, dangerous drugs, and harmful household products (e.g., Drano) around where they can be ingested by children, having loaded guns in the house, living in a home where the child is exposed to pornography, failing to prevent exposure to persons who have threatened or harmed children in the past, and/or where there is intimate partner violence. Not supervising young children who are allowed to cook hot liquids on the stove or in the microwave. Not providing a baby sitter or day care when parent is absent, leaving a young child unattended in a car or apartment, being unconcerned about where children play and what they are doing when out of sight. Roaches, rats, too many pets in home. Matches and lighters easily available. Piles of trash in home; housing condemned or inadequate (boarded windows, falling roof, rotted floors). Child supervision provided by a disabled adult with hearing or vision loss or cognitive impairment. Supervision provided by adult engaged in illegal activities. Illegal activities occurring in the child's home.
Educational neglect	Not requiring children to attend school on a consistent basis (and home schooling or alternate education is not provided). Keeping a child home from school to attend to physically ill persons. Keeping a child from attending school as a punishment. Not providing transportation to child for school.
Medical/dental neglect	Unreasonable delay or failure to seek needed medical or dental attention. Failure to follow recommended plan of care (e.g., not purchasing or administering medications, special diets, and so on).
Shelter inadequacy	Homes that are not clean or safe; lack of shelter (homeless). Not enough beds (e.g., having to share with much older children or adults), not enough bedrooms, not enough bathrooms or inadequate plumbing (e.g., broken toilet or clogged tub or sinks). Unpaid utility bills (e.g., electric, heat, or water) that result in the cutoff of services or the threat of services being cutoff.
Poor hygiene/ inadequate clothes	Children are teased by other children because they smell, are dirty, or always appear unkempt; head lice; clothing inappropriate for weather (e.g., no coat or light coat in cold weather).
Lack of nurturance and affection	Child is ignored, uncared for, abandoned, lied to, not respected.

that's all she bought? Would a parent be neglectful, in your opinion, if the five-year-old got up each morning before his Mom and ate a bowl of ice cream for breakfast? If you were a child protection worker, what would make you concerned?

Regarding the *Shelter Inadequacy* category, toilets, sinks, and tubs can clog no matter where you live. Let's assume that a family might not have money to hire a plumber the same week. At what point does lack of hygiene or cleanliness become neglect? At five days? 10? 14? Would family members having to pour buckets of water down a commode to flush it make you uncomfortable about a child's well-being in the home? What about the single parent who uses candles in a child's bedroom because the electricity bill can't be paid right away? And while it might be possible to get through the spring or fall without heat, when would it strike you as being so cold inside an apartment or house that you think it would be unhealthy for a child to be subjected to that kind of temperature? And how many days should that condition be allowed to continue? Even physical neglect may not always be an easy call to make.

Aside from lack of financial resources to meet a child's basic needs, some forms of neglect may be due to different community or parental perspectives that have been influenced by religious beliefs or even practices from other cultures. For instance, Jehovah's Witnesses do not believe in blood transfusions. This issue sometimes comes to the attention of the child protection authorities when parents of that faith refuse to give permission for a sick child to have a transfusion. Views can vary across cultures and circumstances about what constitutes suitable forms of disciplining a child. What do you think about sending a child to bed without dinner as a punishment? What if it was every night for three days in a row? At what point would you become concerned that the child might be harmed? Could it vary depending on the age of the child? His or her body weight? What other issues might you need to consider?

Similarly, Hornor (2014) also discusses how difficult it is to form an absolute definition of emotional neglect, that is, a standardized criterion to fit every child. Think about a parent's decision to leave a child alone for an extended period. How old might the child have to be? For example, one 10-year-old might be very mature and responsible while another might engage in inappropriate behavior without supervision. One 10-year-old could be comfortable staying alone while another of the same age might be anxious without an adult around. And of course, there are other considerations such as whether the child is left alone everyday (say, during summer vacation) or just once in a while. And then, there are issues about how safe the neighborhood is, whether there are friendly neighbors nearby, the time of day, how long the adult(s) would be gone, and so on. Child protection workers must weigh a number of different variables in deciding what to conclude.

Physical and Emotional Neglect

Often when we hear about a child who has been neglected, at least in the stories reported in the newspaper and on television, the accounts are so awful that they almost defy understanding. For instance in Ontario, Canada, the police rescued a 10-year-old boy who had been kept in a locked filthy room for somewhere between 18 months and two years. The child was tossed fast food twice a day but was malnourished. He was found wearing urine-soaked pajamas and had hair below his shoulders.

In another recent horrendous case, the cousin and caregiver of an autistic 12-year-old girl allowed her to starve to death. Tamiyah Audain was unable to speak or feed herself and went from 115 pounds to 56 pounds when discovered. She had bed sores that exposed bone ("'Tortured' Broward preteen shriveled from 115 pounds to 56 at death," *Miami Herald*, August 27, 2014).

While both cases are examples of the most extreme and severe form of *physical* neglect, neglect cases on the less severe end of the spectrum often involve parents or caregivers who were either inattentive, overwhelmed, or simply didn't understand the risks to their children. For instance, a Florida mother left an eight-year-old, seven-year-old twins, and a six-year-old at a park while she went to a food bank. One of the kids flagged down a police officer when the eight-year-old became stuck in the toddler swing and couldn't get out.

Other cases of this type include parents or caregivers who leave infants in cars unattended while they shop. Sometimes a concerned onlooker calls police as in the case of a foster mother arrested for leaving a 15-month-old in a hot car for 20 minutes while she shopped. Although the child was not seriously injured, he could have been, and the foster mother was arrested. Unfortunately, in other cases infants and toddlers have died when left in cars during summer months.

From this foundation of understanding about child maltreatment, let's now examine some cases where emotional neglect was primary.

Here is an account told to me by "Jerry" (name changed) about his adolescent years:

> **Case Example 7**
>
> My parents paid very little attention to me—where I went, who my friends were, or what we did. When I was 13, I had my first sexual experience with a man. He was 29. We dated off and on for several months. When I was 15, I began to date a 25-year-old man named Darren. He introduced me to a world of drugs, alcohol, and sadomasochism. Sex had no boundaries; pain and pleasure became one and the same. I was taken to parties where young people (mainly boys 13 to 18) were passed around like peace pipes.
>
> I didn't enjoy it much; as a matter of fact, I found it utterly humiliating, but I guess it was my way of getting some attention. At one of these parties, I found myself naked at the bottom of a human pile. I didn't like it and decided to leave. I was forced back down and raped repeatedly by six men. It was my sixteenth birthday.
>
> By the time my relationship with Darren ended, I was an alcoholic. I would start drinking vodka as soon as I woke up in the morning and would take it to school with me. I would drink between classes and during lunch. After school, I would drink until it was time to find a party and then I would drink until I passed out. Then I would start all over again the next morning. My parents never asked where I was going and I don't remember any curfew. It was as if I never existed. The loneliness was unbearable. I hungered for one of them to care about me.

Another account, posted on www.experienceproject.com, poignantly captures the lack of love and the emotional neglect that individuals can feel. The Experience Project is a social networking website where individuals can post their stories anonymously without fear of recognition and correspond with others who have had similar experiences. The story below was posted by an adult about her childhood.

> **Case Example 8**
>
> For a long time, I was in denial about my parents' neglect. So many of my friends came from broken homes or were abused as children, I thought I had nothing to complain about by comparison. My dad provided the basics, right? We weren't cold or hungry or in the street, and no one ever raised their voice unless dad was punishing us for something. Sometimes I wondered, though, why my parents had kids when they acted like they didn't *want* us. Raising us seemed like a chore for them. They wouldn't talk to us or do anything with us. My dad just sat around watching TV, and my mother seemed to resent taking care of my brother and I.
>
> I knew I was transgender from an early age but I could never talk about it. No one talked in my family. Emotions practically didn't exist. My parents were happy if I sat in my room all day and stared at the walls because then I wouldn't bother them. I became severely depressed and suicidal in middle school. After class, my mom would pick me up, and I would just lie down in the back seat, catatonic. She never asked me what was wrong. She acted like I didn't even exist. At the same time, they wouldn't let me do anything. I wasn't allowed to do extracurricular activities at school, I wasn't allowed to see friends, or even cross the street or go next door to visit the neighbors. My parents acted like they didn't trust anyone, and every time I slipped away to be with friends I was punished for it. I started to think there was something wrong with me and I didn't deserve friends.
>
> It was years before I came out of the closet because I thought no one cared. I went to college with financial aid, but my parents didn't care what I studied and never talked to me about what I planned to do with my life, so I ended up with a degree that hasn't really helped me at all. Eventually, my brother and I told them what a worthless job they did raising us, and now we don't see or talk to them unless we have to. There's like a hole there, though, of what my childhood could have been like and how I could have been a more confident, stable person otherwise.

As we learned earlier and will discuss more a bit later, emotional abuse and neglect are often involved with other forms of abuse as well. Although the next account is a bit long, it is a powerful description of the complex dynamics and problems that can occur within a home and aptly portrays how emotional neglect feels. It also was reported on the www.experienceproject.com.

Case Example 9

I was the child that was nagged and pushed until I was brought to tears. I was humiliated, mocked and criticized all my life. I guess that could explain my social anxiety that has developed from low self-esteem. Always felt like the ugly, stupid duckling, I would get yelled at if I spent too much time on my homework and forgot to do the dishes. What I didn't understand is why my mother felt my teen sister could not contribute to doing the dishes while I was busy studying? I'm sure my sister is capable of handling the dishes instead of skimming her phone about gossip while sitting on her ***. I never understood why I took all the blame in the household for all the responsibilities. I always did as I was told even if I was treated unfairly and had to pick up after someone else. I guess I look back at it and am thankful I'm away from that abuse, I wasn't just emotionally or verbally abused, I was also physically abused. I was physically abused until I was 20 years old by my mother and even my younger sister. My mother was abused by my father for no reason so I imagine my mother has been damaged by it. I could lean toward that reason as to why she abused me for no reason. If I answered her back when she asked me a question she would drag me by my hair across the floor while smacking my face with a shoe and hit me all over my body. I remember one time when I was six; I was sitting at the table doing my homework while my mother was helping me. She asked me one of the questions from my homework assignment, I answered it wrong and she grabbed my head by the hair and started slamming my head against the table and she did that about three times until my cousin walked through the garage door. I would assume she wouldn't have stopped if my cousin never came through that door. My sister often resembled my mom in her personality and looks; I always looked more like my father (I would say that had a lot to do with her despising me). My sister absorbed everything my mom said to me throughout my life and repeated it back to me. My sister was a reminder of my mom; she would even come up with her own words to call me, such as trash, no good, low class, ugly, mental, stupid, etc. And she would give me the same look my mother gave me. A look of disgust, as if I was the most ugly creature they ever laid eyes on. When I cried when I was upset or sad they would mock and ridicule me, they had no sympathy for my feelings. If we had a dog, they would consider the feelings of the dog. But me? No never. If I expressed my feelings my mother would call me a great actor. She thought I lied about how I felt; she thought my tears were forced as if I was putting on an act. Isn't that sad? She believed that everything I did was to annoy her. She thought everything I did was directed toward her. She went through my phone all the time as well, up until I was 20. She was paranoid and was hoping to find texts of me gossiping about her. She believed that I deleted the texts about her, when she didn't find anything. I lost all my friends after

> high school so I hardly texted anyone. So when she found no texts she would accuse me of deleting it to hide it from her. Yeah I had no privacy in my life, words can't express the humiliation she put me through in front of my siblings. She never laid one word to rest when it came to arguing. My mother had a difficult time with my brother at the time as well but she always kept her mouth shut with him. She never wanted to lose him, he was the oldest and he was praised for every good deed and accomplishments in his life. My sister was the baby, the tall skinny beauty that resembled her. I was the middle child (black sheep) the one that caused problems in the family, looked down upon, a shame, embarrassment. On the outside we were a happy family in front of our church members and friends. On the inside we were as screwed up as any family out there. Often times when my mother and I argued she would always bring up this phrase, "I'll just send you to your father to live with him, maybe you will live a better life with him". I never understood why she never did send me to him? I'm sure I would have been happier with my father, since he has changed and become a better person. My mother hates my father; she will curse his name to her death bed. I don't blame her for everything he put her and my siblings through, I feel like I am the only one who has forgiven him and his mistakes.

In both of these last two cases one feels the loneliness of the individual, the sense not being loved or cared for, of not being respected as an individual. Such treatment has powerful consequences for the developing child that we will discuss more in-depth in Chapter 3. Before concluding this chapter, we want to examine the estimates concerning how often emotional abuse and neglect occurs.

The Prevalence of Child Abuse and Neglect

The magnitude of children who become victims of abuse is staggering. The estimates provided in this chapter provide a good idea of the amount of work needed to address, prevent, and remediate child maltreatment in our neighborhoods, cities, states, and nation.

The problems associated with adequately defining emotional abuse and neglect become much more evident when efforts are made to determine how many children are mistreated and might be identified as emotionally abused or neglected. Despite what leading experts call "a lack of definitional clarity in the field" (Finkelhor, Vanderminden, Turner, Hamby, & Shattuck, 2014, p. 1429), researchers have sought to provide estimates from large national samples from a cross-section of respondents and families—often called general *population studies*. Excerpts from some of these studies are provided below.

Drawing upon the Fourth National Incidence Study of Child Abuse and Neglect Report to Congress (NIS-4; Sedlak et al., 2010), we learn the following details about the number of children affected by abuse and neglect in the United States using their *Harm Standard*.

- 1,256,600 children were estimated to experience some form of maltreatment during the NIS-4 study year of which 771,700 were neglected and 553,300 were abused
- 360,500 experienced educational neglect
- 323,000 experienced physical abuse
- 295,300 experienced physical neglect
- 193,400 were emotionally neglected
- 148,500 were emotionally abused
- 135,300 were sexually abused.

(pp. 3–4)

If you are a careful reader, you will have noted that the first large estimate (1,256,600) is broken down into six types of abuse and neglect categories used by the NIS-4. This allows us to see that 148,500 children were emotionally abused and 193,400 were emotionally neglected—the best anyone can estimate. The term "estimate" is appropriate since we really don't know how many abused and neglected children never come to the attention of child protective services (CPS) because the maltreatment is hidden from sight (e.g., bruises under a child's clothing) or never occurs in public.

We must also remember that children can be recipients of multiple forms of abuse/neglect. Abuse is seldom "pure." That is, where there is physical or sexual abuse, there is often emotional abuse. Where there is emotional abuse, there is likely emotional neglect.

While the large numbers of children indicated above are difficult to imagine, these estimates are even larger when the NIS-4 *Endangered Standard* is used. This larger grouping includes all of the children who were considered to have been harmed as well as those children not yet harmed but at risk of being harmed. Using this standard, almost three million children (2,905,800) in the United States were harmed or endangered—or about one in every 25 children. Over two million (2,251,600) were neglected, 835,000 abused. Of those abused, 476,000 were physically abused, 302,000 were emotionally abused, and 180,500 were sexually abused. More than one million children (1,192,200) were physically neglected, 1,173,800 were emotionally neglected, and 360,500 were educationally neglected (pp. 3–15).

It can be difficult to comprehend these large figures, and so another way of thinking about the *prevalence* of child maltreatment is to view the problem in terms of percentages of children or rates of those affected. To bring the question down to the local level, we might ask, "What percent of children are emotionally abused in my neighborhood or community?" One survey conducted by the federal government, the Second National Survey of Children Exposed to Violence, provides some useful information. (See Finkelhor et al., 2014 for details about the methodology and a fuller reporting of findings.)

The study, based on a sample of over 4,503 children and youth, found that 5.6% reported emotional abuse in the past year and 10.3% indicated they had been emotionally abused at some point in their lives (the lifetime rate). These rates were determined from responses to a question that asked similar questions of *children who were 10 to 17 years of age* and *parents of children under 10*: "Did you/your child get scared or feel really bad because grown-ups in their/your life called this child/you names, said mean things to this child/you, or said they didn't want this child/you?"

Rates were higher for girls than boys (6.7% vs. 4.5%) and higher for youth ages 14–17 (11.7%). Rates were lower in homes with two biological parents (4.3%). Twenty-three percent of the sample indicated that they were "very afraid" but 40% said they were "not afraid." Only a small portion (28%) of these episodes were known to authorities. Of those persons likely to know about the child's experiences, 19% were teachers, 17% were counselors, and police were specified only 3% of the time.

The emotional abuse rate of 5.6% reported in Finkelhor et al. (2014) is much lower than a previous rate of 19% reported by Straus, Hamby, Finkelhor, Moore, and Runyan (1998); however, the question that provided that rate asked about *any* name calling that left the child feeling scared or really bad.

Finkelhhor and his colleagues are leading researchers in this field. Another national study they conducted (Finkelhor, Ormrod, & Turner, 2009) of 1,467 children involved their caretakers if the child was nine or younger, and the child if 10 to 17 years of age. The social scientists found that respondents to the random digital dialing survey indicated that 7% of the children had been victims of psychological/emotional abuse in the past year and roughly 10% had been victimized at some point during their lifetime. Further, 17% of the children had received emotional bullying in the past year and almost 24% during some point in their lifetime. Respondents in the study were asked about 33 different types of victimization. These categories included such items as being a witness to domestic violence, physical assault, assault with a weapon, witness to murder, exposure to random shootings, etc. Viewed in a cumulative way when all the categories were added together, over two-thirds of children (69%) had been victimized in the past year and almost 80% had been victimized during their lifetimes.

Table 1.3 provides some other estimates that have been made about the number of individuals affected by emotional abuse.

Looking at prevalence rates from another perspective, Chamberland, Fallon, Black, and Trocmé (2011) explored the rates of emotional abuse in child maltreatment investigations in Canada. They found a rate in 2003 of 2.42 investigations of single form (only) emotional abuse per 1,000 children or 6% of all the investigations. In terms of substantiated

Table 1.3 Prevalence Rates for Childhood Emotional Abuse

Men (%)	Women (%)	Study description	Authors
4	8	Emotional maltreatment; 18- to 24-year-olds community survey; random probability sample in the United Kingdom	May-Chahal and Cawson (2005)
10.1	10.5	Psychological/emotional abuse; children 2 to 17 and caregivers if child is under 10; nationally representative sample; United States	Finkelhor et al. (2005)
12.3	15.3	Witnessing maternal battering; adult members of Health Maintenance Organizations (HMO) retrospectively remembering	Edwards et al. (2003)

emotional abuse single form, the rate was 1.51 per 1,000 children or 9% of all the substantiated cases. Co-occurring emotional abuse with other maltreatment was another 5.9 investigations per 1,000 children or 15% of all investigations. And co-occurring emotional abuse represented 13% of all substantiated child maltreatment investigations.

The authors also noted that substantiated single-form and co-occurring emotional neglect had the highest rate of transfer to ongoing services (>70%). Eighty-five percent of emotional neglect cases had been previously investigated. While substantiated co-occurring emotional abuse had the highest rate of physical injury, proportionately more children with substantiated co-occurring emotional neglect were identified by CPS workers as needing treatment for emotional harm.

Child Neglect Estimates

Several items from the Finkelhor et al. (2014) study were used to estimate childhood neglect. These items included such topics as: parental drinking and drug use, being left alone, living in a broken-down home, unsafe or unhealthy conditions, allowing unsafe people to be around, and lack of personal hygiene. When asked about occurrence in *the past year*, the rate was determined to be 4.7% of children. Almost 12 percent (11.7%) indicated that neglect had occurred sometime during the child's lifetime. Of those who reported some lifetime exposure, 73% said that it had happened more than once. Children in homes with two biological parents had the lowest rate of neglect as did those living in higher socio-economic homes. The percent of children "very afraid" was almost the same as those assessed under emotional abuse (24% vs. 23%). Authorities were slightly more knowledgeable about neglect in the child's life than emotional abuse (32% vs. 28%).

The neglect rate of 4.7% was much lower than the previous rate of 27% reported in Straus et al. (1998). In that study 19.5% of the sample indicated that the parent had left his/her child alone at home "even when you thought some adult should be with him/her." Such situations may not always constitute neglect as they depend upon the child's age, maturity, length of time the child was alone, possibility of other resources such as the child's ability to use a phone, the neighborhood, the frequency with which it occurs, and so on.

Additional Estimates

Finkelhor, Turner, Ormrod, and Hamby (2009) have also reported data from a large national telephone survey (the first National Survey of Children's Exposure to Violence) that almost 10% of children had witnessed family assault and 19% witnessed assault in their community in the previous year. Over their lifetimes, 20% witnessed family assault and 29% assault in their community.

Approximately 9% had been threatened in the previous year, almost 16% over their lifetimes; 13% had been bullied in the previous year, and almost 22% at some point over their lifetimes. Twenty percent reported being teased or emotionally bullied (previous year) and this number climbed to almost 30% over their lifetimes.

Children are no strangers to physical assault themselves. Almost half reported being physical assaulted in the prior year, more than half had been assaulted sometime during their lifetime. In the prior year 10% were injured, and 15% reported physical assault injury sometime during their lifetime. The authors concluded that the study "reveals high levels of exposure to violence, victimization, and abuse among a representative sample of American children and youth" (p. 1416) which "are consistent with earlier literature" (p. 1417).

Another set of estimates on emotional neglect comes from a *meta-analysis* of articles on child neglect. A meta-analysis is a study of studies. In other words, the authors (Stoltenborgh, Bakermans-Kranenburg, & van Ijzendoorn, 2013) searched electronic databases and specialized journals (e.g., *Child Abuse & Neglect*) for articles with the terms "incidence" or "prevalence," "neglect," and "child" between the years 1980 and 2008. They found 16 publications meeting their criteria on self-reported emotional neglect; these studies were based on a total of almost 60,000 participants. Based on all those studies from various countries around the world, the combined rate of emotional neglect was 18.4%. For the United States and Canada, it was 14.5% of children.

Thus, the best estimates for *lifetime prevalence* of emotional abuse or neglect in our communities seem to range from about 10% (Finkelhor et al., 2014) to 19% (Straus et al., 1998) with the findings from the meta-analysis at about 15%—almost in the middle.

Targeted Youth in Care

From the studies that started this segment of the chapter, we can see how the specific questions asked and the way they are aggregated can affect the estimates of child maltreatment. That is why some researchers have called for the use of research instruments or scales that have been tested and shown to be highly reliable and valid in studies of prevalence rates. Such a practice would likely improve the accuracy of estimates. Physician Elizabeth Miller and her colleagues (2011) used the Childhood Trauma Questionnaire (CTQ) to assess for the extent of maltreatment in a sample of 1,715 youths who were receiving services in California from one or more public agencies such as child welfare, drug/alcohol treatment, mental health services, juvenile justice, and school services for youth with serious emotional disturbance. The CTQ contains five subscales each containing five items. The five dimensions it assesses are: physical punishment, sexual abuse, emotional abuse, physical neglect, and emotional neglect. An example of the item used to measure emotional abuse is "People in my family called me things like 'stupid,' 'lazy,' or 'ugly.'" Emotional neglect was evaluated with items like "I thought that my parents wished I had never been born." Instructions to participants in the study were to consider the items in terms of "while growing up."

It should be pointed out that these high rates of emotional maltreatment present an *average* for youths of all ages and for both genders. But for any given age or gender, the rates could be much higher. For instance, 86.7% of the female youths receiving alcohol/drug services experienced emotional abuse and 77.3% experienced emotional neglect.

Table 1.4 Proportion of Youthful Public Service Recipients (11 to 18 years of age) Assessed with Emotional Abuse or Emotional Neglect

Type of abuse (%)	Child welfare (%)	Alcohol/ drug (%)	Mental health (%)	Juvenile justice (%)	School services for serious emotional disturbance (%)	Group totals (%)
Emotional abuse	53.5	49.4	38.3	36.7	39.4	41.2
Emotional neglect	58.5	61.2	49.9	52.8	49.9	54.3

Source: Miller et al. (2011).

Understandably, these rates are much higher than those typically reported in community studies because the participants in this study are receiving some form of protective or public service. Analysis of the data revealed that as the age of the young person increased, he/she was more likely to report some form of maltreatment.

Other Sources of Information

Another source of data demonstrating the magnitude of the problem of abuse and neglect in the United States comes from the Department of Health and Human Services, Administration for Children and Families, Administration on Children, Youth and Families. Entitled *Child Maltreatment 2012*, this report provides data collected from 49 states, the District of Columbia, and the Commonwealth of Puerto Rico in the National Child Abuse and Neglect Data System (NCANDS).

In the Federal Fiscal Year 2012, 3.2 million children received either an investigation or alternative response from child protection systems. This translates into about 42.7 children per thousand children in the population. However, children might have been involved in more than one report. Thus, 3.8 million children were investigated during that 12-month period and most of those cases were not substantiated. Roughly 20% of the investigated cases were substantiated or received an alternative response. *Child Maltreatment 2012* states that 9.2 children per 1,000 were victims of abuse or neglect. Of course, this assumes that every victim's case has been reported and substantiated.

Approximately three-quarters (79%) of the child victims were categorized as neglected and 18% physically abused. Nine percent were sexually abused. Medical neglect, neglect, and psychological maltreatment rates were the highest for the youngest children and decreased as the child grew older. For instance, psychological maltreatment of children between one and two years of age was reported to be 21.4%, of children 12 to 14 it was 14.2%, and for teens 15 to 17 it was 10.3%. Older children can spend more time away from home and parent or caregiver tormentors.

The estimates available for understanding the extent of emotional abuse and neglect are like snapshots taken by a group of people—each with a different camera and perspective. That is, survey questions will vary and this affects what is being counted as representing abuse or neglect. Also, the time frames will be different and the individuals in the sample will be different. Therefore, it might make more sense to pay attention to the range of the rates rather than to any one specific rate. Also, keep in mind that the rates presented do not include the number of children who have been victimized and never told anyone—even a researcher. Thus, it is hard to know the number of *unreported* acts of emotional bullying, exposure to domestic violence, and so on. Ideally, we would like to add these to the *known* reports and rates to arrive at the best estimates.

The Problem with Prevalence Estimates

The basic problem with prevalence estimates is that there is no single best way to capture or create the most accurate assessment of child maltreatment. Studies which attempt to arrive at a number of children who have been maltreated are always estimates that derive from numerous methodologies. How they go about the process of collecting the data can differ (do they ask children about their experiences or ask adults to reflect back over their childhoods? Do they use official reports? Are telephone interviews employed or paper-and-pencil questionnaires?) The items used to determine maltreatment may vary from verbal insults and threats to one's safety to witnessing violence and seeing a loved one or pet hurt. Sometimes the authors caution that their way of defining emotional abuse may not be a clinical assessment, and sometimes only one facet of all the ways a child might be emotionally mistreated are examined (e.g., witnessing domestic violence). These different ways of collecting data can make it difficult to make comparisons across studies and to know the "true" prevalence rate of emotional abuse. We'll probably never know the true rate of emotional abuse because human memory is fallible. That is, we all forget things, and sometimes we are motivated to forget hurtful things said and done to us. There is also the issue of not recognizing abusive behavior as maltreatment because of not knowing what constitutes "normal" family life and parental behavior.

Another issue is that sometimes research participants, be they children, youth, or even adults, may not want others to know about the abuse or their home lives. They may share partial information instead of full information to make it appear that there was less abuse than what they really experienced. Or, they may be completely dishonest. Even when actual child protection data is utilized for estimates, official investigations and cases of child maltreatment represent only a small portion of all the actual maltreatment that occurs and goes unreported. Thus, official estimates are always *underestimates* (Anda, Butchart, Felitti, & Brown, 2010). In fact, a 1993 national incidence study found "that only one-third of cases countable under the study Endangerment Standard had been investigated by child protective services" (Fallon, Trocme, Fluke, MacLaurin, Tonmyr, & Yuan, 2010, p. 73).

It is important to remember that emotional abuse will not always be identified as a single type or form of abuse. Indeed, it is much more likely that children who are physically or sexually abused will be reported first for those injuries and then possibly emotional abuse identified as co-occurring. This is discussed in the next section.

Multiple Victimizations, Poly-Victimization, and Multicategory Abuse

There is growing recognition among the scientific community that children residing in dysfunctional families experience multiple, not just single, forms of abuse. Several studies are briefly presented to make this important point. David Finkelhor and his colleagues discussed "multiple victimization" in 2005 and observed that 71% of children and youth who reported a direct or indirect victimization reported an average of three different victimization types (Finkelhor, Ormrod, Turner, & Hamby, 2005). Later, Finkelhor and associates introduced the term "poly-victimization" as a term to focus attention on children who receive a high level of mistreatment in different types of adverse childhood experiences (Finkelhor et al., 2005, 2007; Finkelhor, Ormod, & Turner, 2009).

Similarly, Wright, Crawford, and Del Castillo (2009) found that college students reported being the recipient of multiple types of abuse. The authors observed, for instance, that the correlation between physical abuse and emotional abuse was 0.63—meaning that the two forms of abuse are associated. Or, stated another way, when you see one type of abuse you tend to see the other as well. The authors noted, "various forms of child maltreatment do occur in the same household, even in a relatively high functioning college sample" (p. 65).

Edwards, Holden, Felitti, and Anda (2003) have also talked about "multicategory abuse." They noted that of the 43% of their research participants who reported any childhood abuse, 34.6% experienced at least two types of maltreatment in childhood.

In a study of childhood trauma and alcohol dependence, the authors reported that in their sample of alcohol-dependent individuals, "70% of those who experienced sexual abuse also experienced emotional abuse" (Schwandt, Heilig, Hommer, George, & Ramchandani, 2013, p. 990).

We will be talking more about this notion of poly-victimization in Chapter 3 as we look at its impact and consequences that may be revealed even years later.

A Final Note about the Prevalence of Emotional Abuse and Neglect

Estimates based on official reports like *Child Maltreatment 2012* have at least one major limitation—they are based on cases that come to the attention of child protection agencies and many others go undetected and unreported. Although we will discuss making assessments of abuse and neglect in much more detail in Chapter 4, deciding whether a child is at risk of harm in a volatile situation such as where there is intimate partner violence (IPV) is a complex and complicated decision. According to research reviewed by Hughes and Chau (2013), the presence of IPV in a home may not be enough to initiate action by a CPS worker. Instead, the workers also weigh such considerations as whether the family has had previous CPS involvement, other co-occurring issues (e.g., substance misuse or mental health issues), the severity of the IPV, and whether children were harmed. Some IPV might be viewed as temporary marital discord or disputes rather than domestic violence. Unfortunately, workers may not always have the time they need to fully investigate each family situation. Thus, it is appropriate to speculate about how many cases or how many times CPS workers might miss assessing child emotional abuse and neglect when it was actually present.

Simmel and Shpiegel (2013) have written that "it is essential to note that not substantiating a report is not synonymous with absence of harm to the child, nor is it indicative of no abuse being perpetrated against the child" (pp. 626–627).

Key Chapter Takeaways

- There are various ways to define emotional abuse and neglect.
- Neglect is usually associated with a repeated or chronic pattern of omissions, not a single incident. However, neglect can occur in a single event (e.g., leaving an 11-month-old in a bathtub without supervision).
- To be defined as neglect, there must usually be an omission of behavior that places the child at harm or potential for harm.
- A neglected child is at risk for other forms of maltreatment.
- There are multiple types of abuse and neglect.
- Emotional abuse and emotional neglect unlike, say, a black eye, can be intangible—won't always be recognized by simply looking at a child. They are related but seem to be different forms of maltreatment (Baker & Festinger, 2011).
- The context, situation, and environment are important when trying to assess emotional abuse and neglect.
- The prevalence rates for child abuse and neglect at the national level are staggering and probably vastly underestimate the number of children who are mistreated.

Glossary

Meta-Analysis: This term applies a type of research where studies on a particular topic or phenomenon are collected to see if a pattern emerges. Meta-analyses often attempt to determine the benefit of the program or treatment for participants (e.g., there was a large, medium, or small effect) based on a statistical comparison derived from findings reported in each study.

Population Study: Typically where a representative sample of a community, state, or the nation is drawn (as opposed to a selected group of persons, say, from one treatment program). Sometimes called a community study.

Prevalence: Generally an estimate of the proportion or percentage of individuals who have or have had a particular disease, condition, or risk factor based on a sample from the population.

Class Discussion Questions

1. What would you have done if you had been walking the dog and the mother described earlier in the chapter shouted at her son, "Shut up, you little brat!" Does this one event justify an assumption that the child protection authorities should be called?
2. What do you think is the biggest challenge to understanding the true level of child emotional abuse and neglect occurring within families across the United States?
3. For the city or county in which you live, how might you go about estimating the number of children who possibly are emotionally abused?
4. What, in your opinion, constitutes poor parenting?
5. Do you feel that the prevalence rates for emotional abuse in your community are higher or lower than in surrounding areas? Why? With enough resources at your command, how might you document or determine this?
6. A father takes a young child out into the woods. When she is not paying attention, he runs away from her—leaving her lost and unable to get home. He tells the mother several hours later that they "accidentally" went different ways. He claims his back hurts too much to go out right away to locate the child again. The child is 10 years old. Is the child being emotionally abused?
7. As you look over the case examples in this chapter, what are the key indicators that suggest emotional abuse? What concerns you most in each of the examples?

2
THE UNDERLYING CAUSES OF EMOTIONAL ABUSE

Errors, like straws, upon the surface flow;
He who would search for pearls must dive below.
—John Dryden

Overview: Why do some parents and caregivers emotionally abuse children? This chapter looks at theories and possible explanations. We'll look at certain family and individual characteristics and other circumstances that the research has shown to be associated with child maltreatment.

Perhaps you've already read or heard explanations as to why parents are abusive or neglectful. You might even have a pet theory about these parents. Stop for a minute to think about how you might explain the root cause of child maltreatment to someone from a culture where it didn't occur. What explanation would you offer?

Maybe you've encountered some situations, possibly through friends at school, where a parent had mental illness, or was heavily involved with alcohol or substance misuse, or just never seemed to be available for their children? Perhaps some of these parents you just couldn't figure out or understand. In this chapter we are going to examine a number of explanations and learn that there are many possible contributors to parental or caregiver abuse and neglect behaviors.

Let's start with the *Fourth National Incidence Study of Child Abuse and Neglect (NIS-4): Report to Congress*. This effort is a national needs assessment mandated by Congress periodically. Its purpose is to gather estimates about the number of abused and neglected children in the United States who come to the attention of professionals in the community. From all the counties in the United States, a nationally representative sample of 122 counties was chosen for the 2010 study. From that subset of counties, professionals who often encounter maltreated children were identified from public agencies, shelters for runaways and homeless youth, police and sheriffs' departments, schools, day care centers, hospitals, and so on. These professionals (called "sentinels") from over 1,000 different agencies completed over 6,200 data forms. Standardized definitions were used to count the number of cases and types of maltreatment.

We will draw from the NIS-4 to examine some of the characteristics of those who abused their children. Child protection workers and other professionals must have a good understanding of parental and other factors that put children at risk for harm and neglect. The findings from the NIS-4 are quite comprehensive, as you will see.

In the section below is provided information using the report's *Harm Standard* which means that there was an act or omission that resulted in demonstrable harm to a child. The NIS-4 report also includes data on abused and neglected children using an *Endangered Standard* which uses a wider net in counting children—those not yet harmed but at risk if the sentinel/professional thought that an act or omission was endangering children. Here are some of the characteristics that the report has discussed as associated with child maltreatment.

Family Characteristics

- Parents' employment. Children with no parent in the labor force were 2.4 times more at risk for emotional abuse than children with employed parent(s). Similarly, children with no parent in the labor force were 3.5 times more likely to be a victim of emotional neglect than children with no employed parent(s).
- Socio-economic status. (Low socio-economic status includes those with household income less than $15,000 a year, where parents' highest educational achievement is less than high school,

and any member of the household receiving benefits from Temporary Assistance for Needy Families (TANF), food stamps, public housing, subsidized school meals, etc.) Children in low socio-economic households were five times more likely to be emotionally abused and more than four times more likely to be emotionally neglected.
- Family structure. Children with a single parent with or without a live-in partner were more than 3.5 times more likely to be emotionally abused as children living with married biological parents. Children were most likely to be emotionally neglected if they lived with one parent with an unmarried partner. This group was followed by children living with one parent without a partner. Children living in homes with two married biological parents were least likely to experience emotional neglect.
- Family size. Incidence rates for maltreatment were highest for families with a large number of children (four or more), and generally the lowest for children in families with two children. Children in large families had twice the rate of emotional abuse as "only" children. Emotional neglect also occurred twice as often in large families than with those with "only" children (*Endangerment Standard*).
- Rural status. Children living in rural counties were mistreated at more than twice the rate of those living in major urban counties. This was true for both emotional abuse and emotional neglect.

Perpetrator Characteristics

- Relationship to child. The majority of child victims (73%) of emotional abuse were mistreated by their biological parents, 20% by their nonbiological parents or partners, and 7% by some other person. In cases of emotional neglect, 90% of the perpetrators were biological parents and 10% were nonbiological parents or partners.
- Perpetrator's gender. Emotionally abusive perpetrators tend to be male primarily and almost three-quarters are males when there is a nonmarried parent or partner in the home. With emotional neglect, the vast majority of perpetrators are females.

- Perpetrator's age. For both emotional abuse and emotional neglect, biological parents who are perpetrators tend to be over 35 (slightly under 50% of the time). The youngest biological parents (under age 26) represent a minority of the perpetrators (5 to 8%). Biological parents between the youngest and oldest age groups represent about 38% of the perpetrators. Nonbiological perpetrators tend to be mostly located in the category of over 35 (62–68%).
- Alcohol, drug use, and mental illness. For emotionally abused children, the perpetrators' use of alcohol contributed to mistreatment 21.8% of the time, while 16.7% used drugs, and 16.7% had mental illness. For emotionally neglected children, alcohol was also a factor 20.7% of the time, while 19.9% used drugs, and 13% had mental illness.

The source of all the facts in the beginning of this chapter, the *Fourth National Incidence Study of Child Abuse and Neglect (NIS-4): Report to Congress*, contains quite a bit more information than can be displayed here (such as on physical and sexual abuse, and other types of neglect). You can view the full report at www.acf.hhs.gov/sites/default/files/opre/nis4_report_congress_full_pdf_jan2010.pdf.

Other Studies Examining Risk Factors

Examinations of the causes or reasons that child abuse and neglect occurs (its *etiology*) started, in a historical sense, decades ago with a focus on parental psychopathology. Later studies failed to find a single or specific psychological or personality pattern that fit all or most cases (Stith et al., 2009). Indeed, studies into the root causes of child maltreatment have explored such associations as with maternal age, parental education, income level/poverty/public benefit recipient, social support, domestic violence, mental health, substance abuse, child health and behavior, stress, family size and structure (Slack et al., 2011). Other factors that have been discussed in the literature include isolation and aggressive biases and hostile attributions to the behavior of others (Berlin, Appleyard, & Dodge, 2011). Simonic, Mandelj, and Novsak (2013) have suggested that religious abuse may, in the mind of the perpetrator, justify insults and accusations of an emotional abuse variety that results in instilling feelings of fear, guilt, worthlessness, and shame and even allow for physical abuse.

Stith et al. (2009) have conducted a meta-analysis of risk factors in child maltreatment literature. They identified 39 different risk factors for child physical abuse (**CPA**) and child neglect (**CN**) from 155 studies conducted between 1969 and 2003 meeting their criteria. They grouped the child risk factors that were studied during that time frame as follows:

Parent–Child Relationship Where Parent Reports on Child Behavior
- Parent–child relationship, CPA, CN
- Parent–child interaction (parent perceives child as problem), CPA, CN
- Parent use of corporal punishment, CPA
- Parenting behaviors, CPA, CN
- Parent's stress over parenting, CPA, CN
- Unplanned pregnancy, CPA.

Parent Characteristics Independent of Child
- Parent anger/hyper-reactivity, CPA, CN
- Parent anxiety, CPA
- Parent psychopathology, CPA, CN
- Parent depression, CPA, CN
- Parent (low) self-esteem, CPA, CN
- Parent poor relationship with own parents, CPA, CN
- Parent experienced childhood abuse, CPA, CN
- Parent criminal behavior, CPA
- Parent personal stress, CPA, CN
- Parent (lack of) social support, CPA, CN
- Parent alcohol abuse, CPA
- Parent unemployment, CPA, CN
- Parent (poor) coping and problem-solving skills, CPA
- Single parent, CPA, CN
- Parent age, CPA, CN
- Parent drug abuse, CPA

- Parent health problems, CPA
- Parent gender, CPA
- Parent approval of corporal punishment, CPA.

Child Characteristics
- Child social competence, CPA, CN
- Child *externalizing* behavior, CPA, CN
- Child *internalizing* behavior, CPA, CN
- Child gender, CPA, CN
- Child pre- or neonatal problems, CPA
- Child disability, CPA
- Child age, CPA, CN.

Family Factors
- Family conflict, CPA
- (Lack of) family cohesion, CPA
- Spousal violence, CPA
- (Lack of) marital satisfaction, CPA
- Family size, CPA, CN
- Socio-economic status, CPA, CN
- Nonbiological parent, CPA.

To make sense of the various studies they collected, the authors performed a statistical analysis of the sample of those associated with child maltreatment and compared them to a sample presumed to have no child maltreatment involvement. Because different instruments and measurements were employed in the studies, standard deviations and mean (average) differences were computed and translated into *effect sizes*. This is a way to standardize comparisons and look for statistical significances between the groups. The larger the effect size, the greater the difference between the groups—that is, the greater the likelihood that the risk factor was indeed a potent one.

Of all the variables listed above, Stith et al. (2009) found the *largest* effect sizes for child physical abuse as the risk factors of parent anger/hyper-reactivity, family conflict, and low family cohesion. *Insignificant* effect sizes (meaning that no real differences were found between the abusing and nonabusing groups) were found for seven possible risk factors: parent health problems, approval of corporal punishment, child gender, prenatal or neonatal problems, disability, age, and nonbiological parent in the home.

Five risk factors had *large* effect sizes for child neglect: the parent–child relationship, parent perceives child as a problem, parent level of stress, parent anger/hyper-reactivity, and parent self-esteem. *Insignificant* effect sizes were found for child gender and child age. Table 2.1 summarizes the results.

The meta-analysis shows the difficulty associated with trying to pinpoint an exact cause of abuse or neglect. The strongest risk factors for neglect were parent perception of the child as problem and parent–child relationships. The stronger risk factors for child physical abuse were parent anger/hyper-reactivity, family conflict, and low family cohesion.

The fact that high family conflict and low family cohesion don't show as risk factors in Table 2.1 doesn't mean that they aren't involved as "players" in the dynamics creating situations where child neglect occurs. It simply means that the authors of the meta-analysis did not find any studies where these two factors were examined within studies meeting their seven criteria for inclusion in the meta-analysis. Indeed, it is very possible that a risk factor or risk factors shown as associated with child neglect was also present in many cases of child abuse and vice versa. Also, some of the variables are not independent of each other but nested within or correlated with depression, anxiety, and psychopathology. Another complication is that factors such as the child's *internalizing* and *externalizing* behaviors may actually be an outcome of maltreatment rather than a cause of the child's maltreatment. Lastly, the vast majority of the risk factors do not help us in truly characterizing how abusers may be different from parents who do not abuse.

To further explain, a risk factor should not be interpreted as anything more than a potentiality. It is not a foregone conclusion that a family with one or more risk factors will end up maltreating its children. To take an example or two, there are plenty of large families where there is no mistreatment of children. There are numerous unemployed parents, although not happy about their financial circumstances, who value and cherish their children and never shout obscenities at them or mistreat them in any way.

Familiarity with the risk factors helps child protection workers and other professionals in assessing families' propensity to abuse and

Table 2.1 Overlap of major meta-analysis risk factors for child maltreatment (Stith et al., 2009)

Risk factor	Type of abuse	Effect size*
Parent–child relationships	Child neglect	Large
	Child physical abuse	Moderate
Parent perceives child as problem	Child neglect	Large
	Child physical abuse	Moderate
Personal stress	Child neglect	Large
	Child abuse	Small
Anger/hyper-reactivity	Child neglect	Large
	Child physical abuse	Large
Self-esteem	Child neglect	Large
	Child physical abuse	Moderate
Psychopathology	Child neglect	Moderate
	Child physical abuse	Moderate
Unemployment	Child neglect	Moderate
	Child physical abuse	Small
Depression	Child neglect	Moderate
	Child physical abuse	Moderate
Child social competence	Child neglect	Moderate
	Child physical abuse	Moderate
Child externalizing behaviors*	Child neglect	Moderate
	Child physical abuse	Moderate
Family size	Child neglect	Moderate
	Child physical abuse	Small
Family conflict	Child neglect	—
	Child physical abuse	Large
Family cohesion	Child neglect	—
	Child physical abuse	Large

Note
* See Glossary.

neglect as well as indicating where resources may be applied to minimize future maltreatment. While we will discuss assessment in greater detail in Chapter 4, it is important to gain an understanding of the factors that may be responsible whenever parents and caregivers mistreat children. As suggested in the beginning of this chapter, it is not possible to state a simple cause or explanation for child maltreatment—although in any one randomly selected case we might find what appears to be a single risk factor that is assumed to be primarily responsible. Stith et al. (2009) concluded their study by stating, "The results provide support for the importance of examining child maltreatment from a multi-factorial perspective" (p. 25). Similarly, infant neglect has been described as having a multi-causal nature (Bartlett, Raskin, Kotake, Nearing, & Easterbrooks, 2014), a complex etiology (Dubowitz et al., 2005), and being multiply determined (DePanfilis & Dubowitz, 2005). Indeed, this is the position taken in this book—that many or multiple factors may interact with each other and combine in an unfortunate way that produces maltreatment for children (and possibly other adults in the family).

What are the maltreatment factors in Case Example 10 below?

Case Example 10

John grew up in a home where, after his mother died of cancer, his father would get drunk several times a week and go on rampages breaking furniture and throwing things. After his older brother Will got his nose broken in a violent altercation with their father, Will left home a week later in the middle of the night without telling anyone. A year later, John's father was drinking even more heavily. He screamed curses if there was no beer in the refrigerator, if John hadn't made them something to eat, or if John was talking on the phone when he came home. Before he would pass out, his father sometimes tried to get John to fight with him—"Like me and my father did." When John wouldn't fight, his father called him "Wussy" and "Mama's Boy." After he was fired for drinking on his job as a truck mechanic, John's father would play with an old revolver that he kept loaded beside the couch as he drank. Several times he threatened to shoot John because he believed John knew where Will had gone. One night after his father threw a beer bottle at the television and broke it when there was nothing in the house to eat, 14-year-old John also ran away from home.

As you think about the case example on the previous page, what seems to be primary risk factor? What are other issues?

You may wonder why it seems we have taken a detour from emotional abuse and broadened the discussion to child neglect and child physical abuse with the focus on this meta-analysis. As we discussed in Chapter 1, emotional abuse is almost always associated with other forms of maltreatment—at least when it comes to the attention of those in the community who might be in a position to recognize it and report the mistreatment of children to child protection or civil authorities. And sometimes the research is not specific enough to let us see how factors affect a specific type of child maltreatment. Bartlett and Easterbrooks (2012), for instance, have noted that most studies associated with one theory of child maltreatment (intergenerational transmission) that we'll be examining shortly "do not distinguish among types of maltreatment" (p. 2165).

Let's move on to examine theories that attempt to explain child maltreatment—whether it is emotional or physical abuse, or neglect. One last note, while it is imperative that we remain cognizant of risk factors that may be in families when working with them, it is also important to remember that emotional abuse can occur in homes without any apparent risk factors, in two-parent homes, and in tidy middle-class homes. Emotional abuse can be found in every major income category and neighborhood.

Theories that Try to Account for Child Maltreatment

In the study of social problems, researchers often begin their investigations by becoming well-informed about the existing literature and the theories that have been proposed to explain the existence or continuation of a problem. This is also true in the study of child abuse and neglect. But let's stop for a moment. What good is a theory? Theories attempt to organize information about a phenomenon or problem so that predictions can be made and the phenomenon is better understood and explainable. Sometimes the explanations are relatively simple—for example, pointing to the parent's or caregiver's mental disorder or experience being abused himself or herself as a child. And, as we hope you are learning, the theories that might be more versatile and applicable are likely to be the ones

Case Examples 11, 12, 13

Emotional abuse can be so insidious, stealthy, and hurtful, but not in a direct way that would always register with others as in these examples:

#11 Cindy

I don't think my parents ever liked me. Mom was always pointing out my mistakes and making unfavorable comparisons—comparing me to my "perfect" older sister. I never felt as smart or capable as her, but I managed to graduate from high school with a high "B" grade point average. I remember talking to Mom one day as we were dusting the furniture. I said that I was thinking about going to college. Mom didn't say anything right away and when I turned to look at her she said through clenched teeth, "I have two SONS who need to go to college." The issue was settled. I knew I would have to put myself through college.

#12 Marsha

My father would not tolerate my disagreeing with his point of view. He always had to be the authority. We could be just talking and if I said something that he wouldn't agree with, his face would turn red and he would shout, "You're crazy!" and glare at me until I would apologize. Then, he would return to his newspaper as if we had not been talking at all. He made me think maybe I was crazy, and I began to doubt my honest feelings—never knowing when I had a right to question something I didn't like. I thought there was something wrong with my mind—it seemed to explain why he was so unhappy with me.

My mother had her own ways of putting me down and making me feel useless. She kept comparing me to herself. She liked to show me that I couldn't do things as fast or well as she could. She said she'd always done better than me when she was my age. She made me feel about as valuable as a dirty handkerchief. Anything I did, like vacuuming the carpet, she had to do over again. It seemed like she went out of her way to avoid giving me compliments.

#13 Leigh

One attractive woman told me that in her teens, whenever a date was running late, her mother would say, "If you were only prettier, he'd be on time." While she was growing up, the daughter never believed that she was attractive. Think of the trap in which the daughter was caught—either she trusted what her mother was saying and believed herself to be unattractive, or she had to believe her mother was lying.

(Excerpts from Royse, 1994)

that account for more than one risk factor and complicated situations. Theories inform us about what variables might be important to notice or address—providing clues about where the phenomenon exists and what might be needed to remediate the problem.

What follows in this section is a brief review of some of the relevant theories that have been advanced from studies that have attempted to explain child maltreatment. As you review these, you might ask yourself how each of them might be of use to the child protection worker trying to protect a child or children from maltreatment.

Attachment Theory

Psychoanalyst John Bowlby, often referred to as the Father of Attachment Theory, is noted for his writings suggesting that mental health and behavioral problems can be attributed to disruptions in the instinctive drive within an infant to attach to its mother. From an evolutionary standpoint, he believed that babies who remained close to their mothers had a greater chance of survival. When there is a close bond between mother and child, the attachment relationship provides a secure psychological basis for the child to later become more autonomous and explore the world. When the relationship is disrupted or broken, Bowlby expected irreversible long-term consequences in the child's life. That is, the primary caregiver relationship provides the standard for all other future relationships because of the internal working model that the child forms.

Others have built upon Bowlby's ideas (he died in 1990) and continued to refine and develop attachment theory. Later theorists and researchers have developed the Adult Attachment Interview (the AAI, which requires training to administer; see George, Kaplan, & Main, 1985 for a description of the process and Main & Goldwyn, 1998). The AAI allows designation to one of four classification schemes for the attachment relationship based on the caregiver's ability to attend to attachment-related memories and topics while participating in the AAI. Caregivers who are sensitive and responsive in their caregiving tend to produce *secure* infants. Additionally, there are three types of parental relationships which leave infants insecure. Caregivers who dismiss and reject the child by not allowing emotional or physical closeness tend to produce infants that are *avoidant*—these infants become distant, disengaged. They may defensively turn away and minimize emotion and/or become overly self-reliant. Caregivers who are unpredictable, angry, confused, inconsistently available, or very passive can produce infants who become enmeshed, overly dependent on others, who may exaggerate emotion and become anxious or angry. These infants are classified as having an *ambivalent* internal working model. Lastly, caregivers who are disorganized, disoriented, frightened or frightening, those who make excessive use of alcohol or substances may produce infants with a *disorganized* attachment pattern with no coherent strategy for dealing with the world. They, too, act disorganized, disoriented, and often fearful (Riggs, 2010).

The insecure parental relationships might be just an interesting tidbit of information about the influences affecting a child's behavior except for the research that suggests that insecure parental attachment may provide an explanation for emotionally abusive parenting and continuation of the cycle of emotional abuse. Attachment theory suggests that those with insecure attachment have difficulty regulating negative feedback and expectation and they are then at risk for using alcohol and drugs to cope with their negative emotions (Reinert & Edwards, 2009). Individuals with secure attachment have greater self-efficacy and expect that others will respond to their emotional needs.

In short, the theory proposes that maltreatment would contribute to poor adult relationships. Fearful individuals with low self-esteem distrust others and avoid intimacy out of a fear of being hurt. They may remain disconnected and rejecting—interfering with their ability to form a meaningful relationship with a partner. In fact, research suggests that emotional abuse in childhood may endow interpersonal conflict, hostility and aggression, and partner victimization (see, for example Crawford & Wright, 2007 and Messman-Moore & Coates, 2007). There is substantial evidence indicating the caregiver's state of mind affects attachment with the infant (Zajac & Kobak, 2009).

Attachment theories resonate with many individuals who realize, usually as adults, that they have learned the values, behaviors, and even mannerisms of their parents and have exhibited these to their own children and significant others. And research shows that children who received warm and competent care are more likely to be sensitive and empathetic parents. And on the other side of the coin, children who were abused or neglected when growing up may have increased risks for maltreatment.

Using the Child Abuse Potential Inventory (CAPI), designed to assess the likelihood of possible future abuse, Rodriguez and Tucker (2011) collected a sample of at-risk parents who had taken children with behavior problems to therapy. These parents were divided into four groups: *Low Risk* mothers (no childhood abuse history and low CAPI Abuse Scale scores), *Cycle Breakers* (those with a personal history of childhood abuse but low CAPI Abuse Scale scores), *High Risk* mothers (personal history of abuse and high CAPI Abuse Scale scores), and *Initiators* (those with no personal history of abuse but high CAPI Abuse Scale scores). They found mothers in the Low Risk category reported better attachment than the other three groups and mothers in the High Risk group had the lowest attachment scores. Overall, they concluded that for the sample of 73 mothers, poor attachment to parents was associated with greater physical abuse potential and dysfunctional disciplinary style. Importantly, the quality of the attachment to one's parents was a more powerful predictor of the potential for child abuse than one's personal history of abuse.

What do you think would be a dysfunctional disciplinary style? Do either of the situations in the box below qualify?

BOX 2.1

Reflection Questions

(a) 15-year-old Amanda has her cell phone taken away for a week at a time whenever she breaks certain rules such as not hanging up her bathrobe, combing her hair in the kitchen, or not eating all of her supper. Her stepfather makes her get up at 6:00 a.m. every day—even on weekends.

(b) Stephanie's mother, a hostess at a large restaurant, never comes home in the evening and never provides any discipline or guidance when 11-year-old Josh sleeps in and doesn't go to school or stays out past midnight with some older boys in his neighborhood.

Can you suggest other dysfunctional disciplinary styles?

Attachment theory suggests that mothers of abused children and caregiver grandmothers of abused children will show more disruptions in their own attachment histories (e.g., attachment-related traumas), more insecure adult attachment styles, and more conflicted relationships between mother and child than comparison families (Leifer, Kilbane, Jacobsen, & Grossman, 2004).

It is good to recognize that a history of childhood mistreatment does not deterministically doom one to becoming a perpetrator of mistreatment. However, Bartlett and Easterbrooks (2012) found in a sample of 92 adolescent mothers enrolled in a home-visiting program for first-time young parents that the odds of being neglectful were more than four times greater for those mothers with a history of abuse than for mothers without a history. How might you explain this? Why wouldn't a mother be securely attached to her child? What other factors might need to be considered? Let's take a look at the next theory, the ecological model.

Ecological Model

Ecological theorists Bronfenbrenner (1979) and Belsky (1980, 1993) have had considerable impact on our thinking about the factors influencing child maltreatment. More recently, the Centers for Disease Control has refined the original model and presented it as the social-ecological model with four very similar factors: the *individual* (as in the individual characteristics of the child and parent), *relationships* (as between parent and child, peers, and other family members), the *community* (e.g., lack of social support for an isolated family in the surrounding neighborhood; impoverished neighborhoods and schools), and *societal* (e.g., norms regarding violence and ways to resolve conflict). One's own upbringing and parenting role models as well as interactions with significant persons in one's environment as well as interest in and ability to access information from resources in the surrounding culture also are part of the ecological theories.

Sometimes there is a lack of awareness of having been exposed to poor parenting models and abusive disciplining techniques. Here are some of the words used by parents whose children were at risk for foster care: "Sure, I pop my kids, but I was beat!" Another parent was astonished to learn that her actions would require a report to the child protection authorities. That mother said, "She [the therapist] said 'you know I have to report that to child services' and I said 'You do?'" (from McWey, Pazdera, Vennum, & Wojciak, 2013).

To understand this theory a little better, let's consider a hypothetical adolescent mother. Considered as a group, these mothers are likely to have less emotional maturity and knowledge of child development than women who wait to start their families later. Adolescent mothers may have lower levels of education—especially if they dropped out of high school when pregnant. If a single mother, they may have to live in low-income neighborhoods. Bartlett and Easterbrooks (2012) have made this observation about these mothers:

> In combination with the more normative stress of navigating the developmental tasks of adolescence (e.g., identity, autonomy, peer acceptance) and adjusting to the demands of motherhood, these disadvantages may overwhelm a young mother's personal resources and lead to insensitive or neglectful parenting.... Indeed, young mothers often are less affectionate, flexible, patient, and sensitive with their children than are their older counterparts.
> (p. 2164)

We can make the scenario for an adolescent mother even less rosy. The child may have unique characteristics (e.g., special needs, health issues, etc.) that could require special caregiving that makes it more temperamentally difficult and consumes more of the young mother's time and patience and creates a stressful situation for her. Mothers can have unique characteristics of their own, too. They may be angry that they are burdened with a child while their friends are still enjoying their youth. They can have problematic parenting attitudes and unrealistic expectations of children—sometimes as a result of the caregiver behaviors they experienced as a child. They can lack warmth and empathy due to a lack of positive childhood care. They can be depressed about their life situation, about having to stay home 24/7 to care for an infant.

In terms of community/environmental characteristics, if the young mother is without transportation, she may find it difficult to visit and receive physical or emotional support from friends or family. If she has limited income, she may be forced to live in a dangerous or less than desirable neighborhood where she has few positive relationships. As a result of where she lives, she may be afraid, lonely, and isolated with little hope for the future. The societal factor can exist to the extent that the larger society feels little empathy for or blames the teen mother for getting pregnant, possibly for dropping out of school or not working and then having no choice but to live in an undesirable neighborhood. Prejudice/racist values in society may also prevent the teen mother from certain resources or opportunities if she is a person of color.

As if all of these factors were not enough, the young mother's situation is made even more risky for the child if she is experiencing IPV and/or high levels of conflict with a partner or family members.

Bartlett et al. (2014) examined many of the variables contained in the scenario described above to investigate the risk factors for infant neglect in a sample of 383 mothers requesting a home visiting program for first-time young parents. Here is a quick summary of what they found.

Characteristics of infants and mothers: Low birth weight infants were more likely to be neglected although baby's sex, age, and *Apgar score* did not add more predictive power. Maternal factors associated with infant neglect were maternal smoking prior to and during the prenatal period, a maternal history of maltreatment and having primary caregivers in childhood who exhibited less caring parenting styles, IPV resulting in injury (either as a victim or a perpetrator), and maternal use of mental health services. The neglectful mothers in this study lived in census blocks with lower average incomes than the non-maltreating mothers.

When these risk factors were entered into a multivariate analysis to find the strongest predictors of infant neglect, mothers who had received mental health services since becoming pregnant was the predictor with the highest risk factor. The odds of an infant being neglected by a mother who received mental health services was approximately eight times greater than for those with mothers who had never received these services. Other significant predictors were those mothers who received less than positive caretaker care in childhood, those who were involved with IPV, and those who resided in lower income neighborhoods. The inclusion of other variables did not improve the statistical procedure's ability to make a better prediction for infant neglect.

The authors concluded that "adolescent mothers who face certain adversities have fewer psychological, behavioral, and financial resources to support healthy parenting than do their non-maltreating counterparts" (p. 730). And they noted:

> The early months and years of parenting are challenging, physically, economically, and emotionally for all parents, and being a young parent may add additional layers of complexity, as mothers negotiate potentially unsupportive school environments, or harsh social judgments. Navigating the period of infancy without a healthy "blueprint" for parenting, or a supportive intimate relationship in the context of a traumatic childhood history, might exceed any individual's capacity to parent effectively, especially a young mother. It makes sense, then, that teenagers, who themselves did not receive positive care from caregivers in childhood, are more likely to neglect their infants.
> (Bartlett et al., 2014, p. 730)

Intergenerational Transmission Theory

The theory about intergenerational transmission of maltreatment can be found in the professional literature going back to the pioneering work of Drs. Kempe and Helfer and Steele and Pollock in the 1960s (Renner & Slack, 2006). By reading only the last study previously discussed, one can see how easy it would be to develop a theory of child maltreatment that centers on the notion that poor parenting causes poor parenting. Even lay people without professional training or preparation seem to recognize the power of early developmental influences. In 1732 Alexander Pope is credited with a line that, though it has changed slightly over time, you may have heard, "As the twig is bent, so grows the tree." Jaffee et al. (2013) has written, "There is a widespread belief dating back to the 1960s that 'abuse breeds abuse'—that children who are victims of maltreatment in turn grow up to become abusive and neglectful parents" (p. S-4).

Years before the pioneering work of the early investigators of child abuse, writer Dorothy Law Nolte wrote a poignant and widely circulated poem in 1954 (and later revised in the 1970s), "Children Learn

UNDERLYING CAUSES OF EMOTIONAL ABUSE   53

Figure 2.1 Drawing by a nine-year-old boy (courtesy of the Center for Women and Children in Crisis, Inc., Provo, Utah) (source: Ascione, 1998, p. 129)

What They Live." The sentiments of this poem are relevant for this chapter and its explanations regarding theories about child maltreatment (see Box 2.2).

The poem expresses such good common sense that the notion of intergenerational transmission of child mistreatment seem quite plausible and obvious. We must be cautious, however, in oversubscribing to this notion. Most individuals who were mistreated in childhood do not become abusive or neglectful parents.

Table 2.2 reveals a sampling of studies that have investigated the intergenerational transmission hypothesis. Note that the range of the "cycle of abuse" runs from about 7% to 43% depending upon the sample, the type of abuse, and the period of time covered by the study.

These studies do not focus exclusively on emotional abuse or emotional neglect and vary in the way they define or measure child maltreatment. However, even though the range of percentages for the estimates

> **BOX 2.2**
>
> **Children Learn What They Live**
>
> If children live with criticism, they learn to condemn.
> If children live with hostility, they learn to fight.
> If children live with fear, they learn to be apprehensive.
> If children live with pity, they learn to feel sorry for themselves.
> If children live with ridicule, they learn to feel shy.
> If children live with jealousy, they learn to feel envy.
> If children live with shame, they learn to feel guilty.
> If children live with encouragement, they learn confidence.
> If children live with tolerance, they learn patience.
> If children live with praise, they learn appreciation.
> If children live with acceptance, they learn to love.
> If children live with approval, they learn to like themselves.
> If children live with recognition, they learn it is good to have a goal.
> If children live with sharing, they learn generosity.
> If children live with honesty, they learn truthfulness.
> If children live with fairness, they learn justice.
> If children live with kindness and consideration, they learn respect.
> If children live with security, they learn to have faith in themselves and in those about them.
> If children live with friendliness, they learn the world is a nice place in which to live.

of children who seem to have been affected by intergenerational mistreatment is fairly wide, Schofield, Lee, and Merrick (2013) concluded, regarding research articles in the *Journal of Adolescent Health*, "The collective results from this special issue provide evidence that child maltreatment in one generation is positively related to child maltreatment in the next generation of parents" (p. S36).

In reviewing the articles on the etiology of child maltreatment in the same issue, Etter and Rickert (2013) say this: "substance abuse problems, domestic partner violence, antisocial behavior, and depression have been associated with maintaining the intergenerational cycle of maltreatment" (p. S39). These factors have been reported as contributing to the mistreatment of children in many studies.

Table 2.2 Sampling of studies on the continuity of mistreatment across generations

Study	Findings	Sample/comments
Kaufman and Zigler (1987)	30% of those with a history of being mistreated will subject their offspring to mistreatment	Early review of the literature
McCloskey and Bailey (2000)	Of 54 mothers with a history of childhood sexual abuse, 43% had daughters who were sexually abused. Daughters of mothers with a history of sexual abuse were at 3.6 times the risk of sexual abuse as other girls in the sample. When mother's history was combined with mother's drug use, daughters were at 24 times the risk of sexual abuse as other girls	179 families from Arizona drawn from a study in 1990–1991; battered women were oversampled
Pears and Capaldi (2001)	23% of boys were abused within families; only the parents who experienced both multiple physically abusive acts and multiple injuries demonstrated the highest level of abuse toward their children	109 families where at least one biological parent was present through the boy's eighteenth birthday; boys from inner-city area at risk for delinquency
Renner and Slack (2006)	31% of parents reported for abuse or neglect; 25% of parents physically abused as children, 12% sexually abused, and 8% reported neglect as children. However, no correlation between childhood physical abuse and physical abuse of one's own children	Illinois families receiving Temporary Assistance to Needy Families (TANF); over 1,000 in the sample

Table 2.2 Continued

Study	Findings	Sample/comments
Jaffee et al. (2013)	Of 178 mothers with history of mild maltreatment in childhood, 46% had at least one child who experienced physical maltreatment by the age of 12. Fifty-six percent of mothers reporting severe abuse in childhood had at least one child physically maltreated. These mothers were 5.3 times more likely to have a child maltreated by the age of 12	Nationally representative sample of families in part of the Environmental Risk Longitudinal Twin Study tracking the development of 2,232 British children. Maltreatment was defined as any from the Childhood Trauma Questionnaire (emotional, physical, and sexual abuse as well as emotional and physical neglect)
Berlin et al. (2011)	Of mothers who experienced childhood abuse, 16.7% had children who were mistreated by age 26 months. Of mothers who experienced childhood neglect, 9.4% became victims of maltreatment compared to the rate of 7.7 percent for mothers who were not neglected	499 mothers recruited from prenatal care providers, a large public health clinic and private OB/GYN practices. County records for child maltreatment are reported
Milner et al. (2010)	A history of childhood physical abuse was associated with two to three times higher risk for abusing among Navy recruits and college students and was similar across gender, race/ethnicity, age, and marital parenting status.	Symptoms that were the best predictors of scores on the Child Abuse Potential Inventory were Impaired Self-Reference, Defensive Avoidance, and Tension Reduction Behavior. Note that this study is based on risk, not on actual substantiated episodes of abuse

While Pears and Capaldi (2001) acknowledge "a direct effect for the intergenerational transmission of abuse" (p. 1454) in pointing out that the parents who abused their children were "twice as likely to have been abused themselves" (p. 1454), this finding held only for the parents who received both multiple physically abusive acts and multiple injuries in childhood. Saying this another way, it was not simply the amount or number of times that one was abused as a child, but the extent of the injury or trauma that may have resulted from the abuse that increased the risk of intergenerational transmission.

Other Theories

In this brief presentation of theories, we see, once again, how improbable it is that emotional abuse, or any type of abuse, would have a single cause. The research on the etiology of child abuse suggests that this would be a much too simplistic way to think. Accordingly, there are some other theories that deserve at least a mention before we conclude this discussion.

Biological Theories—A parent shares approximately 50% of his or her genes with his or her children and while that may seem like a lot or a little based on your point of view, even with this model there is recognition of other variables. The genetic inheritance that an individual receives can be considered a potential for expression in the same way that a seed contains genetic material. This material is a mixture of dominant and recessive genes which allows for some variation at the individual level. Environmental variation either supports or prevents the expression of the genetic material. In order for a seed to sprout it needs certain conditions in its immediate environment (e.g., soil, water, light) that activate or allow the genetic potential to be expressed. Genetic material that we inherit may contain factors that seem to be at cross-purposes. For instance, some seeds of the same type might do better in drier rather than wetter conditions and this may be due to interaction of genes, or just randomness in the alignment of the seed's genetic structure. Coming back to a human example, the potential for certain behavior may be expressed differently because of the individual's gender and one's family, friends, partner, and neighborhood.

Social Learning Theory—Albert Bandura (1963, 1976) is a major theorist associated with social learning theory. His notion is that we learn behaviors by observing those around us. We observe what behaviors result in punishment and which ones result in rewards. Thus, children who are mistreated (whether it is emotional or some other form) can learn and acquire these behaviors from adult models and then play them out within their own families when they become adults. *Learned helplessness*, a theory often used to explain why battered women remain with abusive and violent parents, can be classified as under social learning theory.

Renner and Slack (2006) report some support for this theory in that children who experienced physical abuse in childhood were 2.6 times more likely to report, as adults, that they had experienced IPV than respondents who did not identify physical abuse in their childhood. In other words, being abused and exposed to violence as children may create a mindset where individuals learn/acquire the belief or role that they are or should be victims.

Similarly, McCloskey and Bailey (2000) found that mothers with a childhood sexual abuse history place their own daughters at a risk 3.6 times higher than that of other girls. They write in discussing the intrapsychic and environmental factors that seem to contribute to this situation:

> It is possible that women who have been sexually abused develop an "internal working model" of sexual relationships that encompasses exploitive, coercive, and domineering behavior among men. If such a "template" results from early exposure to sexual abuse, then these women might be more tolerant of men either in their households or their social spheres who are potential abusers of their daughters ... it is possible that this heightened risk of sexually abused women's daughters could be explained through extended family relationships that include the mothers' family members. That is, women might sustain contact with their family of origin despite prior sexual abuse experiences perpetrated by family members, and this continued contact places their daughters at the same risk to which they were once subjected.
>
> (p. 1032)

In another example, Berlin et al. (2011) have reported that a mother's childhood abuse predicted social isolation and social isolation predicted victimization of their offspring. Also, mothers' childhood physical abuse predicted aggressive response biases which predicted victimization of their offspring. Thus, social learning might be one mechanism that helps to explain intergenerational transmission of child maltreatment.

Not All Doom and Gloom

The purpose of this chapter has been to share some of the vast literature available on risk factors associated with child maltreatment to educate the reader about findings that may possibly guide investigators when a child is thought to be in peril. Past history does not dictate future behaviors. Anyone with child maltreatment in his or her past should not conclude from the discussion of risk factors that he or she is doomed to become a perpetrator of child abuse. Many, many very successful people including famous actors, writers, performers, and even U.S. presidents experienced conditions that were abusive and/or neglectful and they did not grow up to abuse their children. Having a rough start growing up does not prevent one from being a marvelous parent and living a life full of love and generosity.

Don't miss the message here. No one is suggesting that risk factors absolutely determine or cause poor parenting. Risk factors alone do not make someone a bad parent. And it is possible to be a happy and successful individual and parent, even if one's childhood was not just unpleasant but downright unfortunate.

Two studies have indicated that the intergenerational transmission rate is actually pretty low. Dixon, Browne, and Hamilton-Giachritsis (2005) found a rate of 6.7% in Essex, United Kingdom and this rate was "very similar to a 7.6% rate in a 5-year prospective study of newborns in Surrey" (p. 53). Thus, as we have pointed out previously, only a small proportion of adults who were abused as children may become abusive to their own children.

Further, as compelling as anecdotal accounts of intergenerational transmission of abuse/neglect may be, a *systematic review of the literature* on the cycle of child maltreatment by Thornberry, Knight, and Lovegrove (2012) observes that the notion that mistreated children grow up to mistreat their children has been primarily based on methodologically weak studies. Creating 11 methodological criteria necessary to be a strong study in this area, the authors found that four studies provided general support for the cycle of abuse, three provided "very limited support" for only one type of maltreatment, and two provided no support at all. Thus, they concluded that there is "likely to be a significant association between maltreatment in the first generation and maltreatment in the second generation but, at the present time, there is insufficient scientific evidence to draw a definitive conclusion about the cycle of maltreatment hypothesis" (p. 145).

Dixon et al. (2005) concluded that three risk factors provided a partial explanation for intergenerational transmission of abuse. These were: being a parent under 21, having a history of mental illness or depression, and residing with a violent adult. Such parents were 17 times more likely than nonabusive families to maltreat their children. It is very likely that those adults with a history of abusive behavior who do not go on to become abusers have some resources available to them lacking in the other families. Emotional support from friends or significant others, stable intimate relationships, safe, secure home environments, and psychotherapy for depression and other mental health problems seem to buffer or neutralize some of the harmful effects of childhood abuse.

Final Chapter Note

Can there be a single theory that would explain all child maltreatment? While it may seem that we understand a great deal about the mechanics involved with childhood abuse and neglect, there is still much we don't know. While a personal history of childhood mistreatment may greatly increase the potential for mistreatment of one's children, it does not explain why the vast majority of those who were mistreated do not become abusers as parents. However, it is logical to assume, even if we start with the intergenerational transmission model, that attachment theory, social learning, biological/genetic theories, and a multi-factor explanation such as ecological theory can all offer something valuable (Renner & Slack, 2006). Depending upon the particular case or situation, it may be that one theory does seem to "fit" the circumstances better than another.

Although there seems to be a reasonable amount of empirical support for an intergenerational transmission theory, most persons who experienced childhood abuse or neglect do not perpetrate maltreatment. Individual risk factors interact with other factors in the social environment. Factors like the quality of adult relationships/social support available to the parent of a child (think safe, stable, nurturing) might help to neutralize individual factors that could put the child at greater risk. Families that were able to break the cycle of abuse were the ones where there appeared to be none or little domestic violence—making the mothers feel safe and where relationships "between mothers and children and mothers and their partners were nurturing" (Jaffee et al., 2013, p. S8).

Kerr, Capaldi, Pears, and Owen (2009) use the term "interplay" to describe a "multiagent" theoretical model based on a dynamic developmental systems approach. In their 2009 article, they describe their investigation of the transmission of fathers' constructive parenting instead of focusing on the cycle of abuse. What is of interest to us at this point is their description of the systems they identified as being involved in parenting behavior: biological systems (e.g., genetic influences), individual characteristics (e.g., temperament), contextual factors (e.g., neighborhood and family resources), socialization experiences (e.g., coercive family processes), and social influence (from peers and romantic partners) explaining risk behaviors.

Is there evidence of intergenerational transmission of problem behaviors that mistreat children? The answer is yes, there are many studies which indicate that at least some potential for maltreatment may be passed from one generation to the next generation. For instance, Kim (2009) utilized data from the National Longitudinal Study of Adolescent Health conducted between 1994 and 1995 when the respondents were in grades 7 through 12. They were interviewed again when they were 18 to 26 years old. Of those who had become young parents, respondents who reported being neglected in their childhood were 2.6 times more likely to report their own neglectful parenting behavior and twice as likely to report their own physically abusive parenting behavior as those who indicated having no maltreatment in childhood. Respondents who said there was physical abuse in their childhood were five times more likely to report that their own parenting behavior had been physically abusive at times. However, 71% of those who had been mistreated in childhood had neither neglected nor physically abused their own children. And only 40% of the young parents who had been multiply mistreated in childhood with physical abuse, neglect, and sexual abuse reported mistreating their children.

Key Chapter Takeaways

- Child maltreatment is multiply determined; it would be unrealistic to look for a single explanation that would apply all of the time.
- Multiple theories have been proposed to explain child maltreatment.
- Several theories seem to complement each other. For instance, social learning theory may work well together with intergenerational transmission.
- While each case of child abuse/neglect will be a little different, individual, family, neighborhood, community, and cultural factors should be considered.

Glossary

Apgar Score: This is a quick assessment of a newborn baby usually made at one minute and five minutes after birth. The child is rated on whether the skin color is normal, the pulse regular, whether the child is taking deep breaths and crying, and so on. The score, generally from one to nine, indicates whether the child might need emergency treatment because of heart or breathing difficulties or other serious medical conditions.

Effect Sizes: This is a statistical term computed by subtracting the mean (average) score obtained in one group on some measure from another comparison mean score (say, looking at improvement in self-esteem for children before and after an intervention) divided by the pooled standard deviation. The effect size (large, moderate, or small) informs us as to how potent the intervention was for bringing about change among the study's participants.

Etiology: This term refers to efforts made to understand what causes or leads to a disease or problem. Hypothesized variables are examined as part of the investigation of how they may affect health or mental health.

Externalizing Behavior: Behavior that acts upon the external environment in a way that is often destructive or violent. Individuals with externalizing behavior may be verbally or physically aggressive in threatening or harming others. They can be viewed as disruptive or defiant and exhibit such behaviors as running away or engaging in underage drinking, etc.

Internalizing Behavior: Behavior that is inwardly focused as when a child is feeling sad, fearful, lonely, or anxious. Such individuals may be characterized as inhibited or depressed; they can engage in problematic eating—either too much or too little. They may have suicidal thoughts.

Systematic Literature Review: These are very specific searches for literature focused on a specific research question where the methods of searching, the terms used, and inclusion/exclusion criteria are stated so that the process is transparent and others can replicate it if they wish. Effort is often made to synthesize the findings based only on studies of high quality.

Class Discussion Questions

1. When you review the family characteristics and perpetrator characteristics from the NIS-4 presented as risk factors for child maltreatment in this chapter, which of them strike you as more important?
2. Of the 39 risk factors that Stith et al. (2009) identified in the child maltreatment literature, many were found in studies of physical abuse of children. Which of these variables would you want to examine if you were designing a study of children who have been emotionally abused?
3. Various theories are presented in this chapter to try and explain why child abuse occurs. Which theory or combination of theories do you think offer the best and most credible explanation?

4. Choosing one of the theories from this chapter, discuss a macro intervention that you would design to minimize or prevent child maltreatment in society.
5. Most of us have friends who have survived less than optimal childhoods. What traits or qualities do you see in these friends that might have given them a certain resilience?
6. Reflect for a moment and examine your biases about who you think is most likely to emotionally abuse a child. When might your biases cause you to miss clues in families that you didn't think would be abusive?
7. What dysfunctional disciplinary styles have you observed or know about?
8. What possible indications of emotional abuse do you see in Figure 2.1? Which of the APSAC types of emotional abuse does the figure best represent?
9. As you look over the case examples in this chapter, what are the key indicators that suggest emotional abuse? What concerns you most in each of the examples?

3

THE EFFECTS OF EMOTIONAL ABUSE

There's a phrase, "the elephant in the living room", which purports to describe what it's like to live with a drug addict, an alcoholic, an abuser. People outside such relationships will sometimes ask, "How could you let such a business go on for so many years? Didn't you see the elephant in the living room?" And it's so hard for anyone living in a more normal situation to understand the answer that comes closest to the truth; "I'm sorry, but it was there when I moved in. I didn't know it was an elephant; I thought it was part of the furniture." There comes an aha-moment for some folks—the lucky ones—when they suddenly recognize the difference.

Stephen King

Overview: Why do we need to be concerned about emotional abuse? How harmful is emotional abuse to children? Do negative effects continue into adulthood? This chapter will provide answers to these questions.

As the opening quote at the top of the chapter suggests, for some individuals their mistreatment is so much a routine of daily life that it came to be regarded not as exceptional cruel acts but as a part of normal life.

For these individuals, episodes of maltreatment may not have been viewed as all that bad or harmful because "that's just the way Dad was" or "Mom was just too stressed out" or "my older sister Carol just kept us all constantly reeling from the chaos she created in our home." The point is, surveys that ask adults about the amount of mistreatment they received as children are usually viewed from their perspective of what constitutes "normality." Being told to "Shut up, Stupid" might not register on the individual's radar screen as emotional abuse because "that's what Dad called all of us kids."

Studies of Adverse Childhood Experiences (ACE)

Our knowledge about the effects of maltreatment on children is informed by a number of studies that have used a common data collection instrument and a very large sample as part of the Adverse Childhood Experiences (ACE) Study which began in the late 1990s with adult members of the Kaiser Permanente Medical Care Program in California. Adults were offered a free comprehensive medical exam that included standardized health appraisal questionnaires that also probed 10 ACE categories (emotional, physical abuse, and sexual abuse, emotional and physical neglect, witnessing of domestic violence against mother or stepmother, residence with someone who used drugs or who had mental illness, separation or divorce of parents, and residence with a household member who had been incarcerated; see Box 3.1). See the phrasing of the questions that captured information about these ACE categories in Strine et al. (2012, p. 410).

BOX 3.1

Adverse Childhood Experiences (ACE)

Emotional abuse	Physical abuse
Sexual abuse	Emotional neglect
Physical neglect	Witnessing of domestic violence
Living with someone who used drugs	Household member had mental illness
Parental separation or divorce	Incarcerated household member

As you read further in this chapter, you will discover a number of different studies that have made important findings and connections about emotional abuse, emotional neglect, and so forth using the ACE instrumentation and data. One summary of this body of research (McLaughlin, Green, Grukber, Sampson, Zaslavksky, & Kessler, 2012) states: "Childhood adversities (CAs) are among the most consistently documented risk factors for psychiatric disorders. Research has shown that several different CAs, including parental death, abuse, neglect, and family violence, are strongly related to mental disorders" (p. 1151).

While these childhood adversities may occur singly, they often co-exist. Indeed, in a large survey of thousands of American adults, parental substance abuse, criminality, domestic violence, and abuse and neglect were shown to cluster together in a factor that was labeled maladaptive family functioning (Green et al., 2010). The authors found that when one type of childhood adversity was experienced, it was also common for other adversities to occur so that the average number of adversities in their sample of respondents, when there was at least one, was three. Further, the childhood adversities were able to statistically predict 41% of disruptive behavior disorders, 32% of anxiety disorders, 26% of mood disorders, and 21% of substance use disorders among the respondents—explaining 45% of childhood-onset disorders, and 32% of adolescent disorders.

The research is abundantly clear—children and adolescents who are mistreated are severely affected. While some children may be resilient enough to spring back and show little evidence of being harmed, there is strong scientific evidence that child abuse has lasting consequences and can result in suicide attempts, drug use, mental disorder, and a range of other problems that you may have never considered.

Mental Disorder/Mental Health

There are many possible ways that child maltreatment can affect the child, the adolescent, and later even the individual in adulthood. Experts in child and adolescent psychiatry at the University of Massachusetts Medical School and the University of Connecticut School of medicine have written:

> The consequences of exposure to interpersonal trauma vary from individual to individual and also, over time for the same individual. Many traumatized children do not develop PTSD or any other disorder. Nevertheless, individuals who experience interpersonal trauma in childhood are at increased risk for numerous psychiatric disorders, including attachment disorders, PTSD, depression, and anxiety disorders, oppositional and conduct disorders, eating disorders substance abuse, a dissociative variant of PTSD, and personality disorders. Traumatized children also are at risk for self-harm, sexualized behavior, anger, poor impulse control, and attention difficulties. Revictimization is common in maltreated children and adolescents, is associated with increased risk for PTSD and other comorbidities, such as depressive and substance use disorders.
>
> (Dvir, Ford, Hill, & Frazier, 2014, p. 151)

A great deal of the research on the effects of child maltreatment has focused on types of abuse that might be easily labeled traumatic—such as sexual abuse and the easily identifiable (such as physical abuse). However, emotional abuse often occurs with other types of maltreatment. Some might argue that emotional abuse is not a "trauma" in the strictest sense of the word because the term generally implies a single terrible event like a rape or seeing someone killed right in front of you. However, children can be traumatized by seeing their mothers slapped or punched and cursed, when one's favorite brother or sister is kicked out of the house late at night after an argument, when the father turns the supper table upside down in a fit of rage and everyone goes to bed hungry, or when the family pet is kicked in the ribs and hurt—simply for being in the house. Dysfunctional homes regularly generate conditions that over time traumatize children by their lack of sensitivity to the personhood of those in the family. The cruelty experienced may never be displayed outside the home and may reside just below the horizon of what is considered child maltreatment.

Wright et al. (2009) referenced Feiring (2005) on the emotional maltreatment of children and observed, "Emotionally abusive or neglectful parental treatment conveys the message that the child's core self is a disappointment because he or she has not lived up to expectations, or is simply not worthy of love and attention" (p. 65). When we think about the damage done when a child does not think he/she is worthy of love, shouldn't that be considered a trauma?

Let's further delve into the effects of emotional abuse by examining a systematic literature review and meta-analysis by Norman, Byambaa, De, Butchart, Scott, and Vos (2012). You'll remember that a systematic literature review is a comprehensive attempt to learn about a specific problem or intervention with a rigorous search for relevant studies. A systematic literature review identifies the specific search methodology so that it can be reproduced by others (one of the expectations of good science) and includes standards that might exclude, for instance, weaker and less scientific studies. Often the purpose of the systematic review is to summarize what we know on a particular topic and to identify the strengths and weaknesses of the literature available. A meta-analysis is like a systematic review except that the purpose is to identify studies and then to determine, mathematically, how groups are different or which programs can be shown to be more successful (to have a larger effect) than no treatment or treatment with another program.

Using a broad search strategy (for example, searching for articles with "psychological abuse," "emotional abuse," "child abuse," "child maltreatment," and "risk" and "harm," etc.), Norman et al. (2012) located 124 studies meeting their inclusion criteria. These articles showed a relationship between non-sexual child maltreatment and health outcomes. Here is a quick summary of the findings from the Norman et al. (2012) meta-analysis regarding the category they called mental disorder:

- Emotionally abused and neglected individuals had a greater risk of developing depressive disorders than nonabused individuals.
- There was also a *dose–response* relationship—meaning that more emotional abuse made the health outcome of depression more likely.
- Emotional abuse also was associated with a significantly increased risk of anxiety disorders.
- Emotionally abused individuals were 2.5 times more likely to develop eating disorders than nonabused individuals and more

likely to have problem drinking behaviors (1.27 times more likely) and drug use behaviors (1.4 times more likely).
- Finally, individuals who had experienced emotional abuse were more than three times more likely to attempt suicide.

One study of early trauma and suicidal behavior reviewed by Jeon et al. (2009) involved all of the medical students in South Korea. Over 14,000 of these students answered questionnaires that asked whether they had been physically, emotionally, or sexually abused and whether they had seriously thought about committing suicide, made a suicide plan, or attempted suicide. Of those who had reported any of these suicidal behaviors, 46% of them had an early history of emotional abuse. This prevalence of suicidal behavior was greater than the group who reported physical abuse (28%), sexual abuse (36%), or other childhood traumas such as the death of a parent (32%). The authors of the study, Jeon et al. (2009), reported that emotional abuse was more strongly associated with suicidal behavior than factors such as poor physical health, poor economic status, being female, or heavy stress. Medical students with early emotional abuse were 4.1 times more likely to attempt suicide than students without that kind of maltreatment. Breaking down the items that went into the measurement of emotional abuse, the authors found that being treated with a continuously cold or uncaring parental attitude had a stronger association with suicidal behavior than having parents who didn't understand the individual's needs, who ignored, or who often put down or ridiculed the child.

Karen Ritchie and colleagues (2009) investigated the effect of childhood abuse on persons late in life (over the age of 65) in France. All of the participants were examined by a neurologist and a nurse or psychologist. In this population of persons with an average age of 72, exposure to physical, sexual, or verbal abuse (any one) contributed to these individuals being 2.28 times more likely to experience late-life depression. Those experiencing verbal abuse from parents were 2.9 times more likely to have late-life depression, while those with humiliation, harassment, or mental cruelty in their backgrounds were 4.3 times more likely to be depressed. Once again, the emotional abuse in childhood seemed more impactful than physical and/or sexual abuse. Emotional abuse put the

French elders at a 2.67 greater risk for late-life depression. Having maternal or paternal affection and/or availability of an adult friend seemed to decrease overall risk. The authors stated: "We conclude from this study that certain types of early childhood trauma continue to constitute risk factors for depression in old age, their effect outweighing more recent life events and other proximal causes of depression" (p. 1287).

Unlike most of the studies in this chapter, researcher Richard Liu and colleagues (2009) identified 165 college freshmen who scored in the most positive or most negative quartiles on both the Cognitive Style Questionnaire and the Dysfunctional Attitudes Scale and who had no psychiatric diagnosis. These two groups constituted individuals who were either at low or high cognitive risk for depression. The researchers then collected data from these college students every six weeks (the students were paid for their time) for 2.5 years. The findings of this prospective study revealed that prior emotional maltreatment predicted a shorter amount of time to development of a major depression, minor depression, or hopeless depression. Emotional maltreatment by peers and authority figures was also found to be associated with a shorter time to onset of new hopelessness depression episodes.

Two features that give strong credibility to research showing the harmful effects of emotional abuse and dysfunctional families are:

1. the findings are not based just on Americans, but can be found in many different nations; and
2. the large sample sizes associated with the studies.

In a unique study of over 7,000 pairs of mothers and their children, Australian researcher Ryan Mills and colleagues (2013) were able to follow individuals in their study even 14 years later and to link child protection agency data with scores on an instrument, the Youth Self-Report, that assessed for internalizing and externalizing behaviors. The authors found that both neglect and emotional abuse were associated with externalizing and internalizing behaviors even after adjustment for *socio-demographic* variables such as gender, age at completion of the Youth Self-Report, race, mother's age, marital status, family income, and maternal education. A strength of this study was that it was not affected by recall bias where individuals may forget important details or even key events. Recall bias was not present because data from the child protection agency established the maltreatment—the 14-year-old research subjects were not asked to recall and self-report on such events. The authors concluded that "emotional abuse and neglect appear to be more consistently correlated with adverse psychological outcomes in adolescence than sexual abuse" (p. 300).

In a study of over 2,700 men and women in South Africa between the ages of 15 and 26, the researchers reported that women who experienced emotional neglect "often" were five times more likely to have suicidal thoughts than those who did not have emotional neglect in their lives. These same women were 1.82 times more likely to be depressed and 1.82 times more likely to abuse alcohol. Men in the study who reported "often" emotional neglect were 3.4 times more likely to be depressed, and almost two times more likely to be abusing drugs. Those who were emotionally abused were 1.48 times more likely to be abusing alcohol (Jewkes, Dunkle, Nduna, Jama, & Puren, 2010).

A study of over 7,000 residents of the Netherlands revealed similar patterns as previously discussed. That is, individuals with psychological abuse in their backgrounds were 2.8 times more likely to have *suicide ideation* than those without psychological abuse. Individuals who experienced emotional neglect were 3.78 times more likely to report suicide ideation even after controlling for socio-demographic factors like age, gender, marital status, education, work status, and urbanicity. Similarly, adults who experienced psychological abuse were four times more likely to attempt suicide and those with emotional neglect in their backgrounds were 3.6 times more likely to attempt suicide than persons who didn't experience emotional neglect. This study also showed with a large, nationally representative sample that the total number of adversities experienced by a child are also important. For instance, individuals who reported five or more adversities were almost 10 times more likely to attempt suicide (Enns, Cox, Afifi, De Graaf, Ten Have, & Sareen, 2006).

A separate study conducted in the Netherlands of persons with depression (Major Depressive Disorder, Dysthymia) and anxiety (Panic

Disorder, Agoraphobia, Social Phobia, or Generalized Anxiety Disorder) found that persons with "regular" emotional neglect in their background were two times more likely to have depressive and anxiety disorders two years after the initial assessment of childhood life events and childhood trauma. Interestingly, adverse life events like parental death, divorce, or other forms of parent loss were not associated with chronicity of panic and anxiety disorders. The authors concluded that "the quality of the childhood holding environment is more important than life events per se" (Hovens et al., 2012, p. 206).

Back in the United States, Thompson et al. (2012) conducted an innovative study that identified children in five different geographic regions of the country who were at risk of maltreatment or who had been maltreated by the time they were four to six years old. Then every two years interviews were conducted with the children and their primary caregivers as well as an ongoing review of CPS records. By age 16, 740 youth had supplied information on suicidal ideation. Those individuals who experienced psychological abuse were 3.66 times more likely to have suicidal ideation compared to those with no psychological abuse and those with physical abuse were 2.6 times more likely to have suicidal ideation after controlling for other risk factors.

It is not unusual for those who were emotionally abused in childhood to not see the connection between earlier life experiences and adult health symptoms. Spertus, Yehuda, Wong, Halligan, and Seremetis (2003) studied 203 female patients between the ages of 19 and 82 who made appointments at a women's primary care practice in New York City. Fifty-one percent requested a regular or gynecological checkup and the rest had general complaints such as allergies, follow-up appointments, infections, and behavioral problems (diet, eating, anxiety, etc.) The vast majority (83%) had never received treatment for a psychiatric problem. The sample was described as "comprised primarily of highly educated persons in an urban professional community" (p. 1256).

However, using such instruments as the Childhood Trauma Questionnaire (CTQ), the Trauma History Questionnaire (THQ), the Symptom Checklist-90R, and the Revised Civilian Mississippi Scale for PTSD

(PTS), the researchers found that 42% of the women reported childhood emotional abuse and 43% reported emotional neglect. More interestingly, emotional abuse and emotional neglect in their childhood predicted trauma episodes in their lives (e.g., the summed number of such events as muggings, sexual assaults, physical assaults, accidents, witnessing someone injured or killed, etc.). Further, childhood emotional abuse and neglect were significant predictors of anxiety, somatization, depression, and PTSD symptoms even when their physical abuse, sexual abuse, and trauma scores had been accounted for. Emotional abuse and neglect were also significant predictors of the number of visits to the doctor over the past year. Unlike some studies which have been conducted with low-income populations, this study derived its data from "a non-clinical, high functioning sample" (p. 1256). The authors concluded, "These findings demonstrate that it is not only the more severe and overt forms of abuse that have implications for adult health" (p. 1256).

Consistent dose–response relationships with repeated, frequent, or severe abuse have been reported for mental disorders and emotional abuse in two different studies. The Norman et al. (2012) study stated:

> there is evidence to suggest that experiencing multiple types of maltreatment may carry more severe consequences, with those exposed to multiple types of abuse at increased odds of developing mental disorders… and the risk increases with the magnitude of multiple abuse.
>
> (p. 22)

The findings reported above have "persisted across different study designs, samples, and geographic regions investigated" (p. 22) and are based on multiple studies. Further, there are numerous other research efforts that have investigated health outcomes with specific populations that aren't reflected in the Norman et al. (2012) study.

In the next section, we will continue to examine published studies presenting relevant research on how emotional abuse and child maltreatment has been shown to affect individuals. If you want to know more than the brief summary provides, you may wish to see if you can access the particular journal articles from your university library.

Substance Use/Alcohol Dependence

Strine et al. (2012) found that adults who reported any ACE had more self-reported alcohol problems than those without ACE. The psychological distress caused by ACE were associated with increased risk of self-reported alcohol problems. Children growing up in a home with an alcoholic parent or parents are hit with doubly bad luck. Not only do they experience the stresses of living with individuals who can be insensible, unresponsive, or easily provoked, angered, and outrageous, and certainly unpredictable at times, there is also a genetic component to alcohol dependence—estimated to be about 50% (Goldman, Oroszi, & Ducci, 2005). This suggests that many of them will inherit a tendency to be at risk for heavy use of alcohol.

Existing studies suggest that adverse childhood experiences contribute to the risk of alcohol dependence (Schwandt et al., 2013). It is difficult to explain how/why some individuals seem to be more affected by the risk factors of *heritability* toward alcoholism and living in a home influenced by alcohol (and/or other substances) than others. As has been mentioned earlier, human behavior is complex and other factors interplay even with these two dominant ones. For instance, the effect of heritability toward alcoholism and living in a home influenced by alcohol (and/or other substances) could be reduced by having other caring, supportive individuals in the child's life. While genetic inheritance can seem to stack the deck against one (and note that the heritability for cocaine may be as high as 70%, Goldman et al., 2005), they do not absolutely determine behavior—human choice is still involved. There is zero risk of becoming cocaine dependent if one never tries the drug experimentally or recreationally.

Ystrom, Kendler, and Reichborn-Kjennerud (2014) have noted in their own study of Norwegian twins that the heritability for alcohol use disorders (AUD) is 62% and for early age of alcohol initiation (AAI) it was 37%. Surprisingly, environmental factors for early age of alcohol initiation were "trivial risk factors for AUD" (p. 1830). The heritability findings were consistent with other researchers who have reported the heritability of AUD between 50 and 60%. While early age of alcohol initiation (AAI) is a "strong risk factor of genetic liability to AUD" the authors concluded that "interventions only targeting adolescent environmental factors impacting upon AAI will probably not succeed in preventing the development of AUD" (p. 1830).

Timko, Sutkowi, Pavao, and Kimerling (2008), in a sample of almost 7,000 California women who were assessed for symptoms of PTSD and child and adult aversive experiences, found that even after considering adulthood factors, living with someone in childhood who abused substances or who had mental illness was associated with binge drinking. Those individuals who were emotionally abused by an adult in the childhood home were 1.5 times more likely to be a binge drinker than those not emotionally abused.

Drawing again on the sample of adults enrolled in the Kaiser Permanente health plan who answered questions about adverse childhood experiences, Dube, Felitti, Dong, Chapman, Giles, and Anda (2003) discovered that for every ACE, there was a greater likelihood of initiation of illicit drug use during the early years of adolescence, in mid-adolescence, and adulthood. Further, with a greater number of aversive experiences was an increase in "the likelihood of ever having drug problems, ever being addicted to drugs, and *parenteral drug use* in a dose-response manner" (p. 567).

The authors go on to say that "approximately two-thirds (64%) of the parenteral drug use is attributable to the types of abusive or traumatic childhood experiences" (p. 568). They explain drug use due to the cumulative effect of multiple ACEs this way:

> Children and adolescents, who are exposed to the types of childhood experiences that we examined, may have feelings of helplessness, chaos, and impermanence and may have problems self-regulating affective states. Thus, illicit drug use may serve as an avenue to escape or dissociate from the immediate emotional pain, anxiety, and anger that likely accompany such experiences.
>
> (p. 568)

Participants in the study who were emotionally abused or emotionally neglected were 2.4 times more likely to initiate illicit drug use by age 14 than adults who did not experience emotional abuse or emotional neglect in their childhoods.

More recently, a Schwandt et al. (2013) study involved 280 individuals seeking help from a 28-day inpatient treatment program and a comparison sample of 137 men and women with no past or current alcohol disorders. The researchers found that the sample of those seeking treatment for an alcohol disorder were 11.5 times more likely to have indicated they experienced emotional abuse as a child than the adults without an alcohol disorder and five times more likely to have been emotionally neglected (both traumas revealed from their completion of the CTQ). The treatment-seeking individuals as a group also experienced more than one trauma type *and* more of each type of trauma (Emotional, Sexual, and Physical Abuse, Emotional Neglect, and Physical Neglect) than the comparison group. The researchers found that emotional abuse was a key predictor of severity of the Alcohol Disorder even when other forms of abuse and neglect were controlled statistically. In this study, 70% of those who experienced sexual abuse also experienced emotional abuse. The authors concluded that "exposure to emotional abuse correlated with neuroticism, which in turn correlated with greater severity of AD. This 'negative affect' pathway is likely to involve mood-related drinking motives, that is, drinking to cope with negative mood" (p. 991).

A 2012 study of outpatients 16–24 years of age in a treatment program for substance use concerns found that emotional abuse and emotional neglect significantly predicted severity of substance use problems while physical and sexual abuse were not significant (Rosenkranz, Muller, & Henderson, 2012).

A final study that we will be reviewing in this section (and please remember that we only have the space in this book to cover a tiny selection of all the possible studies in the literature) involved 41,482 Marine recruits under the age of 21. Young, Hansen, Gibson, and Ryan (2006) reported the strongest association with risky drinking behavior was early age at first alcohol use. Those who started at 13 years or younger were 5.5 times more likely to be a risky drinker. They also found an increased risk of problem drinking behavior when the recruit grew up with a problem drinker or someone with mental illness. Childhood emotional abuse and sexual abuse were independently associated with risky drinking behavior.

Physical Health Impact

In the developing country of the Philippines, a group of researchers have examined the impact of adverse childhood experiences on a wide range of health-risk behaviors. In a community sample of persons living in Metro Manila, they found that individuals reporting psychological abuse were 2.1 times more likely to use illicit drugs, to have had more than three intimate partners, and 2.2 times more likely to have had an unintended pregnancy. Those who reported psychological neglect were 1.6 times more likely to have used illicit drugs, and two times more likely to have had multiple intimate partners. However, perhaps the most dramatic effects were seen with children who grew up with a depressed or mentally ill person in the household. These individuals were 5.1 times more likely to use illicit drugs, 3.8 times more likely to begin early sex (age 16 or earlier), 3.8 times more likely to have a pregnancy by age 18, and 11.9 times more likely to attempt suicide. Of those physically abused, 93% also experienced emotional or psychological abuse (Ramiro, Madrid, & Brown, 2010).

Somewhat along this line, Jewkes et al. (2010) conducted a study in villages and townships located in South Africa. Participants between the ages of 15 and 26 were part of a larger study to evaluate an HIV prevention intervention. Jewkes et al. (2010) have written that women who reported receiving emotional abuse "often" were 1.96 times more likely to be at risk for an HIV infection than women who experienced no emotional abuse. Men in the study who responded "often" to being emotionally abused were 1.48 times more likely to have alcohol abuse in their past and 1.98 times more at risk for abusing drugs if they replied "often" to emotional neglect. Emotional neglect "often" was also associated with the women being at greater risk for alcohol abuse (1.82 times) and suicidal ideation (five times more likely when compared to women with no emotional neglect).

Obesity

The Norman et al. (2012) meta-analysis found that emotionally abused children are at a slightly greater risk for obesity (1.24 times more likely to develop it) than nonabused individuals. More recently, a group of

Swedish researchers, Hemmingsson, Johansson, and Reynisdottir (2014), conducted a meta-analysis of all the research they could find on "childhood abuse," "childhood adversity," "childhood trauma," and "childhood neglect" that also dealt with "obesity," "overweight," or "weight gain." From 391 possible studies, they eliminated 368 that didn't meet their inclusion criteria and ended up with a sample of 23. The basic finding emerging from that set of studies was that adults who were exposed to childhood abuse were significantly more likely to develop obesity than adults who reported no abuse. In terms of the overall statistical *odds ratio*, abused individuals were 1.34 times more likely to be obese as adults.

The authors also calculated the odds ratio for obesity associated with various types of abuse (physical, emotional, sexual, and general). For only the studies where emotional abuse was specifically measured, the finding still holds and emotionally abused individuals were 1.36 times more likely to be obese. In terms of the dose–response effect, severely abused individuals were 1.50 times more likely to be obese when compared to those reporting light/moderate abuse. How reliable are these findings? The meta-analysis involved over 112,000 research participants from seven different countries and the association between abuse and obesity was similar across age groups and gender. The authors concluded that the association between childhood abuse and adult obesity was "robust"—which indicates that the researchers view this finding as strong and established, not very likely to be a fluke or to have happened by chance or sloppy investigation.

Eating Disorders

Canadian researchers (Groleau et al., 2012) interviewed women in a specialized Eating Disorders Program in Montreal and found that 81% of the women with bulimia-spectrum disorders (BSDs) reported childhood emotional abuse. The authors suggested that "experiences of childhood emotional maltreatment significantly impact a person's self-esteem, to the point that such an individual might be drawn to engage in eating-disordered behaviors to compensate for feelings of inadequacy" (p. 330).

The percentage of emotional abuse victims among those with eating disorders was similar to a study reporting that 76% of women struggling with bulimia nervosa (or recovered from it for at least one year) also reported psychological abuse. That American study, published 18 years earlier, decided that suffering from multiple forms of abuse had an addictive effect (Rorty, Yager, & Rossotto, 1994). Another study found 71% of those in an overweight/obese *control group*, 79% of those in a night-eating syndrome group, and 82% of those with binge eating disorder had high rates of childhood emotional abuse, physical neglect, and other forms of childhood maltreatment (Allison, Grilo, Masheb, & Stunkard, 2007).

Cancer Risk and Other Diseases

A number of years ago researchers began documenting a possible link between adults who developed cancer and other leading causes of death due to ACEs. Felitti et al. (1998), as part of the early ACE study previously mentioned, drew upon the 13,494 Kaiser Health Plan members who completed medical evaluations and standardized questionnaires that captured information about exposure to psychological, physical, and sexual abuse, and household dysfunction (e.g., substance abuse, mental illness, mother treated violently, criminal behavior). They found a clear and statistically significant dose–response relationship between the number of adverse childhood exposures and *ischemic heart disease*, cancer, chronic bronchitis/emphysema, hepatitis/jaundice, skeletal fractures, and poor self-rated health. Note, however, that "The clear majority of patients in our study who were exposed to one category of childhood abuse or household dysfunction were also exposed to at least one other" (p. 251). For those who were psychologically abused, 52% were also victims of physical abuse.

Exposure to a higher number of adverse childhood experiences made it more likely that these individuals would begin smoking by the age of 14, become chronic smokers as adults, and then be at risk many years later for the diseases of chronic bronchitis/emphysema, cardiovascular disease, and cancer of the lung.

The authors found a strong dose–response relationship between a higher number of childhood exposures and a greater risk for a serious disease that could lead to their death.

The study also found that individuals with a higher exposure of childhood adverse events had much greater odds for having a whole range of other problems—many of which have already been discussed previously. See Table 3.1 presenting the odds (risks) for acquiring health problems targeted in their study (e.g., obesity, alcoholism, drug abuse, depression, suicide attempts, having sex with 50 or more partners, acquiring a sexually transmitted disease and others).

Table 3.1 Problems and diseases linked to Adverse Childhood Experiences (Felitti et al., 1998)

Problem/disease	Odds ratio for those with four or more ACE*
Ever attempted suicide	12 times more likely than individuals reporting 0 ACE
Ever injected drugs	10.3 times more likely than individuals reporting 0 ACE
Considers self to be an alcoholic	7.4 times more likely than individuals reporting 0 ACE
Two or more weeks of depressed mood in the past year	4.6 times more likely than individuals reporting 0 ACE
Chronic bronchitis or emphysema	3.9 times more likely than individuals reporting 0 ACE
Had 50 or more sex partners	3.2 times more likely than individuals reporting 0 ACE
Ever had a sexually transmitted disease	2.5 times more likely than individuals reporting 0 ACE
Current smoker	2.2 times more likely than individuals reporting 0 ACE
Ischemic heart disease	2.2 times more likely than individuals reporting 0 ACE
Any cancer	1.9 times more likely than individuals reporting 0 ACE
Severe obesity	1.6 times more likely than individuals reporting 0 ACE

Note
* Odds ratios adjusted for age, gender, race, and educational attainment.

The authors state that the "linking mechanisms" are behaviors such as smoking, alcohol/drug use, overeating, and/or sexual behaviors that provide psychological or pharmacological benefit for coping with and regulating anxiety, anger, and/or depression (Felitti et al., 1998).

While it might seem easy to dismiss a study that was conducted in 1998, it was a very rigorous study that has been cited by other researchers and authors (as of this writing) over 1,600 times—which is an incredible record. Additionally, there are still other studies connecting child maltreatment to such diseases as cancer. For instance, Kelly-Irving et al. (2013) examined a cohort of persons born in Great Britain who self-reported on cancer and ACE in their lives. The large sample of 6,138 persons were between 33 and 50 years of age. The authors found that:

> psychosocial adversity in childhood was related to cancer incidence before 50 years among women, after adjusting for prior confounding factors and potential mediators, in a large prospective cohort. An accumulation of ACE remained a strong predictor of cancer in women, after taking important mediating factors at age 23 into account, including smoking and drinking. Women who experienced two or more ACE doubled their risk of having a cancer before 50 relative to women who had had no childhood adversities.
>
> (p. 7)

The authors explain that the lack of discovery of this association in men is likely due to the much lower incidence of cancer in men up to age 50. Men tend to develop lung and prostate cancer after age 50.

Other more recent studies have also investigated the link between childhood adversity and cancer. Morton, Mustillo, and Ferraro (2014) also found that additive childhood adversities could predict cancer—but for men, not women. For men who were physically abused by their fathers, the risk for obtaining adult cancer was 2.5 times greater as compared to men who were not physically abused by their fathers.

For women, physical abuse by the mother was the only type of ACE that predicted cancer occurrence in adults (2.2 times more likely). Their data showed that for men reporting frequent emotional and physical abuse by either parent, the risk of cancer was 3.2 times greater than for those individuals who reported no childhood abuse. For men who reported one type of parent abuse "rarely," the odds were still greater (2.384) than expected for those who reported no abuse. For women, age and experiencing frequent emotional and physical abuse were associated with increased cancer risk even when the data were adjusted for demographic, lifestyle, and psychosocial factors.

Ischemic Heart Disease

A study by Dong et al. (2004) also supported part of the Felitti et al. (1998) study presented earlier by examining ACE and ischemic heart disease (IHD)—a life-threatening problem when too little blood gets to the heart. This study, once again based on the large sample (n = 17,337) of adults having medical examinations at Kaiser Permanente's Health Appraisal Center in San Diego, California, found that persons with seven or more ACEs were three times more likely to report having IHD. Individuals who recognized that they had been emotionally abused as a child were 1.7 times more likely to have indicated that they "have been told they were having a heart attack (coronary)," "got pain or heavy pressure in their chest from exertion," or "use nitroglycerine." The authors discovered that for every increase in the ACE score, the likelihood of reporting IHD increased by 20%. This relationship between ACE scores and risk of IHD was somewhat reduced but remained significant even after controlling for psychological and traditional risk factors such as depressed affect, anger, diabetes, hypertension, being a smoker, being obese, and physically inactive.

Also supporting a portion of the Felitti et al. (1998) study is one by Morton et al. (2014) of over 3,000 U.S. adults contacted initially by random digit-dialing. The authors found a higher risk of acute myocardial infarction (heart attack) among respondents with higher levels of "childhood misfortune" (p. 139).

Educational Achievement

Perez and Widom (1994) have noted that "evidence for the long-term consequences of childhood victimization on measured intellectual functioning and academic outcomes is fairly sparse.... In the earliest work, intellectual and neuromotor handicaps of abused children were documented (Martin, Beezley, Conway, & Kempe, 1974)" (p. 617).

The authors go on to review the literature and say:

> Most of the studies of physically abused and neglected children report significant differences in IQ scores between maltreatment and control groups.... Other studies have reported on *reading ability* ... and academic outcomes.... The majority of these studies found significant differences between abused and neglected children and controls across a variety of age groups.
> (Perez & Widom, 1994, p. 618)

In their own study, Perez and Widom (1994) identified a large group of children 11 years old or younger who had been substantiated as cases of childhood physical and sexual abuse and/or neglect and then followed them, interviewing them 20 years later. A control group of similar children was also created who were matched on age, sex, race, and social class. Using a Quick Test IQ measure, it was learned that abused and neglected adults had significantly lower IQ scores than their comparison group (with no abuse or neglect). And similarly, their reading scores as measured by the Wide Range Achievement Test-Revised (WRAT-R Level II) were significantly lower and comparable to a sixth grade reading level. Further, these abused and neglected individuals actually completed fewer years of school than the control group. Fifty-eight percent of the abused and neglected individuals did not complete high school compared to 34% of those in the comparison group. Because of the statistical analysis performed, the authors were comfortable in saying that:

> decreased intellectual functioning observed in the abused and/or neglected subjects in young adulthood remained significant despite controls for economic status and other variables. Thus, it is unlikely that the differences between groups are primarily a function of economic disadvantages suffered by abused and/or neglected children.
> (p. 624)

Another group of researchers (Porche, Fortuna, Lin, & Alegria, 2011) investigated the relationship between high school dropouts and abused or neglected children using three large nationally representative household surveys developed under the sponsorship of the National Institute of Mental Health. While the researchers did not isolate or separate emotional abuse from other abusive events, they did ask 2,532 young adults who were 21 to 29 years of age if they: "*ever witnessed serious physical fights at home, like when your father beat up your mother,*" if they "*were ever badly beaten up by your parents or the people who raised you,*" or if they "*were ever sexually assaulted or raped.*" While 13% of the respondents without any trauma before the age of 16 had dropped out of school, almost one-third of those who had experienced child physical abuse (31%) had dropped out and 26% of those who had witnessed domestic violence.

In a study drawing from Minnesota's Department of Human Services Social Service Information System, youth who were involved in an accepted child protection investigation or assessment case were divided into three groups: those with out-of-home placement (OHP), those with child protection remaining in their homes (CP), and those in the general population (GP) attending public school who did not have a history of CPS involvement. These students in grades K-12 were compared on the state's achievement tests in reading and math (the Minnesota Comprehensive Assessment II tests). Approximately 396,000 students contributed scores to the GP math database and 411,000 to the reading database. Over 6,000 students in the CP group completed the math and reading tests and approximately 2,000 students in the OHP group completed the required tests.

The authors (Piescher, Colburn, LaLiberte, & Hong, 2014) have reported that the highest proficiency scores in math and reading were obtained by the GP group (67% and 73% respectively), followed by the CP group (41% and 48%), and the lowest scoring group, OHP, was only 34% proficient in math and 43% in reading. In other words, less than half of the students involved with CPS were proficient in math or reading and their scores decreased as the extent of involvement with CPS increased.

However, there were also differences when comparisons were made to students who were eligible for and ineligible for free or reduced school lunches. That is, students who were eligible for free/reduced school lunches had lower rates of proficiency in every group when compared to students ineligible for free/reduced lunches. The authors conducted further statistical analyses and concluded:

> Even after controlling for socioeconomic status and race, the academic achievement of youth in CPS was significantly lower than for youth in the general population who had not experienced CPS involvement. Therefore, we can argue that independent risk factors associated with involvement in CPS create a unique and significant achievement gap. This finding is consistent with other maltreatment and OHP studies that found evidence of an achievement gap after controlling for socioeconomic status and race.
>
> (p. 413)

Just to make sure this point is understood, the study does not suggest that involvement with child protection authorities is responsible for children and teens performing poorly on standardized tests. Rather, it is the students' own families, their living situations, neighborhoods, and possibly, to some extent, their schools which may not have the resources to target and give low achieving students more help.

Understanding these findings requires that we not immediately believe that maltreated children perform poorly in school simply because they have been mistreated. Other conditions contribute, too. As Aikens and Barbarin (2008) point out, we must consider their families, their environments, and the resources available to them. First, there is *the home literacy environment* which can be described as how often a parent jointly reads with the child, how often children read books outside of school, how often household members visit the library with the child, and even how many books are owned by the family. There's the variable of *social relationships within the home*, where maternal warmth and positive parent–child interactions occur to a greater or lesser extent. A third variable is the *parents' involvement with the school* which can be shown by attending parent–teacher conferences, parent–teacher association (PTA) meetings, open houses, other school events, and participation in fund-raising or volunteering. And then *schools* differ in terms of teachers' experience and preparation, in the frequency with which they have children participating in literacy-related activities, and they vary in terms of the number of the child's peers reading below grade level. Both number of peers reading below grade level and the number of low-income peers have been associated with children's poor reading outcomes.

Aikens and Barbarin (2008) conclude their study by noting:

> Our analyses also suggest a compounding effect of low quality environments. Children from low-SES homes grow up in home environments poor in literacy experiences. However, their disadvantage does not stop there. These children will often enter schools that have a higher proportion of poor children and those with low reading skills.... Each of these factors is associated with poorer reading outcomes.... Schools may be overwhelmed in trying to serve concentrations of children who require considerable attention and resources.
>
> (p. 249)

Violence

In an early study of men who were receiving treatment from a domestic violence treatment program (each had at least four instances of domestic violence), the researchers discovered that the batterers were more likely than men in the control group to have experienced physical or emotional abuse as a child and were less likely to be married. They also had significantly higher acting-out hostility scores than men who were not batterers (Else, Wonderlich, Beatty, Christie, & Staton, 1993).

Years later, different investigators collected a sample of over 400 youth aged 14 to 17 involved with child protection in a large urban center. Over two-thirds of the females indicated that their parents had said hurtful things to them and over half of the males responded in that way. Responding on the Conflict in Adolescent Data Relationships Inventory (CADRI), 44% of the males indicated that they had perpetrated violence on a date (either verbal violence, physical violence, or had threatened the date) and 49% said that they had been the victim of dating violence. Sixty-seven percent of the females said that they had perpetrated violence and 63% had been victimized. The researchers found that the males' scores on the CTQ emotional abuse factor score significantly predicted violence perpetration on the CADRI. Females' scores on the CTQ physical-emotional abuse factor score significantly predicted victimization on the CADRI. The study authors (Wekerle et al., 2009), note: "Thus, dating can provide an opportunity for maltreated youth to repeat historical relationship experiences, characterized by violence and dynamic roles as victim and/or victimizer, perhaps as a form of re-enactment" (p. 46). And later they explain this a little more fully:

> Social learning theory (SLT, Bandura, 1973, 1977) emphasizes the importance of observational learning in the acquisition of interactional skills. SLT, in the context of childhood maltreatment, suggests that modeling in the maltreatment environment is such that it promotes violence as a means of appropriate communication, rather than the more adaptive verbal and non-hostile forms of communication. Further, aggression as an appropriate interpersonal response (and counter-response) may be directly reinforced by maltreating caregivers, as when the child and parent enter into an escalating aversive pattern or when encouraging siblings to fight to solve their differences or enlisting them as co-abusers.
>
> (p. 47)

In study of 268 college students, Allen (2011) found that childhood psychological abuse significantly predicted participants' self-reported aggression (physical aggression, verbal aggression, and aggressive attitude). Here is his explanation:

> It is possible that the experience of child maltreatment, psychological abuse in particular, teach the child ineffective ways of relating to others. As a result, the child develops poor relationship skills that then increase the likelihood of interpersonal problems as an adult. These problematic relationships most likely result in situations with an increased likelihood of verbal

and/or physical aggression. Similarly, maltreating experiences during childhood may result in the failure to acquire adequate emotion regulation skills that increase the risk that a person will be unable to rid themselves of negative feelings of anger, predisposing them to overt forms of aggression.

(p. 2105)

Adolescent perpetration of violence has also been explored by researchers using information gathered from sixth, ninth, and twelfth grade students in Minnesota. Capturing data on six adverse childhood experiences (physical abuse by household adult, sexual abuse by family member, sexual abuse by non-family, problem alcohol use by family member, problem drug use by family member, and witnessing physical abuse by a family member on another family member), perpetration of violence (delinquency, bullying, physical fighting, dating violence, weapon-carrying on school property), and self-harm behavior (self-mutilation, suicidal ideation, suicide attempt), the researchers found that adverse childhood experiences were associated with increased risk for suicide, self-mutilatory behaviors and bullying, fighting, dating violence and weapon-carrying. In fact, they said that, "When adolescents with 4 or more events were compared with those who reported no adverse-event exposure, the likelihood of female perpetration increased 2- to 7-fold (bullying and suicide attempts, respectively) and male perpetration increased 2.7 to 10 fold" (Duke, Pettingell, McMorris, & Borowsky, 2010, p. e782).

Notice that perpetration of violence was directed at both others and self with both genders. Males who witnessed physical violence among family members were more than seven times more likely to have engaged in dating violence than males who had not witnessed family violence. Also, both males and females who had witnessed family violence were more than three times more likely to have engaged in self-harm, suicidal ideation, and to have made a suicide attempt (3.55 for females, 4.85 for males). Clearly, their dysfunctional home environments had a major effect upon the children.

In one last study, Renner and Slack (2006) contacted over 1,000 women receiving TANF and found that all forms of interpersonal violence including witnessing parental interpersonal violence as a child "increase the risk of this adult outcome by 200 to 300%" (p. 608).

The Double Whammy

Children who grow up in dysfunctional homes do not have an easy time in life—it almost goes without saying. As mentioned earlier, an alcoholic or addicted parent can provide genetic structure that makes the child more vulnerable to alcohol or substance use disorders, and poor parental role models put the child at greater risk for maltreating his or her own child and at a disadvantage in social/intimate relationships. Along with the health and mental health effects and other problems that the child from a dysfunctional home may have as an adult, there are other hardships that may be associated with the family origin.

For instance, there are documented economic consequences:

> In a prospective study of court documented cases of childhood maltreatment and community-matched controls, significantly more of the abuse and neglected individuals were in menial and semi-skilled occupations than were controls (62% vs 45% at 29 years of age), and fewer had remained in employment during the past 5 years (41% vs 58%).
> (Gilbert, Widom, Browne, Fergusson, Webb, & Janson, 2009, p. 74)

Even earlier, in a state-wide survey of adults regarding traumatic experiences within the family while growing up (death of a family member, parents unhappily married, serious or life-threatening illness, family break-up, alcoholism or drug addiction, emotional problems, child abuse or neglect), individuals reporting one or more of the childhood events lived in households with significantly lower family income than those who reported none of the experiences. Further, a significantly greater percentage of those who experienced a childhood trauma did not own their own homes compared to those who experienced none of the traumas.

And when respondents were grouped in terms of those having no traumatic experiences, those having one, and those having two or more types of trauma, the respondents rating their Life Satisfaction the highest were from those who had not experienced any trauma followed by those experiencing any one type of trauma. Those with two or more types of trauma were the least satisfied with their adult lives (Royse, Rompf, & Dhooper, 1991).

Why is childhood emotional abuse/neglect so powerful and such a force in causing unhappiness and even physical illness among its victims? Wright et al. (2009) described the home life where childhood maltreatment occurs as a "pathogenic relational environment." All three words are important to our understanding. The child is born into or at some point is brought into an environment where relationships with primary caregivers are not as nurturing, supporting, and warm as they should be. Instead of a relationship that allows the child to develop self-confidence and a sense of self-worth, interactions with the child are toxic, poisonous—disease-producing.

While traumatic events like physical and sexual abuse tend to be episodic, perhaps occurring only a few times in a child's life, or at least not very frequently, emotional abuse is often an almost daily, chronic event occurring in a venomous household that slowly and consistently grinds away at the child's sense of self and well-being. Changes in the child occur slowly, almost invisibly, as the negative messages and actions subtly communicate that the child is not valued. Sometimes, in the most toxic of these environments, children are made to feel that everything in the family would be better if the child would just die or somehow disappear from the face of the earth. How do you think coming to this conclusion daily over a number of years would affect a child?

Key Chapter Takeaways

This chapter has discussed the possible effects of child maltreatment generally, and emotional abuse more specifically when that information was available. Here are some of the points made:

- The effects of ACE are insidious and stealthy. They may show up years later when the individual is in adulthood.
- Not every child is affected in the same way.
- Maltreatment can be thought of in a dose–response manner. The greater the frequency of abuse, the greater the effect.

- Children who are abused physically or sexually are also very likely to be abused emotionally (including emotional neglect).
- Experiencing multiple types of maltreatment seems to increase the odds for more severe problems.
- Findings on the effects of child maltreatment have been shown with different kinds of problems, different types of research designs, and in many different geographic regions.

Glossary

Control Group: A comparison group that does not receive any special treatment.

Dose–Response Relationship: When more of an event or stimulus produces more of an effect.

Heritability Study: An attempt to estimate the extent to which genetics may create a tendency, vulnerability or liability for a particular characteristic.

HMO: Health Maintenance Organization, a type of self-funded insurance plan where members receive health care benefits from health professionals who work for the organization often in one facility.

Ischemic Heart Disease: Otherwise known as a heart attack; caused when not enough blood gets to the heart and portions of the heart muscle die.

Odds Ratio: A way of reporting the results of a statistical procedure known as logistic regression which attempts to predict how much selected variables contribute toward prediction of a special outcome.

Parenteral Drug Use: Drugs that are injected into a vein (same as intravenous injection).

Socio-Demographic Factors: These are the variables such as age, gender, race, educational level, and usually income level. Researchers try to control these or neutralize them with statistical techniques when there are differences among the research subjects so that comparisons are like apples to apples, not apples to oranges.

Suicide Ideation: Thinking about committing suicide; such as considering when or where one might do it and with what method.

Class Discussion Questions

1. Which type of abuse do you think would be most damaging: a single severe episode that perhaps required hospitalization or almost daily harassment over years? Explain your reasoning.
2. Why do you think that some victims of child emotional abuse develop cancer, while others have heart attacks, and still others struggle with obesity?
3. Of all the harmful effects caused by child maltreatment, which type do you think has the most damaging effect upon the individual? Why?
4. Give an example of a hurtful, emotionally abusive statement that you may have heard as a child directed either to you or to someone else. What would or could you say to that person now if you heard the same statement?
5. How is a child in an emotionally abusive family like a prisoner in a concentration camp?
6. Discuss the dose–response relationship relative to Case Examples 7, 8, 9, and/or 13. Would emotional abuse have been easy to detect early in the child/adolescent's life?
7. Discuss why some individuals who have had emotionally abusive childhoods might, as adults, be more at risk for suicide.

4
ASSESSMENT OF EMOTIONAL ABUSE

My mother told me that I started drinking when I was a year old. My dad took care of me during the day while she worked. He put whiskey in my bottle to keep me quiet. When I was in elementary school, my teacher discovered whiskey mixed with my milk. She took it away, and I went into DTs.
—Heidi from *Silent Voices: People with Mental Disorders on the Street* by Robert Okin (2014, p. 70)

Overview: How do child protection workers determine and document the presence of child abuse/neglect in their investigations? What tools exist to assist them in identifying emotional abuse? This chapter discusses the assessment process and available tools.

Poor Versus Dysfunctional Parenting

It is vitally important that child protection investigators keep several things in mind as they attempt to assess the child, the family, and the family's home environment whenever there is an allegation of child abuse or neglect.

First and foremost, the vast majority of parents have said hurtful things to their children and been emotionally insensitive occasionally—and especially when under stress. Straus and Field (2003) used five items to assess "psychological aggression" toward children ("shouted, yelled, or screamed," "threatened to spank," "swore or cursed," "called name," and "threatened to kick out of the house"). They reported:

> even infants were not immune from being yelled at in anger by parents, and by ages 2–4, almost all parents reported yelling, screaming, or shouting as a method of correcting or controlling the behavior of the child. By the teen years, about half of all parents reported using one or more of the three severe behaviors in the Psychological Aggression scale.
>
> (p. 805)

However, there is a difference between poor parenting which occurs occasionally (and possibly in most families) when an adult yells at a child, insults or hurts the child's feelings, or even threatens a child, and parental behavior that can be identified as emotional abuse.

To take an example, when I was a child, the next-door neighbor's small son would occasionally get into mild trouble and his mother would say something like, "You'd better stop that right now, or I'm going to eat you alive." None of us children were scared by the threat (although it could be pretty scary if interpreted literally) since the mother said it without any anger and usually with a smile on her face. All of us recognized that she was simply trying to set some boundaries on her child's behavior. Even if she had raised her voice and yelled these words at her son on occasion, I'm not sure any of us would have been threatened or considered it abusive since she was warm and fun and we all felt comfortable around her. Sometimes parents are simply at a loss for how to redirect a child's behavior. Parents can respond in anger without thinking how their words or actions might feel to the child.

Wolfe and McIsaac (2011) differentiate poor or dysfunctional parenting from parenting that constitutes emotional maltreatment this way: Emotionally abusive parenting forms a pattern that is "chronic, severe, and escalating" (p. 806). The authors further suggest that in emotionally abusive parenting behavior toward the child is "extreme, appalling, or disturbing" (p. 806). Because emotional abuse is chronic and severe, there is a great likelihood of psychological harm and possible developmental disruptions due to the stress that interferes with the child's ability to establish emotional regulation. Wolfe and McIsaac (2011) have outlined, in Figure 4.1, a continuum of parenting emotional expression and sensitivity from the appropriate and healthy in the left column, to the poor/dysfunctional in the middle column, and the emotionally abusive, neglectful in the right column.

The healthy parenting column can be thought of as child-centered, the middle column as parents who could benefit from instruction and assistance. Such behaviors do not typically trigger a child welfare response. However, parental behaviors in the right column rely upon verbal harassment, are ineffective forms of discipline, and they are harsh and insensitive to the needs of children. Living in households with rejection and lack of love or ambivalent feelings toward meeting the child's needs denies the child a chance to develop normally and would concern and involve child protection authorities.

While Figure 4.1 may provide some assistance in understanding the boundary between abusive and poor parenting techniques, it alone is not sufficient for making the determination of child maltreatment.

The second thing that child abuse investigators must keep in mind is that there is an orderly process which must be followed. One cannot make snap decisions except perhaps in the most flagrant, extreme cases. Most often with emotional abuse, time is needed to gather sufficient information to complete the investigation. At the end of that process, the child protection worker must make a thoughtful and considered determination about the evidence available and the welfare of the child. The investigation may conclude or substantiate a case of child abuse, neglect, or dependency. Dependency is a term indicating that the caregiver does not have the capacity to meet the needs of the child (e.g., incapacity due to illness or frail health or even death of the caregiver). It does not include situations resulting from intentional acts of harm and it also applies in situations where the infant or child's special needs have not been met and when it has been abandoned. Note, though, that child protection authorities are subject to their own state's statutory and regulatory definitions of abuse, neglect, and dependency. States will have similar laws that will vary somewhat when compared side by side.

Most positive ⇅ Most negative

Positive, healthy parenting style

Stimulation and emotional expressions
provides a variety of sensory stimulation and positive emotional expressions
expresses joy at child's effort and accomplishments

Interactions
engages in competent, child-centered interactions to encourage development
friendly, positive interactions that encourage independent exploration

Consistency and predictability
demonstrates consistency and predictability to promote their relationship

Rules and limits
makes rules for safety and health
appropriate safeguards for child's age

Disciplinary practices
occasionally scolds, criticizes, interrupts child activity
teaches child through behavioral rather than psychological control methods

Emotional delivery and tone
uses emotional delivery and tone that are firm but not frightening

Poor/dysfunctional

Stimulation and emotional expressions
shows rigid emotional expression and inflexibility in responding to child
seems unconcerned with child's development/psychological needs

Interactions
often insensitive to child's needs; unfriendly
poor balance between child independence and dependence on parent

Consistency and predictability
often responds unpredictably, sometimes with emotional discharge

Rules and limits
unclear or inconsistent rules for safety and health

Disciplinary practices
frequently uses coercive methods and minimizes child's competence
uses psychologically controlling methods that confuse, upset child

Emotional delivery and tone
uses verbal and non-verbal pressure, often to achieve unrealistic expectations

Emotionally abusive/neglectful

Stimulation and emotional expressions
expresses conditional love and ambivalent feeling towards child
shows little or no sensitivity to child's needs

Interactions
emotionally or physically rejects child's attention
takes advantage of child's dependency status through coercion, threats, or bribes

Consistency and predictability
responds unpredictably, accompanied by emotional discharge

Rules and limits
sporadic, capricious
exploits or corrupts for parent's benefit

Disciplinary practices
uses cruel and harsh control methods that frighten child
violates minimal community standards on occasion

Emotional delivery and tone
frightening, threatening, denigrating, insulting

Figure 4.1 Continuum of parental emotional sensitivity and expression (source: Wolfe & McIsaac, 2011, p. 807. Permission granted Elsevier Ltd.)

Unfortunately, there are no diagnostic criteria for child emotional abuse although the American Psychiatric Association provides criteria for child physical abuse, sexual abuse, and neglect (Marshall, 2012).

Overview of the Basic CPS Investigative Process

Allegations of child abuse or neglect may be made anonymously by the public. Reports can be made in person, directly communicated over a CPS special 1–800 phone number, or left on voice mail. They are always treated confidentially. While persons making allegations of child maltreatment may remain anonymous if they choose, they are usually encouraged to leave contact information so that the CPS agency can follow-up if more information is needed or questions arise. What all CPS agencies have in common is a quick response to every alleged case—generally within 72 hours. While each state may define child maltreatment somewhat differently, essentially the same investigative process is followed.

A CPS investigation must begin within 24 hours and usually includes these steps and considerations from a brief summary from Michigan showing the typical process:

1. Face-to-face interviews with the alleged child victim(s). (How much pain or impairment has the child experienced?)
2. Face-to-face interviews with the child's caretaker(s), the alleged perpetrator(s). (What is their explanation of the incident?)
3. Viewing the family's home conditions. (Are home conditions dangerous or unhealthy?)
4. Reviewing any necessary documents, such as police reports, criminal history, medical reports, school reports, prior CPS history, etc. (Was there a failure to follow prevention or aftercare planning from a prior episode?)
5. Interviewing school personnel, neighbors, friends, relatives, or professionals that have had contact with the family. (What has been seen, heard, or experienced and by whom?)
6. An assessment of the child's safety. This involves observations and interviews but can also include use of questionnaires, rating scales, and standardized measures. (Do caregivers have problematic

attitudes, behaviors or lack knowledge about children? Have children been adversely affected? Is maltreatment likely to reoccur?)
7. An assessment of the child's future risk of abuse and/or neglect. This may involve conferring with others such as co-workers, supervisors, or experts.
8. An assessment of the family's needs and strengths and development of a report.

The younger the child's age, the greater the risk to the child; children with special medical or physical needs are at greater risk.

Here's a list (also from Michigan) of the factors to be considered during an investigation:

- Are there alternative explanations to the allegations?
- What are the family dynamics and family circumstances?
- Who is making the complaint?
- Is there corroborating evidence? (For example, witness statements, findings during a home visit, etc.)
- Should there be a medical exam of the child?
- Does the child have an injury? If so:
  - What is the explanation of the injury?
  - Is that explanation feasible?
  - Where is the injury located?
  - Is there more than one injury at different stages of healing?
- What is the condition of the home? (For example, cleanliness, safety hazards, etc.)
- What is the condition of the child? (For example, appropriately dressed, cleanliness, etc.)
- Are the child's basic needs being met?
- Is there adequate supervision?
- Are the caretakers emotionally/mentally abusing the child?
             (www.michigan.gov/dhs/0,4562,7-124-7119_
                 50648_7194-159484-,00.html)

There are differences in the forms and assessment tools agencies use to assess and document child maltreatment. However, many of the same issues are also dealt with in other countries, too. For instance, Barker and Hodes (2007) have described a Common Assessment Framework used in England that, like a triangle, has three sides: Family and Environmental Characteristics (e.g., parental strengths and difficulties, who is living in the household and their relationships, basic amenities), the Child's Developmental Needs (e.g., the nature and quality of attachments, affectionate relationships, sense of belonging and acceptance, interaction with other children), and Parenting Capacity (e.g., able to provide basic care and safety for the child, able to set boundaries, to provide stimulation for the child's cognitive development, provision of stability). This is just another way for a CPS worker to conceptualize what is needed and what might be missing from a child's life.

At any rate, after the investigation a determination must be made as to whether or not the bulk of the evidence supports a conclusion that child abuse or neglect occurred. The alleged case is then handled based upon the decision and its assignment to a particular category. This is referred to as making a disposition.

In most states, the case can be assigned to one of several categories which could indicate, on one end of the spectrum, that there was no abuse/neglect, that the family couldn't be located, or that the case was presented to the court but no order was issued to require the family to cooperate. On the other end, the preponderance of evidence could lead the CPS to go to the court and file a petition to protect the child by mandating services for the family or removing the child/children from the home temporarily and utilizing foster care or relative care.

In between these two categories, there are other case dispositions where, for instance, there could be some evidence or risk of abuse/neglect and where the child's family could agree to voluntarily participate in community-based services. In some situations, there is a preponderance of evidence of abuse/neglect in the home but a risk assessment suggests that the risk of harm to the child is fairly low. (For example, the abuser may have left the family, could be in jail, etc.) Families in this group could also receive a referral to community-based services. In those families where there is strong evidence of abuse/neglect and the risk for additional abuse/neglect remains high, the CPS may decide to allow the child to remain in the home but could ask the court to mandate that the family receive community-based services (see Table 4.1).

Generally speaking, for substantiation of child abuse or neglect, there must be evidence that the basic needs of the child were not met and/or the injury or risk of injury to the child was not an accident; this means the injury or risk of injury was deliberately inflicted or resulted from omission of supervision or care. In other words, a caretaker was responsible.

Caregiver Behaviors/Issues and Abuse/Neglect Types

Before we begin to address the assessment of emotional abuse, we'll briefly examine other types of child maltreatment and ways it can be flagged during a standard CPS investigation (commonwealth of Kentucky's Cabinet for Health and Family Services Standards of Practice Online Manual[1]). The CPS investigator may find that despite detection of detrimental emotional abuse, other forms of maltreatment may be easier to document. For instance, with **physical abuse** of children there can be observable injuries (e.g., welts, bruises, broken skin, etc.). Of special concern are children who have been hit, punched, or kicked in the head, neck, genitals, or abdomen and children who have been strangled, shaken, punched, kicked, suffocated, or punished in bizarre or cruel ways (e.g., when inappropriate restraint has been used). The worker must consider the age of the child (especially the very young under the age of four), the severity of the injury, whether the child has increased vulnerability (e.g., a disability). Adolescents injured in altercations with the caretaker will need to be interviewed out of the hearing of the caregivers and possibly in a safe location (like school). The CPS worker will want to know if the family has previously been reported to the child protection agency and will look for any prior involvement.

Sexual Abuse. CPS workers must investigate allegations of sexual abuse which includes acts of rape, sodomy, incest, sexual penetration with foreign objects, exhibiting of the genitals in a sexual manner, touching or fondling that is sexual in nature, kissing a child in an intimate manner, allowing or forcing a child to witness sexual activity, children being used in the making of pornography, or allowing children to view pornography. Sexual abuse is also considered when invasive,

Table 4.1 Typical case dispositions following a CPS investigation

CPS case disposition	CPS involvement after disposition	Evidence of abuse/neglect	Family's responsibility
Case closed; unsubstantiated	None	None or questionable; family not in need of services	Nothing mandated
Case opened	CPS assists with referral to services and monitors participation	Some evidence but low risk, no preponderance of evidence; family is assessed but full investigation may not be needed	Voluntarily agrees to participation in community-based services
Case opened	CPS monitors participation in community-based services	Preponderance of evidence; court may not be involved	Family mandated to receive community-based services
Case opened	CPS monitors participation in community-based services; agency may remove children from home	Preponderance of evidence; court involved with possible removal petition	Family must cooperate with CPS and community-based services if children are to be returned home

coercive sexual suggestions are made to children or adolescents. A child may be at risk of sexual harm if the caregiver has committed sexual abuse previously, or if the child is left in the care of a person suspected to be or actually listed on a sexual offender registry. Symptoms of sexual abuse can include reports of the child being observed masturbating or acting in a sexual manner (e.g., with dolls, peers, animals, or adults).

Neglect. There are many types of neglect which may come to the attention of the CPS worker and each state may define these slightly differently. Each type of neglect places the child at some risk of harm or potential harm. Several types of neglect are outlined below (summarized from the commonwealth of Kentucky's Cabinet for Health and Family Services Standards of Practice Online Manual).

Abandonment/Supervisory Neglect occurs when a child is found in an unsafe location, is without supervision, or has inadequate supervision (e.g., a child of seven years of age babysitting a two-year-old). The length of time the child is unsupervised, the age of the child and his/her maturity level, safety hazards in the home, and so forth are some of the key factors that must be considered.

Neglect Related to Substance Use/Abuse can be documented when the caregiver is found operating a motor vehicle while under the influence with a child present, when a medical or qualified mental health professional is concerned about the caregiver's use of alcohol, drugs, or medication and whenever these substances impair the caregiver's ability to provide a safe environment or to meet the child's needs.

Environmental Neglect may be found when the child is exposed to chemicals such as those used to make methamphetamines or when illegal drugs are in the home. Children with unsupervised and unsafe access to prescription and nonprescription medicines can also be a concern as well as environmental poisons (e.g., for ants, mice, or drain cleaners, antifreeze, etc. found on the kitchen table or floor, etc.) that children could easily obtain and ingest. Housing infested with rodents or roaches, too cluttered (e.g., where there is hoarding), inadequate because of broken windows, exposed wires, lack of heat, and other conditions that pose a serious health or safety risk where the caregiver is not taking appropriate action to improve upon the problem provide a basis for concern.

Hygiene and Clothing Neglect is found when physical conditions resulting from inadequate care require medical management such as when there is severe diaper rash, scabies, sores from lice, and multiple insect bites. The CPS worker should also be alert to children who smell of urine, feces, or strong body odor. Additionally, the child's clothing may not be sufficient for the weather (e.g., the child has no coat in the winter) and particularly of concern would be a child with an injury due to exposure to harsh weather (e.g., frostbite).

Food Neglect is an issue for CPS workers when children are dehydrated, malnourished, or appear to have not been provided with an appropriate amount of food for their age, height, and weight or when they have special dietary needs that are not met. The lack of food in the home is indicative of a problem that must be immediately addressed.

Medical Neglect may be established when a child does not receive treatment for an injury (e.g., dog bite or broken limb), illness, or disability that could be life-threatening, result in permanent impairment, or when that untreated condition could interfere with normal, physical functioning and worsen without treatment. This can include *mental health neglect* when a child has a serious emotional/behavioral problem as in cutting himself/herself, suicide attempts, depression, drug or alcohol problems, etc.

Educational Neglect occurs when the caregiver prevents a child from attending school or receiving appropriate education (e.g., frequently removing the child from school to babysit for younger siblings or care for an older adult) and the child is not being home-schooled. Note that abusive caregivers sometimes keep children from attending school when the children have significant injuries (e.g., visible bruises).

Risk of Harm Neglect is a broad category some states use to protect children when, for instance, a health provider indicates a child is born exposed to drugs or alcohol, or when someone in the neighborhood or family reports that a child or adolescent is permitted to use drugs or alcohol frequently. Equally bad would be when a parent knows that an adolescent is high and spending money on drugs but does nothing about it.

Case Example 14

A Portion of a Suicide Note Posted by Zander Mahaffey, a Transgender Youth

My mother is physically disabled. She has seizures and strokes and a hurt ankle and a bad knee and she is morbidly obese, the list goes on. She has anxiety. In fact she takes xanax for the anxiety. That's where I got it from. I'm sure she can just get more.

But even with her disabilities ... she hurts me. Not physically, no she doesn't have the capability to do that. But emotionally and mentally. I try, I try so hard sometimes. I'm not a perfect human, okk??? I MAKE MISTAKES. A lot of mistakes. And I get yelled at. I get yelled at and it hurts so bad. It hurts so bad for your "mom" to tell you she's going to kill herself over her cheating ex boyfriend. It hurts so much for her to accuse you of doing sexual things to people for money. It hurts so much for her to accuse you of stealing money from her, only to find out she had just misplaced it and doesn't even apologize. It hurts so much to have a panic attack and her say "stop acting retarded". It hurts so much for her to mention the man that raped you, even though she knows it makes you angry and sad. It hurts so much for her to yell at you till you cry, for you to be sobbing, tears pouring down your face, and then ask you why are you crying. MAYBE YOU SHOULD STOP FUCKING YELLING AT ME, THEN.

It hurts so much to hate your mother. It hurts so much for your mother to act so two faced. It hurts for you to actually have a nice time, to talk and smile and laugh together, and then it all does [goes] back to hell, and the illusion shatters, and you remember about all the horrible things she still does. It hurts to not know what it's like to have a "mommy", to know what a mothers love is, to feel cared for by a maternal figure.

To my mother, one of us was gonna die and I guess it is gonna be me. I hope you're life from here on is MISERABLE. I hope you realize how MUCH YOU NEEDED ME AND TREATED ME LIKE GARBAGE. I want you to BEG FOR ME TO COME BACK, FOR MY FORGIVENESS. But I won't. I want you dead. I wanted you to DIE FOR SO LONG, DO YOU KNOW HOW MUCH I HATED THAT?? WHY DID YOU DO THIS TO ME, YOU ARE MY MOM!! YOU WERE SUPPOSED TO LOVE ME AND MAKE ME FEEL BETTER, NOT MAKE ME KILL MYSELF!!!!!! You're a two faced pathetic excuse for a parent. You may be my mother but you are not my mom. I certainly won't miss you. Goodbye forever, you abusive piece of shit.

(http://hipopatmus.tumblr.com/post/111113295034/suicide-note)

> **BOX 4.1**
>
> **Reflection Questions**
>
> 1. What strikes you about Zander Mahaffey's suicide note?
> 2. What convinces you that she felt her home life was less than optimal?
> 3. What are the signs someone is thinking about suicide?
>
> (See www.afsp.org/preventing-suicide/suicide-warning-signs and www.helpguide.org/articles/suicide-prevention/suicide-prevention-helping-someone-who-is-suicidal.htm. Also, the National Suicide Prevention Life Line is at 1–800–273-TALK if you need to refer someone or talk to someone yourself.

The child is at risk of harm if there is domestic violence in the home that places the child in a dangerous position such as when weapons are used threateningly, items are thrown, the perpetrator assaults individuals holding or protecting the child, when the child intervenes in the situation, and when the child is restrained or restricted from leaving during interpersonal violence in the home. The child is also considered at risk of harm if anyone in the home has made a suicidal or homicidal statement, when physical altercations in the home are frequent and result in injury, and whenever there is a violation of emergency protective orders or domestic violence orders. Children are at risk of harm when he or she or any other family member is threatened with bodily harm or has a fear of death to self or others. Other concerns are bizarre behavior by the caregiver that could result in harm to the child (e.g., punishing the child by having her stick her head into a gas oven and turning on the gas). The CPS worker must be concerned about any previous behavior by the caregiver which resulted in injuring a child or a child's death, and self-reports by caregivers that they may be unable to take adequate care of the child.

When it comes to emotional abuse, many states follow the guidelines of the American Professional Society on the Abuse of Children (APSAC) in defining types of emotional abuse (which will be reviewed below). However, the APSAC's *Handbook on Child Maltreatment* notes that:

> Despite the fact that PM [psychological maltreatment] is widespread and has consequences that can be just as serious as other types of maltreatment, very few court cases allege only PM. The government attorney who files the case nearly always accuses the parent(s) of some form of maltreatment *in addition* to PM. Attorneys are reluctant to allege only PM because this form of maltreatment can be difficult to prove in court. Thus, to increase the probability that the judge will approve intervention, the attorney alleges a type of maltreatment that is "easier" to prove. PM can "tag along" with the other form of maltreatment. Once intervention is approved, the judge has the authority to order programs to reduce PM.
> (Hart, Brassard, Binggeli, & Davidson, 2002, p. 135)

Simmel and Shpiegel (2013) have reported that the odds of a case being substantiated were significantly increased (over 20 times) when there was domestic violence in the home and almost 40 times when there was alcohol abuse. Historically, situations of emotional abuse alone have rarely resulted in state child welfare intervention (Hart et al., 2002).

Categories of Emotional Abuse for CPS Investigators

Not every state relies upon the definitions created by APSAC, but some states do and here is a brief abstraction from one of those states (commonwealth of Kentucky's Cabinet for Health and Family Services Standards of Practice Online Manual):

Spurning: Terms capturing this notion would be verbal harassment, scapegoating, insulting, disparaging, depreciating, resentful, and/or angry speech, hurtful name calling, cursing the child, humiliating the child. For example, it would be humiliating when an eight-year-old wets the bed and then the wet sheets are thrown at her in front of other family members or her friends. To take a storybook example, treating Cinderella differently than her stepsisters is an example of giving differential care to favored children and denying or mistreating another—which is spurning. As with other types of emotional abuse, a single incident or even several incidents may not be enough to establish emotional abuse. The more often this type of behavior or disparaging speech is made, the stronger the case for emotional abuse.

Terrorizing: These are acts or threats that create fear or anxiety in the child. The fear may arise from the threat of potential physical harm to self or others—such as being in a chaotic or dangerous environment where others are beaten or injured (as when there is active domestic violence). The child may become anxious about bodily harm or worry about destruction of beloved possessions and/or injury to pets. Again, a single argument or even a violent altercation between caregivers may not be sufficient to make a case for terrorizing. What the CPS worker must assess is whether the home environment is safe for children. It might not be safe for the child if the caregiver has explosive anger and goes out of control with some regularity (as when he or she drinks too much). An example of a father who terrorized his children and family again and again is well portrayed in Pat Conroy's book and in the movie *Prince of Tides* (1991). More recently, the movie *Precious* (2009) is a powerfully visual story of a dysfunctional abusive mother who mistreats her daughter horribly and continually from the age of three to 16. Such chronic mistreatment can be contrasted with a single episode as when a mother fires a shot through the front door in an attempt to kill a boy's father (Hart et al., 2010).

Exploitation/Corruption: These are adult behaviors which encourage or allow a child to develop inappropriate behaviors that might be criminal, deviant, antisocial, or simply maladaptive. A child might be taught or encouraged to steal, be truant from school, or misrepresent a medical condition. Adults might also exploit or corrupt a child when they lie about the other parent or caregiver in order to manipulate the child or authorities. Children are exploited/corrupted when they are taught or instructed to lie or misrepresent matters (e.g., when they are involved in a scam about having nothing to eat or needing to buy medicine for a grandparent). They are exploited when kept from doing normal activities that children do and kept in subservient roles (e.g., being the primary caregiver for an elderly family member with dementia).

Isolating: Examples of this form of emotional abuse include periods of long confinement in a playpen, crib, car seat, being locked in a room for extended periods, restriction of peer or school contacts such that the child is prevented from having friendships or social relationships, and can include confinement of relationships to a specific group with unorthodox beliefs or values (e.g., a cult), and unreasonable restrictions of a child's movement within the home (such as making the child sleep in the bathtub). This form of emotional abuse is not placing a child in "time out" or sending him or her to their own room after dinner occasionally for punishment. It is a regular, often, and sometimes severe limitation on the child's ability to interact with other people—both within and outside the family or small group.

Denying Emotional Responsiveness: Children who are denied emotional responsiveness usually are not shown affection; that is, not hugged or appropriately touched, or given attention. The caregiver may avoid the child, not speak to the child or speak minimally, without affection. The child is not nurtured with healthy and supportive interactions and may be made to feel unwanted, unloved, or a burden. A parent who goes days without speaking to a child, sometimes as a punishment for the child, is denying emotional responsiveness. While parents may not have grown up in homes themselves where there was a lot of hugging or supportive affirmations, they ought to communicate positive pronouncements to their children. This is what Covitz (1986) wrote a number of years ago: "Parents should express their positive feelings about their regard for their children, saying, for example, 'I like to be with you' and 'What you just did was wonderful,' showing excitement about the child's experiences" (p. 144). Not hearing positive affirmations during a home visit, does not, however, make the case for emotional abuse or denying emotional responsiveness.

According to the guidelines established by APSAC, the assessment of emotional abuse should be based on the following severity factors:

- The intensity/extremeness of the abuse
- The frequency
- The chronicity of the abuse
- The extent to which the maltreatment affects the caregiver-child relationship

- The forms of psychological maltreatment that have been or are being inflicted on the child
- Influences that might buffer the child from the abuse
- The developmental periods during which the abuse occurs
- The probability of the child developing with negative outcomes from the abuse.

Greater detail for the assessment of psychological mistreatment of children and adolescents can be purchased from the APSAC website.

Assessing Emotional Abuse in Preschool Children from Their Emotional, Behavioral, and Developmental Features

Even very young children who are not all that verbal will exhibit recognizable signs of emotional abuse and neglect. Naughton, Maguire, Mann, Tempest, Gracias, and Kemp (2013) provided the following information from their systematic review:

Children 0 to 20 months: Passive, withdrawn behavior, early developmental delay in cognitive skills, more likely to demonstrate language delay.

Children 20 to 30 months: Negativity in play, reduced social interactions, may be avoidant of mothers, possible deficits in memory.

Children three to four years: Delays in language development, more anger than other children, negativity in play, difficulty in emotion discrimination.

Children four to five years: Fewer interactions with other children, more aggressive, more disruptive behavior, delays in complex language, difficulty with discrimination of emotions; helpless outlook.

Children five to six years: Low self-esteem, insecure-avoidant attachment, poor peer relationships, angry, oppositional.

Other indicators in children may include:

- Daytime anxiety and unrealistic fears
- Irrational and persistent fears, dreads, or hatreds
- Sleep problems, nightmares
- Behavioral extremes

- Biting, rocking, head-banging, or thumb sucking in an older child.

(www.dcf.ks.gov/services/PPS/Documents/
GuidetoReportingAbuseandNeglect.pdf)

Parents' behaviors can be revealing, too. Naughton et al. (2013) identified these behaviors in the adult care providers of very young children: hostility, lack of interest and involvement, lower maternal sensitivity. These parents/caregivers speak less, give less positive feedback, and direct fewer commands or questions to the child: "emotionally abusive mothers persistently found fault with their children, ignored their child's cues for assistance in problem-solving tasks, offered no encouragement if the child failed, and even looked comfortable if the child began to look frustrated" (p. 772).

Marshall (2012) provides this overview of the developmental effects of maltreatment on children and youth:

> Preschoolers who experience emotional abuse are more likely to display negative affect, be avoidant, and be noncompliant with requests. These preschoolers are also more likely to experience internalizing and externalizing problems, including increased physical aggression. Children who experience emotional abuse in middle childhood and early adolescence are more likely to display socioemotional problems, experience peer rejection, have low self-esteem, have conduct problems, suffer from depression, and be aggressive with peers. Adolescents who experience psychological maltreatment were more likely to suffer from dissociative symptoms and increased risk of suicide attempts, delinquency, substance use, and personality disorder symptoms.
>
> (p. 74)

BOX 4.2

Reflection Question

What makes emotional abuse so difficult to document, so tough to convince a skeptical person that it is real and not made-up?

Investigative Assessment Procedures

Even though the caregiver(s) may engage in one or more of the categories of emotional abuse (spurning, terrorizing, exploiting/corrupting, isolating, and denying emotional responsiveness), the CPS worker must still establish that the child's emotional or mental well-being has been harmed or that the child is at risk of being harmed. Thus, the CPS worker must observe or have reason to believe that the child has a substantial impairment in his/her ability to function normally with regard to age, development, culture, or environment. Further, the emotional injury to the child must have been inflicted intentionally by parents or caregivers by non-accidental means. In some states, the burden of establishing emotional injury is so complicated that the child must be referred to a Qualified Mental Health Professional (QMHP) who then evaluates the child and documents injury or risk for injury if the behavior continues. Note that emotional abuse can occur without a QMHP being able to conclusively state that there was emotional injury.

Risk of injury or actual emotional injury is but one part of the equation. CPS workers must also weigh parental capacity and family and environmental factors along with the developmental needs of the child in the assessment process (Horwath, 2007). In discussing the assessment of neglect, Horwath offers this wise advice:

> Practitioners also need to balance what they observe with what the family tells them. There is a danger that carers and children may be over-optimistic in their responses when answering questions from professionals as they have a vested interest in creating particular impressions of the situation.
>
> (p. 162)

Multiple sources of information are generally needed to form the most accurate impressions. And multiple observations may be needed of the person suspected of being an abuser.

Brassard and Hart (2000) provide a set of questions that can be asked of parents/caregivers, neighbors, family members, and older children to assist with the assessment of emotional maltreatment. For instance, one can ask, "In the past month, how often have you done (or have you seen [name of the caregiver] do) the following":

- Swore at the child or called him or her a swear name
- Called the child demeaning names, such as stupid, loser, or lazy
- Threatened to kick the child out of the house or send him or her away to foster care
- Threatened to hit or spank a child but didn't do it
- Blamed an adult's drinking, marital, or mental health problems on the child
- Acted too busy to pay attention to the child
- Ignored a child's request to be helped when he or she was crying, hurt, or frightened
- Failed to show needed/desired affection to the child (kisses, hugs, and playful gestures).

(p. 218)

Brassard and Hart (2000) also caution that:

> observations should be done on several occasions to obtain a representative sample of caregiver-child behavior and to detect chronic behavioral patterns.... Single observations have limitations because some parents may not behave in their typical manner. Reported observations by one caregiver or the other, or by relatives or acquaintances, in most cases will bring suspected cases under consideration. These original reports should be carefully and thoroughly explored. Interviews with the caregiver and child, records review, collateral reports from siblings, neighbors, relatives, school and day-care personnel, and others can provide useful information.
>
> (pp. 215–216)

Good record-keeping is a necessity for every CPS worker. The investigative worker must record information such as the date, time, and location of the interview as well as the full names and relationships of everyone interviewed. The steps taken to gather information must be detailed. All of the children's full names and dates of birth are recorded and social security numbers of caregivers. Information may be gathered from multiple sources such as from alleged victims, alleged perpetrators, neighbors, other family members, teachers, or others who may have information about the child and the family. In some cases, alleged victims, alleged perpetrators, and witnesses may be asked to make written statements. If there are injuries or deplorable living conditions, pictures may be made for the file. Where additional consultation is sought from other professionals, this information should also be folded into the official record.

Next, the worker must identify all of the risks and safety issues existing in the home and make a determination. As discussed earlier, typically the worker can decide that a report of child maltreatment is unsubstantiated if there is not enough evidence or an inability to document it. In order to substantiate a report of abuse, neglect, or dependency or make a finding that the family is in need of services, the CPS worker must decide: that the injury or risk of injury or omission of care was deliberate (not accidental), or that the basic needs of the child are not being met, and that the caregiver was responsible. Caregivers who allow a child to be harmed even if they had no direct role are viewed the same as those who inflict harm. Caregivers and parents have a responsibility to protect the children in their care.

When the investigation has been concluded, the caregiver and alleged perpetrator are provided with written notice of the outcome of the investigation and are provided with information regarding their rights in appealing the findings of the investigation.

If a case is substantiated, the intake/investigative CPS worker's assessment is concluded. The incident or case being investigated then becomes an open case within the child welfare agency and a prevention plan is put in place. If the risk of harm has been significantly reduced (e.g., an emergency protective order is in place or the child goes to live with another family member), then the case might be closed. When the involved child is under three years of age, it is likely a referral will be made for early intervention services.

All of the substantiated cases are recorded in an official state database that will go by different names such as the Child Protection Registry

(Vermont) or the Child Abuse and Neglect Registry (Connecticut). This information may help future CPS investigators in that state when deciding the level of risk and harm to children in a home. Obviously, risk for future reoccurrence is high if there are previous reports and/or court adjudications for similar caregiver conduct in the past.

When a case is unsubstantiated—possibly due to lack of clear evidence—the worker may write an aftercare plan for the family. Or, the case may be closed after documenting why the case was unsubstantiated and the family is not in need of services.

In some cases where the CPS worker decides that the criteria for opening a protection case are not met but that there is a potential risk for maltreatment—generally of a low risk variety—families can be identified as in need of services. In these cases, the assessment may be closed and an aftercare plan developed to link the family with community resources that could reduce the chances of future maltreatment.

Community resources may not always be helpful in the identification of abuse and neglect. For instance, in some school districts there is a policy which prohibits school personnel from directly reporting suspected cases to child protection authorities. In situations where a child reports abuse/neglect to a teacher or other school personnel and it is then reported "up" the system to the principal who does nothing about it, both the principal and teacher (or other personnel) could be charged with failure to report as mandated by state law. Approximately 20% of the school sentinels indicated school policies preventing the direct reporting to CPS authorities in the *Fourth National Incidence Study of Child and Abuse and Neglect (NIS-4)*. Further, the executive summary of that study stated that "the majority of maltreated children do not receive CPS investigation" (p. 21).

The Importance of Getting It Right

Even though the odds of a child dying from emotional abuse (when assessed as a single type, not when co-occurring with other types of abuse or neglect) may be very remote, nonetheless 1,640 U.S. children died in 2012 from abuse or neglect (www.childwelfare.gov/pubs/factsheets/fatality.cfm). At least two studies have suggested that many of these children, perhaps 30 to 40% of them, were known to child protection agencies before their deaths (Anderson, Ambrosino, Valentine, & Lauderdale, 1983; Beveridge, 1994). Emily Douglas has conducted research in this area and estimated, using 2009 data, that 531 to over 700 CPS workers that year might have experienced a child fatality on a case known to them. Further, since each worker would have had a supervisor, then between 1,062 and over 1,400 child welfare workers (3.2 to 4.3% of the child welfare workers in the United States) might be affected annually by child fatalities (Douglas, 2013).

In Douglas' convenience sample of child welfare workers and managers, over one-third had experienced a child fatality of a client and 27% of the respondents indicated that the death occurred on an open, active case. Contrary to public opinion, these incidents did not happen to the youngest, most inexperienced child welfare workers. Douglas (2013) reported that the average age of the workers was 38, they had worked in child welfare for about six years, had a caseload of approximately 25, and slightly over half of them had a master's degree. Perhaps more importantly, 84% felt confident in handling the case.

Child welfare work is serious, demanding, and, at times, very stressful. Parents can refuse to cooperate with the treatment recommendations, legally challenge the child protection worker's assessments, and frustrate the system by missing appointments and moving frequently or to completely different geographical areas. CPS workers must be good at asking questions, evaluating evidence, and advocating for the child when necessary. Because children's lives hang in the balance, assessment instruments can be helpful to bring nonbiased, objective information to the CPS workers' decision-making process. The next section will review assessment instruments that may be useful for documenting child emotional abuse.

Tools to Use for Assessing the Emotional Abuse of Children

A. Structured Interview Schedules
Personal interviews constitute the most common approach used to assess child abuse and neglect. Structured interview guides provide the interviewer with consistency in asking the questions the same way and in the same order. This provides a degree of fairness and professionalism that gives the interview greater credibility. At the same time, a skilled

interviewer can observe if a child or person being interviewed is struggling with the questions and can adapt the language if necessary or provide a context to help the individual understand a specific term or question.

Numerous researchers have created structured interview instruments to assist with identifying the extent of emotional abuse that children may have experienced. In fact, a study in 2010 (Tonmyr, Draca, Crain, & MacMillan, 2011) found 144 articles written between the years 2000 and 2010 that provided some psychometric information (discussing the technical features of an instrument's reliability and validity) about instruments designed to measure child emotional abuse. Of those articles, 45 articles had been written about 33 different measures that met the initial inclusion criteria. Of the measures that were structured interviews, four were found to have high internal consistency for use with children (see Box 4.3) but of the four singled out, three were conceptualized as assessing neglect and not emotional abuse. The fourth interview schedule, the Early Trauma Inventory (ETI), was developed with adults and not children. However, the authors of the ETI did create an emotional abuse scale.

BOX 4.3

Structural Interview Schedules with High Internal Consistency for Interviewing for Child Maltreatment from Tonmyr et al. (2011)

The Mother-Child Neglect Scale (see Lounds, Borkowski, & Whitman, 2004).
Multidimensional Neglectful Behavioural Scale (see Kaufman-Kantor et al., 2004).
Emotional Distance & Parental Involvement (see Kirisci, Dunn, Mezzich, & Tarter, 2001).
Early Trauma Inventory (see Bremner, Vermetten, & Mazure, 2000)

CPS agencies are likely to have their own assessment tools or forms for assessment that would prohibit an individual worker from adopting one that he or she liked better. Still, the reader who is looking for an interview schedule to begin using in a child welfare or health/mental health setting is certainly not limited to the four instruments mentioned above. Numerous instruments have been created and can be located in the literature; however, space limitations allow us to only highlight a few of the many available. Note, though, that most are broader than just emotional abuse and may assess physical, sexual, and emotional abuse as well as other dimensions such as exposure to family violence, neglect, etc.

One shouldn't adopt an interview schedule without examining it carefully for the way the items are presented and the dimensions or factors being assessed. Sometimes the instruments are attempting to provide a clinical diagnosis of PTSD or other psychological problems. Several instruments have been described in the literature as "lengthy." Here are some other examples of structured interview schedules available:

- Child Abuse and Neglect Interview Schedule-Revised (CANIS-R) Administered to adults (Ammerman, Hersen, Van Hasselt, Lubetsky, & Sieck, 1994). The CANIS-R can be obtained from Dr. Robert T. Ammerman at Cincinnati Children's Hospital Medical Center; Phone 513–636–4336 or email robert.ammerman @cchmc.org.
- Childhood Maltreatment Interview Schedule (CMIS)
  The longer version of the CMIS is available from Dr. Briere's book (Briere, 1992). The short form (CMIS-SF) of the longer interview schedule is free and available from John Briere's website. This is what the author says about the CMIS on his webpage www.johnbriere.com/cmis.htm:

Like most traumatic event reviews, there are no studies known to the author regarding the overall reliability or validity of CMIS-SF. This is partly due to the fact that, other than the Psychological Abuse subscale (the sum of all scores within item number 7), all items simply ask about potential maltreatment experiences, are not summed to form scales, and can be used by various researchers in different ways according to their interests. There are, however, data on the Psychological Abuse subscale (e.g., Briere & Runtz, 1998, 1990) suggesting reasonably good alpha reliability. Further, the successful use of the CMIS-SF in various studies suggests predictive and construct validity.

B. Self-Report Instruments for Children

Tonmyr et al. (2011) also identified several self-report questionnaires with high internal consistency in child populations that have been used frequently by researchers and practitioners investigating child maltreatment. Self-reports are typically paper-and-pencil questionnaires that the child or adolescent would complete on his or her own. Although with very young children, an adult could be present to assist if questions or problems arose. Self-report instruments are efficient in the collection of information as they ask the same questions in the same way each time. However, practitioners may not always be able to use these instruments with the youngest of children. Knowing the child's maturity level and reading ability are important considerations.

Experts in the field seem to be of the opinion that age 12 may define when a child can handle a self-report questionnaire/instrument without difficulty (Knight et al., 2000, as cited by Portwood, 2006). Kirisci et al. (2001) suggest that even younger children may provide good information. They state, "it would appear that by age 10, children are accurate informants for screening parental neglect and determination of the need for intervention" (p. 252). Portwood (2006) has cited Hamby and Finkelhor (2000) in noting that children as young as age four have been shown to be more than 90% accurate in forensic interviews in cases of sexual abuse. Briere's Trauma Symptom Checklist for Children (TSCC) has been designed for children eight to 16 years of age.

Murray Straus and colleagues at the Family Research Laboratory have developed the **Multidimensional Neglectful Behavior Scale** (MNBS) with subscales for physical needs, emotional needs, supervision, and cognitive needs. Versions are available for children six to nine and 10 to 15 years of age on the computer. Cards and paper-and-pencil versions can also be obtained (see http://pubpages.unh.edu/~mas2/Mul.htm).

The MNBS and the Angie/Andy Child Rating Scale described immediately below, suggest another consideration in selecting an instrument. That is, any one instrument may not serve all purposes that the practitioner or researcher has in mind. The MNBS, for example, is better at capturing information about emotional neglect than emotional abuse. And, if one is interested in assessing PTSD or sexual abuse, there are a number of other instruments designed for those purposes. There is no substitute for doing one's own research and reading about each instrument that one might consider using in his or her practice.

Practitioners may find that there are instruments with child-friendly formats as the **Angie/Andy Child Rating Scale (A/A CRS)** which uses cartoons to measure the extent of various types of abuse including witnessing family violence and community violence. This self-report and many others suitable for children can be found in a collection of instruments for assessing violence within the family (see Feindler, Rathus, & Silver, 2003). Other examples from the Feindler et al. handbook will also be discussed below.

Childhood Trauma Questionnaire (CTQ). This instrument has been described as "by far the most widely used measure of PM [psychological maltreatment] and it does contain separate emotional abuse (EA) and emotional neglect (EN) subscales in later versions" (Baker & Festinger, 2011, p. 2297). The short form of this instrument (28 items) takes 5–10 minutes for a respondent to complete.

The CTQ (short form) contains five subscales designed to measure emotional abuse, emotional neglect, physical neglect, physical abuse, and sexual abuse. Five items provide information on emotional abuse and five are used to assess emotional neglect. It also contains a minimization/denial scale to indicate if individuals are underreporting their experiences. Scoring uses a five-point format with a range from *Never True* (scored one) to *Always True* (scored five) which creates a scale range from 5 to 25. (Example: someone who reported a five on each of five items would have a score on one of these subscales as 25.) Scoring allows for the categorization of maltreatment as none, low, moderate, and severe for each of the five domains. Cut-off scores have been suggested such that 13 or greater would indicate moderate to severe emotional abuse and scores of 15 or more may reflect moderate to severe emotional neglect.

The CTQ is appropriate for individuals age 12 and up. It is copyrighted and must be purchased through www.pearsonclinical.com. A manual is also available for additional information on the CTQ. Early references on this instrument were written by the authors: Bernstein et al. (1994) and Fink, Bernstein, Handelsman, Foote, and Lovejoy (1995).

Internal consistency has been shown to be strong for university students ($\alpha = 0.86$ for emotional abuse and $\alpha = 0.97$ for emotional neglect); for a mixed sample of persons aged 14 to 44 years of age ($\alpha = 0.91$ for emotional abuse and $\alpha = 0.94$ for emotional neglect) [cited in Tonymyr et al., 2011] and $\alpha = 0.94$–0.95 in a sample of adolescent psychiatric patients 12 to 17 years of age (Bernstein, Ahluvalia, Pogge, & Handelsman, 1997).

A few years ago researchers Baker and Maiorino (2010) identified 69 studies that used the 28-item version CTQ in North America and have noted that "the CTQ has become a leader in the field of measurement of adult recall of childhood abuse of all types" (p. 741). "Since its creation, the CTQ has been the subject of extensive psychometric analyses, producing consistently excellent psychometric properties" (Baker & Maiorino, 2010, p. 740).

A recent search of the literature found that psychometric information has been reported on the short form version of the CTQ as it has been translated into Korean, Swedish, German, and Spanish. Also, studies have used the longer form in Canada, Brazil, and Turkey. Advantages of this instrument have been described as being "easy to administer, relatively noninvasive, less time-consuming, and offers continuous rather than dichotomous (present-absent) ratings" (Feindler et al., 2003, p. 160).

The Child Abuse and Trauma Scale (CATS). This instrument has been used with adolescents and the original article by Sanders and Becker-Lausen (1995) has been cited over 100 times in other articles found in the Web of Science database. Respondents use a five-point response scale and report their experiences with both parents combined. The authors discuss three different subscales: negative home environment/neglect, sexual abuse, and punishment. From the original 38 items developed by Sanders and Becker-Lausen (1995), researchers Kent and Waller (1998) identified an emotional abuse scale (the CATS-EA) from seven items (see Box 4.4). However, note that Baker (2009) reports that "utilization of the emotional abuse subscale is much less common and there is no cut-off to differentiate maltreated from non-maltreated samples" (p. 709).

> **BOX 4.4**
>
> **Items Constituting the Emotional Abuse Scale (CATS-EA)**
>
> Response Key: 0 = Never, 1 = Rarely, 2 = Sometimes, 3 = Very Often, 4 = Always
>
> | | | |
> |---|---|---|
> | 1. | Did your parents ridicule you? | 0 1 2 3 4 |
> | 2. | Did your parents insult you or call you names? | 0 1 2 3 4 |
> | 3. | Did you feel disliked by either of your parents? | 0 1 2 3 4 |
> | 4. | How often did your parents get really angry with you? | 0 1 2 3 4 |
> | 5. | Did your parents ever verbally lash out at you when you did not expect it? | 0 1 2 3 4 |
> | 6. | Did your parents yell at you? | 0 1 2 3 4 |
> | 7. | Did your parents blame you for things you didn't do? | 0 1 2 3 4 |

Considerations in Selecting Assessment Tools

A great deal of research has been conducted on the objective assessment of psychological maltreatment. This next section will present information on the tools that have been developed to identify emotional abuse primarily among adults. (Note: In most states CPS workers also investigate abuse/neglect of older, vulnerable, and frail adults.) One strength of paper-and-pencil measurement is that as self-reports from those harmed or alleged to have been harmed they are not influenced by the practitioner's biases or potentially erroneous information contributed by caregivers, feuding family members, and so forth.

On the other hand, one needs to recognize that assessment instruments can approach the task from very different perspectives. For instance, in a review of 14 measures used with adults to assess childhood emotional/psychological maltreatment, only three contained separate subscales distinguishing the spurning/commission type of behavior usually recognized as emotional abuse from the lack of emotional responsiveness/omission type of behavior usually identified as emotional neglect (Baker & Festinger, 2011). Thus, most of the instruments are designed to measure only or mostly the spurning/terrorizing/exploiting type of emotional abuse and may not match up well with the APSAC categories. Research findings from two different studies appear to offer some support for the notion that emotional abuse and emotional neglect are "related but distinct forms of psychological maltreatment" (Baker & Festinger, 2011, p. 2300).

A second strength of paper-and-pencil measures is that some of them suggest cut-off points—allowing investigators to distinguish caregivers who may be maltreating a child from caregivers who are not emotionally abusive. The provision of cut-off points further enhances the investigator's confidence in making a decision affecting the family and child. This is possible because prior research on the instrument has established data for comparison on "normal," non-maltreating samples of adults.

Unfortunately, not every standardized instrument comes with cut-off scores and so may not be as useful as others. Amy Baker (2009), affiliated with the Vincent J. Fontana Center for Child Protection in New York City, conducted an "extensive review of the literature based on numerous searches of PsycInfo" (p. 707) and located 15 instruments. It should be pointed out that one limitation of this set of instruments is that they all have been designed for administration to adults who were asked to recall or remember maltreatment in their childhood or adolescence. Thus, while the instruments may contain individual, specific items that might be suitable for children to use to describe the amount of emotional abuse they have experienced, that was not the population that the authors of the instruments were attempting to obtain information from. However, these tools may be quite useful for clinicians who are treating adults who experienced child emotional abuse/neglect.

Additional Tools Used to Assess Emotional Abuse

Of the 15 instruments examined by Baker (2009) for adult recall of abuse, several have been used much more often by researchers and their results reported in the literature. Two instruments have been used hundreds of times, the previously discussed Childhood Trauma Questionnaire (CTQ) and the Conflict Tactics Scale (CTS).

The Conflict Tactics Scale (CTS) has also been employed in hundreds of studies exploring domestic and interpersonal violence. For adult partners (marital, cohabiting, dating), the instrument captures psychological and physical violence. Straus published the original study on the instrument in 1979 and has continued to refine it through several versions. The revised 20-item short version, the CTS2S, can be viewed in Straus and Douglas (2004).

Perhaps of more interest to those needing to assess child maltreatment, there is a Conflict Tactics Scale: Parent-Child Version (CTSPC) that is an adaptation of the CTS (see Straus et al., 1998). It contains such scales as Nonviolent Discipline (four items), Psychological Aggression (five items), Minor Physical Assault (six items), Severe Physical Assault (three items), Extreme Physical Assault (five items) and supplemental questions for assessing Neglect and Sexual Maltreatment. Anyone wishing to use one of the Conflict Tactics Scales or obtain the *CTS Handbook* on the instruments needs to purchase them through Western Psychological Services (www.wpspublish.com). You may wish to note, though, that much less research has been conducted with the CTSPC than with the other versions.

A selection of other instruments relying upon adult recall reviewed by Baker (2009) are identified below. Still other assessment instruments are found in Appendix A.

The Parental Acceptance/Rejection Questionnaire (Rohner & Khaleque, 2005) is used frequently in cross-cultural studies. The PARQ has 60 items rated on a four-point scale and respondents record their experiences separately for mother and father. The instrument contains four subscales: Warmth/Affection (20 items), Aggression/Hostility (15 items), Neglect/Indifference (15 items), and Rejection (10 items). This instrument and greater information can be obtained from the cited reference (above); the *Handbook for the Study of Parental Acceptance and Rejection* must be obtained digitally from Rohner Research Publications (www.home.earthlink.net/~rohner_research/handbook.htm).

The Early Trauma Inventory—Self-Report contains 62 items with four subscales: General Trauma (31 items), Physical Abuse (nine items), Emotional Abuse (seven items), and Sexual Abuse (seven items). See Bremner, Bolus, and Mayer (2007) for the initial study prepared by the instrument's authors.

The **Negative Life Events Questionnaire**, constructed by Pitzner and Drummond (1997) is one of the longer instruments at 74 items. However, 18 items can be used as a Psychological/Verbal Abuse Scale and 10 of them group together as a Control subscale. The instrument uses a five-point scale to rate each item in terms of a significant person's harmful behavior. No cut-offs have been identified.

The **Childhood Experiences Questionnaire** is a 30-item instrument designed by Ferguson and Dacey (1997). To capture information on psychological abuse, an 11-item subscale was created.

Tips For Locating Assessment Instruments

Each instrument has certain weaknesses and strengths. Sometimes, none of those available captures exactly what one has in mind. Thus, it would not be unusual for a student or practitioner to ask, "How do I find assessment or research instruments that I have heard or read about?" Typically, when an instrument is reported in a research article, the original source of that article is cited and one would go to the list of references in the back of the article and then locate the original article cited. Sometimes, the author is able to provide enough description of the items and the response set that the scale or scales can be constructed without going further. Sometimes, though, one might have to go back several years to earlier works to get the exact wording of the items as later articles may be concerned with more recent analyses or validation efforts.

Sometimes conducting a literature search for articles which compare or evaluate several types of instruments will identify a helpful review. An example mentioned in this chapter is the article by Tonmyr et al. (2011).

Using Google or other search engines can sometimes conveniently identify a resource such as *Child and Adolescent Trauma Measures: A Review* that can be found at https://ncwwi.org/files/Evidence_Based_and_Trauma-Informed_Practice/Child-and-Adolescent-Trauma-Measures_A-Review-with-Measures.pdf.

Lastly, a useful reference for finding multiple scales for assessing problems with children, couples, and families is Kevin Corcoran and Joel Fischer's (2013) *Measures for Clinical Practice and Research: A Sourcebook* (5th edition). This two volume set contains many scales that could be helpful in trying to obtain an objective measurement of some problem that children or adults might have. Examples of several scales that might be of assistance to CPS workers include the Child's Attitude

Towards Father and Child's Attitude Towards Mother. These brief scales are designed to measure the extent of problems that a child (12 years of age or older) has with the particular parent. The 25-item instruments have excellent validity and are very reasonably priced (available from www.walmyr.com). Clinically significant cut scores can be identified. The author, Walt Hudson, also created the Index of Family Relations which can "characterize the severity of family problems in a global fashion and can be regarded as an overall measure of intrafamilial stress" (Corcoran & Fischer, 2013, p. 360). Again, scores above 30 suggest the presence of a clinically significant problem. Another example from the reference work is the Parenting Scale, "a 30-item instrument designed to measure dysfunctional discipline practices in parents of young children" (Corcoran & Fischer, 2013, p. 418).

Criticisms of Self-Report Instruments

Attempting to design an instrument which will accurately capture all of the various behaviors and attitudes and expressions that might be abusive or neglectful is a formidable task. One issue is whether the instrument captures just a few of the facets of the problem being assessed or is broader and covers most of the concept. And there are definitional problems. Some individuals may not recognize that they were abused but could give a different answer if they were asked if specific behaviors occurred in their homes (Portwood, 2006). A related problem is that some individuals may be ashamed of their mistreatment or wish to protect a family member and will minimize problems or indicate that there were no problems. On the other hand, given a range of response choices, individuals can also exaggerate poor treatment to give the impression that things are worse than they are. (Sometimes these problems are referred to as "faking good" or "faking bad.")

Portwood (2006) also notes that measuring the severity and frequency of a particular behavior is complicated. She writes, "For example, how many times must an act such as screaming at a child occur, and/or what must the nature of screaming be for it to be considered abusive?" (p. 235).

And, there is the problem of fallible human memory. Sometimes our memories are just imperfect as to dates or times or even years. To complicate matters even more, some individuals are motivated to forget—they don't want to remember harsh or painful incidents from the past.

Perhaps there is a way to improve upon our assessment of children who have been maltreated; perhaps you can be part of that process!

Glossary

Alpha (Cronbach's Alpha): An expression of how well the items on a test, scale, or measurement instrument correlate with the dimension being measured. This also referred to as internal consistency and generally means, when the alpha is above 0.70, that responders/participants typically interpret and answer the questions reliably in an expected way. When items are reliable, they aren't usually misinterpreted or found to be confusing or difficult to understand.

Internal Consistency: See alpha.

Psychometric Information: Consists of two components: reliability and validity. Reliability can be thought of as a numerical expression of how dependable the instrument is to make consistent assessments (e.g., like a dependable watch that keeps good time). Validity comes from efforts to show that the instrument measures the concept that was intended and not some other unintended concept. Information about both reliability and validity are needed for practitioners and researchers to have a good understanding of what the instrument can be depended upon to provide.

Class Discussion Questions

1. What constitutes poor parenting other than abusive or neglectful parenting practices? Discuss some possible examples.
2. In conducting an assessment of alleged child maltreatment, what would you do if the information provided by a parent differed significantly from the child's account?
3. Of the APSAC categories of emotional abuse, which one do you think is most damaging to the child? Why?
4. Closely examine the emotional abuse scale (CATS-EA) contained in this chapter. Discuss how confident you would feel in

using this instrument to assess a child's emotional abuse. When might it work well and when might it not?
5. Are there more pluses than minuses in using paper-and-pencil instruments to assess emotional abuse? What are your thoughts about the matter?
6. Having read this chapter, what concerns do you have regarding the assessment of child emotional abuse? What ideas do you have for accurately assessing it?
7. Which of the assessment instruments described in this chapter would you like to know more about? Why?
8. Would you be comfortable asking a 13-year-old the questions contained in the emotional abuse scale (the CATS-EA) shown earlier in the chapter?
9. As you look over the case example in this chapter, what are the key indicators that suggest emotional abuse? What concerns you most in the example?
10. Go to youtube.com and watch the movie trailer for *Precious* (www.youtube.com/watch?v=LpU8rJ_ZwOs). What does her mother say that is emotionally abusive? What about her mother's tone and manner of speaking?

Note

1. In this section of the chapter I have drawn heavily upon the commonwealth of Kentucky's Cabinet for Health and Family Services Standards of Practice Online Manual. It is, of course, much more detailed than what I have presented here. Any important omissions or misrepresentations are not the fault of the Cabinet but mine alone.

5
INTERVENING AND TREATING EMOTIONAL ABUSE

Sarah Ascienzo
(University of Kentucky)

Happy families are all alike; every unhappy family is unhappy in its own way.

—From Leo Tolstoy's *Anna Karenina*

Overview: So far we have examined definitions of emotional abuse, prevalence and incidence rates, contributing and causal factors, and assessment procedures, but all of this begs the question: *so now what?* How do we help? How do we intervene in cases of emotional abuse and how do we prevent it from occurring in the future? And, so, this chapter provides a foundation for understanding interventions for emotional abuse.

Introduction

Given the multitude of contributing factors and the complexities associated with emotional abuse, approaches to intervention are wide-ranging in their scope. It is not enough to solely provide intervention services to a child who has suffered emotional abuse: it is also crucial to deliver programs aimed at preventing abuse from occurring, to moderate the duration of abuse through community-based responses, to enhance protective factors, to develop effective policy around the issue, to enact advocacy campaigns, and to change larger societal structures and values which enable emotional abuse to continue. Intervention efforts therefore include both prevention and treatment programs and can be directed at individuals, families, organizations, or the larger community.

Treatment programs intervene in cases where emotional abuse has already occurred. The four overarching goals of these interventions are to:

1. enhance and restore the psychosocial functioning of children affected by emotional abuse;
2. change social conditions that impede functioning, such as maladaptive or abusive parenting;
3. improve interactions between children and their environment, and particularly with parents who inflicted the abuse; and
4. in the case of community, organizational, and national efforts, to create policies which promote achievement of these goals.

Prevention programs aim to avert emotional abuse from occurring in the first place through the provision of campaigns geared toward the larger population, through community-based programs which seek to reduce risk factors and enhance protective factors, and by providing services to high-risk families.

This chapter begins with a discussion concerning the lack of available interventions designed specifically for emotional abuse, and then outlines a theoretical framework for intervention. Three types of treatment approaches—parent-focused, child-focused, and parent–child focused—are presented, and examples of empirically supported interventions for each type of approach are provided. We then discuss universal, selective, and targeted prevention programs, and conclude by presenting an initiative that seeks to create better systems of care for children and families.

Applying Child Maltreatment Interventions to Emotional Abuse

This text focuses on emotional abuse, but as you know from prior chapters, no single agreed-upon definition of emotional abuse exists, and it frequently co-occurs with other forms of child maltreatment (e.g., physical abuse, sexual abuse, neglect, etc.). It may be helpful to return to previous chapters to review those acts of omission and commission that constitute emotional abuse, as well as the specific behaviors, relational dynamics, and risk factors that the interventions presented in this chapter seek to address.

Additionally, despite the prevalence of emotional abuse and the research on its long-lasting harms, there remains scant literature on empirically supported treatments and prevention efforts specifically for this type of maltreatment (Barlow & Schrader-McMillan, 2009; Hart et al., 2010; Leeson & Nixon, 2010). This is of concern given the profound impact emotional abuse has on children and especially in light of evidence which suggests that emotional abuse may predict poor adjustment to a greater extent than exposure to other types of child maltreatment (Briere & Runtz, 1990; Glaser, 2002).

In the absence of interventions specifically designed for emotional abuse, clinicians currently utilize interventions developed for other types of maltreatment, and there are two main reasons to believe that these interventions are effective in treating emotional abuse. First, given the high co-occurrence of emotional abuse with other forms of abuse and neglect (see Claussen & Crittenden, 1991; Crittenden, Claussen, & Sugarman, 1994), many effectiveness studies that focused on other forms of maltreatment likely included a subset of children who also experienced emotional abuse (Cicchetti, Rogosch, & Toth, 2006). It is therefore plausible that these findings are generalizable to children who experience emotional abuse. Iwaniec (1997) writes, "Emotional maltreatment is at the core of all major forms of abuse and neglect" and contends that all other forms of child maltreatment to some extent contain elements of emotional abuse (p. 370).

Second, although families are unique in their experiences and children are differentially affected by emotional abuse, there is a substantial degree of overlap concerning the ways children react to traumatic experiences of an interpersonal nature. Consequently, some researchers argue that interventions developed to treat mental health problems in children exposed to one form of maltreatment (e.g., physical abuse, sexual abuse, exposure to domestic violence, neglect, etc.) are also effective in treating other or multiple forms of maltreatment (Cohen, Mannarino, Murray, & Igelman, 2006).

The treatment and prevention programs outlined in this chapter were developed for other forms of child maltreatment, but are included based on their empirical support and relevance to the specific needs of families where emotional abuse is the primary presenting problem.

Theoretical Perspectives Informing Emotional Abuse Intervention

As a result of the complex factors contributing to emotional abuse, a theoretical framework is needed which utilizes an ecological and developmental perspective, is child-centered, *trauma-informed*, strengths-based, and culturally competent. These are briefly summarized below.

Ecological Perspective

Intervention and prevention efforts must conceptualize human behavior and social functioning within a person-in-environment framework. Emotional abuse occurs in the context of a relationship and is influenced by innumerable individual, family, community, societal, and cultural variables. An ecological perspective underscores the importance of considering all of these complex contributing and interdependent factors not only when providing interventions to children and families, but also when developing policy and larger-scale initiatives to combat and treat emotional abuse.

Child-Centered

A child-centered approach places the needs of children at the forefront of decision-making. Children are vulnerable by virtue of their developmental level and dependency on adults for safety, love, and survival. Adopting a child-centered approach means that the emotional and physical safety, well-being, and welfare of children serve as the primary considerations in selection and delivery of interventions.

Developmental Perspective

A developmental approach necessitates an understanding of growth and development from a life span perspective (DHHS, 2006). It examines individuals and families interacting with their environments over the course of time and molds interventions based on their developmental needs. Interventions with children and adolescents must be informed by a developmental perspective as practices and strategies that may be appropriate with a 3-year-old are unlikely to be as effective with an 8-year-old or 15-year-old. Social workers, psychologists, medical professionals, and others who work with these children must be knowledgeable concerning cognitive, social, and intellectual development in order to delineate appropriate expectations, to assess current functioning, and to determine the best intervention method and strategies.

Trauma-Informed

Complicating this consideration of development is the profound manner in which exposure to emotional abuse and other types of maltreatment can negatively impact development in multiple domains of functioning. As outlined previously, the effects of emotional abuse are far-reaching in their scope and can result in a wide range of difficulties. The impact on development varies depending on the age and developmental level of the child when the abuse occurred, the chronicity, duration and severity of the maltreatment, and other risk and resiliency factors (Cook, Blaustein, Spinazzola, van der Kolk, & the Complex Trauma Task Force, 2003). As a result, a developmental perspective within the context of trauma is necessary. Clinicians need to be well-versed in trauma theory, knowledgeable regarding the direct and indirect consequences of traumatic exposure, and utilize a trauma-informed lens when conceptualizing problems and solutions.

Strengths-Based Approach

A strengths-based perspective refers to practice methods and strategies that recognize the strengths of children, families, and communities and seek to enhance them. This approach focuses not just on deficits and problems, but also acknowledges existing strengths and then tailors intervention strategies to build upon those strengths. A comprehensive approach to the intervention and prevention of emotional abuse demands not just a reduction of risk factors, but also an enhancement of protective factors which can moderate the development of more significant symptoms or problems in later life. Dennis Saleeby, one of the early pioneers of the strengths-based approach, explains it this way:

> The strengths perspective demands a different way of looking at individuals, families and communities. All must be seen in the light of their capacities, talents, competencies, possibilities, visions, values, and hopes, however dashed and distorted these may have become through circumstance, oppression, and trauma.
>
> (1996, p. 297)

When applying a strengths-based approach, Saleeby (1996) notes there are also certain imperatives that need to be met, including the use of empowerment, resilience, and membership. *Empowerment* means assisting clients in discovering and using the tools within and around them, while *resilience* denotes those skills and abilities that accumulate over time as people surmount adversity. *Membership* means that people feel part of a larger community and are valued within that community.

Culturally Competent Practice

Culturally competent practice is the recognition of clients' cultures as well as the development of skills, knowledge, and policies which promote the delivery of effective services to children and families from diverse backgrounds (Korbin, 2002; Sue & Sue, 1999). As Korbin (2002) notes, cultural competence also speaks to the need to promote empowerment and the inclusion of culturally diverse professionals.

Cultural competence requires practitioners to understand the perspectives of children and families who come from culturally diverse backgrounds and to adapt clinical practices to meet their needs. It necessitates not only knowledge regarding diverse cultures, but also consideration of power differentials between providers and families that are inherent in child maltreatment work, and an understanding of structural inequalities that exist within society. Given research which has shown cultural disparities in health care treatment (see DHHS, 2001), and that maltreated children of color may suffer more deleterious consequences of abuse and neglect (see Cohen, Deblinger, Mannarino, & de Arellano, 2001), cultural competence is a necessity when delivering interventions to children and families.

Decision-Making and Evidence-Based Practice

Child protection workers, clinicians, medical professionals, and others who work within child welfare have an ethical obligation to provide competent services to children and families. Throughout the intervention process, clinicians are charged with synthesizing complex information from a variety of sources and repeatedly must make difficult decisions that necessitate strong critical thinking skills. The evidence-based practice model (EBP) can serve as a useful tool when making these practice decisions.

EBP originated out of concerns regarding the wide variations found in practice, gaps between research findings and what was occurring in the field, economic pressures, the development of systematic reviews, concerns over how research was being disseminated, and the proliferation of the Internet, which increased accessibility to information regarding clinical practice (Gray, 2001). Sackett, Straus, Richardson, Rosenberd, and Haynes (2000) define the model as one which requires the integration of the best research evidence, practitioner expertise, and a client's unique values and circumstances when making decisions.

A crucial component of EBP is the utilization of treatment approaches that are evidence-based and have research demonstrating their effectiveness. In line with this model, the interventions included in this chapter have demonstrated positive outcomes in research studies. Additionally, the California Evidence-Based Clearinghouse on Child Welfare (CEBC) evaluates child welfare programs and assigns them a score on a rating scale of one (well supported by research) to five (a concerning/risky practice). The CEBC rating is provided for each intervention presented in this chapter. The National Child Traumatic Stress Network (NCTSN) also offers resources on its website regarding empirically supported treatments for child trauma. Last, the Substance Abuse and Mental Health Services Administration (SAMSHA) offers a registry of evidence-based interventions on its website that includes a critical appraisal of the research evidence for each treatment. You are encouraged to visit all three websites for more information regarding the criteria used to rate programs and to explore the array of resources they provide.

Although EBP has sometimes been misconstrued as synonymous with solely the use of empirically supported treatments, this is a misrepresentation of the model (Shlonsky & Gibbs, 2004). McCracken and Marsh (2008) agree, and contend that EBP is a process-oriented approach that requires the interchange between client values, practitioner expertise, and applicable research that is reliant upon reflection and critical thinking on the part of the clinician. The needs of children and families will vary considerably, and the use of empirically supported treatments and the application of the EBP model should not be misunderstood as a one-size-fits-all approach. EBP is a process by which practitioners utilize their expertise (and supervision) to weigh the research evidence in light of child, family, and environmental factors in order to make informed decisions through a collaborative process with the family (Thyer & Pignotti, 2011).

Common Factors Found in Effective Interventions

Common factors are those personal and interpersonal components that have been associated with positive outcomes across a wide range of intervention approaches (Grencavage & Norcross, 1990). The concept of common factors emerged from research which found that psychotherapy is generally more effective than no therapy at all, and that clients often make positive changes when exposed to a variety of different practice models and theoretical approaches (Lambert & Ogles, 2004). This has led many researchers to conclude that a portion of the positive change that occurs during an intervention is due to common factors, as opposed to solely reliant upon the specific practice approach or theory employed.

Practitioner factors include those qualities and interpersonal skills that are conducive to developing effective therapeutic relationships (Grencavage & Norcross, 1990). Factors include clinicians' responsiveness, warmth, acceptance, genuineness, and empathy. The latter three personal attributes were originally identified by Carl Rogers (1957) in his person-centered theory, and research has consistently shown the importance of these qualities in forming therapeutic alliances and in predicting positive outcomes (Norcross, 2001). Although these qualities may seem common sense, it is important not to underestimate their importance in intervention work.

Client factors that are associated with positive outcomes include hope or an expectation of change, clients' willingness to be actively involved in the work, and clients' view of the clinician as credible and competent (Cameron & Keenan, 2010). Although these qualities may need to be developed during the course of the therapeutic work, a process known as engagement, there is evidence that these factors predict positive outcomes (Orlinsky, Rønnestad, & Willutzki, 2004).

Relationship factors speak to the importance of the client–clinician relationship. The strength of this relationship, commonly referred to as the therapeutic alliance, has a strong correlation with positive outcomes (Horvath & Bedi, 2002; Orlinsky et al., 2004). Relationship factors include mutual engagement in the change work, effective direct and indirect communication, the degree of agreement on problems and treatment goals, and collaboration (Cameron & Keenan, 2010). Both the interpersonal skills of clinicians as well as the willingness and ability of clients to engage greatly influence the therapeutic alliance. Forming a strong therapeutic alliance with both children and parents can be challenging in these cases. Parents who are court-mandated to participate in treatment and who have been perpetrators of emotional abuse may be defensive, not see any need to change, or have mistrust of the child welfare system. Children who have suffered emotional abuse may not be as open to forming new relationships or may lack the skills to do so. Despite these challenges, clinicians need to utilize effective engagement strategies to form relationships with all members of the family, who may have varying—or even conflicting—perspectives, needs, and goals.

Practice factors are effective treatment practices that cut across different intervention approaches and models (Chorpita, Daleiden, & Weisz, 2005; Grencavage & Norcross, 1990). Practice factors include skills like providing reflective feedback, facilitating exploration of thoughts and feelings, building self-awareness, providing psychoeducation, developing coping skills, and offering positive reinforcement (Cameron & Keenan, 2010). Clinicians choose practice strategies that best fit a particular client, problem, and practice context and then utilize them throughout the course of the work.

Finally, **social network factors** include environmental contexts which allow productive therapeutic work to occur. These would include factors such as adequate funding, appropriate policies, supportive values, sufficient knowledge, and organizational support, all of which are necessary in order to provide effective services (Drisko, 2004).

Interventions Targeting Emotional Abuse

Types of Intervention Approaches

Intervention approaches for emotional abuse and child maltreatment are often divided into three different categories: parent-focused, child-focused, and parent–child-focused. Parent-focused interventions are services directed at the parents that aim to change some aspect of their well-being, address environmental factors impacting their ability to parent, and/or correct the abusive behavior. Child-focused approaches are those services delivered to the child that focus on healing the effects of the abuse. Parent–child-focused interventions seek to improve parent–child interactions, and also include treatments that are delivered to the entire family.

The three types of intervention approaches each have a primary focus on different aspects of the problem and the work is therefore directed toward different individuals within the family system. However, since emotional abuse occurs within an interactional context, it is difficult to address problems with parents or children without involving the other to some extent because treatment needs to focus on the relational dynamics at some point in the process. As a result, despite the distinctions that are made between these different approaches, you will notice a substantial degree of overlap amongst them.

Responses to emotional abuse are also typically *multimodal* in that they demand multiple interventions that target different aspects of the problem, and *multidisciplinary* in that they are delivered by a variety of different disciplines or agencies. As Iwaniec and Herbert (1999) note:

> Intervention and treatment strategies should be based on comprehensive assessment, addressing the needs of children as well as parents and the communities they live in; choosing methods, approaches and services which will provide healing for the child; acceleration of developmental attainments; change of parental

attitudes towards a child; better understanding of children's developmental needs; promote better informed child-rearing practices; as well as helping parents with many difficulties, such as poverty, social isolation, dysfunctional marital relationships, depression, alcoholism, family violence, immature personality and so on.

(p. 369)

This is no simple task and the information collected during the assessment process will help inform the appropriate selection of therapeutic interventions, family support services, and/or protective measures.

What's the Threshold Needed for Intervention?

Clinical interventions are typically those delivered by a master or doctoral level clinician, usually with a background in social work, psychology, child development, or other related behavioral health field. These interventions can be provided in the home or in a community setting such as a mental health center or school. The majority of the interventions in this chapter require clinical training, although there are a few that do not (e.g., parent training programs and some home visiting programs); however, all of the interventions require strong helping skills and necessitate training specific to the model.

Child welfare interventions are those services provided by CPS. The child welfare investigative and assessment process outlined in Chapter 4 constitutes one form of intervention. It is important to note that because states vary in how they consider emotional abuse, the difficulties involved with proving that it has occurred, and the threshold of abuse required to trigger child welfare intervention, CPS rarely intervenes in cases where emotional abuse is the only form of maltreatment. More typically, these cases are diverted to community-based services where eligibility focuses on the mental health and resource needs of children and families rather than on whether or not a certain threshold of abuse has occurred. Additionally, families where suboptimal parenting exists can also receive clinical and community-based interventions that are specifically geared toward improving parenting skills and interactional dynamics. In these cases, the clinical assessment will help to determine what issues need to be addressed and which type of intervention is most appropriate. (See Appendix C for greater detail in conducting a biopsychosocial clinical assessment.)

CPS is more likely to intervene in cases where emotional abuse co-occurs with other forms of maltreatment. The provision of services that follows often involves a combination of intervention approaches that are provided by CPS and community-based providers. Several different interventions often occur concurrently, and while the specific goals of various agencies and interventions may differ (e.g., the goal of CPS may be to change harsh parenting practices whereas the goal of the child-focused work may be to reduce the child's symptoms), the overarching aim of these different interventions is congruent. The point is not so much *who* the service is brokered through, but whether or not there is a coordinated and collaborative response adequately addressing the family's needs.

What is the Presenting Problem and Who Should be the Focus of the Intervention?

A primary step in developing a treatment is to determine the desired goals of the intervention. For example, is the goal to ensure the immediate safety of the child; to target maladaptive or coercive parenting practices; or, to counteract the effects of the abuse on the child? This will inform the answers to crucial questions such as: who needs to be the focus of the intervention, are multiple interventions approaches needed, and should the parent be included in the child's treatment and if so, at what point in the process? Information resulting from the assessment process will aid this decision-making process, but particular attention needs to be paid to whether the child feels physically and emotionally safe enough to engage in therapeutic work with the parent, and whether the parent is able to participate in treatment with the child in a productive manner.

Additionally, Danya Glaser and colleagues (Glaser, Prior, & Lynch, 2001; Glaser, 2002, 2011), have developed a conceptual framework termed FRAMEA that is geared specifically toward emotional abuse and has some preliminary empirical support (see Glaser, Prior, Auty, & Tilki, 2012). The FRAMEA model outlines four tiers of concern (tier 0—social and environmental; tier 1—parent risk; tier 2—parent–child interactions; and tier 3—child's functioning) and a framework for determining where to start with families depending on the type of harmful child–parent interactions that are present. Glaser (2011) notes that if there are substantial social and environmental or parental risk factors (tiers 0 and 1), it is necessary to intervene with these issues before it is possible to embark upon meaningful interventions focused on child–parent interactions. For example, if a parent has substance misuse problems, referrals need to be made to acquire adequate services for the parent prior to starting conjoint work. Similarly, if a family is homeless, referrals need to be made to assist in securing adequate and safe housing prior to execution of interventions explicitly targeted at the emotional abuse. Glaser (2011) offers the following principles of intervention according to the different categories of emotional abuse:

Category 1: Emotional Unavailability

Glaser (2011) writes that these parents are "often troubled by their own difficulties which stand in the way of attending and responding to the child's emotional needs" (p. 872). As a result, intervention is initially parent-focused and directed at any parental risk factors (e.g., mental health treatment, domestic violence treatment, substance abuse treatment, etc.) and often involves individual therapy. This work is then followed by treatment with both the child and parent (i.e., parent–child-focused) that is targeted toward improving their interactions.

Category 2: Negative Attributions

Because hostility toward the child is often based on the parent's negative beliefs about the child's temperament or characteristics, interventions for this category also begin with individual parent-focused work. Glaser (2011) suggests that the therapy should focus on exploring with the parent the child's own view of him or herself, which has presumably been negatively impacted by the emotional abuse, and how this might be shifted by interacting in a more positive manner. These interventions might include parent training on more appropriate ways to discipline and interact with the child.

Category 3: Inappropriate Developmental Expectations, Inconsistent and/or Harsh Parenting, and Exposure to Domestic Violence

Glaser (2011) notes that parents who fall into this category are often unaware of the child's developmental needs for consistent, non-punitive boundary setting and rewards, and for protection from domestic violence or high levels of adult conflict. These parents may also be unfamiliar with age-appropriate developmental expectations. Consequently, the initial approach here is parent-focused and geared toward providing psychoeducation regarding child development and effective parenting approaches.

Category 4: Using the Child for the Fulfillment of the Parent's Needs

These parents are unable to differentiate the psychological boundary between the child and themselves, and consequently often use the child for fulfillment of their own needs without meeting the emotional needs of the child. Glaser (2011) finds that emotional abuse of this type is often found in parents with high levels of partner conflict, or amongst those with unresolved child maltreatment histories which have led to traumatic stress reactions impacting their ability to form and maintain effective interpersonal relationships. Notably, more substantial unresolved conflicts may necessitate extensive individual work with the parent prior to addressing the abusive behaviors. When the focus shifts toward the emotional abuse, the parent will need to explore those factors which create unhealthy interactions with the child, and what it would mean for the parent if those interactions changed (Glaser, 2011). It is also useful to provide the parent with an understanding of the child's perception of these interactions, as he or she may not be able to acknowledge the child's own thoughts and feelings without therapeutic guidance (Glaser, 2002).

Category 5: Failure to Promote the Child's Socialization

The FRAMEA framework suggests that parents that fall in this category are "unlikely to have considered the effects of their interactions with the child on the child's own experiences and interactions within the child's peer and educational environment" (Glaser, 2011, p. 873).

Glaser (2002) also notes that cultural factors may play a part in the failure to adequately socialize a child. Accordingly, a psychoeducational approach is often the best place to start with the parent and includes providing information about social development and the importance of different avenues for socialization, while also exploring the parent's reticence or barriers to promoting the child's socialization. This work also may be supplemented by connecting the child to activities and programs which could provide positive socialization experiences.

> **Case Example 15**
>
> Kyle, age seven, lives with his father, Matthew; his stepmother, Samantha; and two half siblings, Zoe, age two and a half, and Nevaeh, who is seven months old. Samantha, age 25, is the biological mother of Zoe and Nevaeh and is the primary caregiver for all three children. Kyle's biological mother is currently incarcerated for methamphetamine use. He has not had contact with her since he was an infant. Matthew works as a construction laborer and when he has jobs they often taken him away from home for long periods of time. The family struggles at times to make ends meet, and their lack of financial resources places additional stress on both Matthew and Samantha.
>
> Samantha, who admits that she only ever wanted girls, reports that Kyle "just doesn't like me." She states that he often
>
>> does things just to be mean to me. I have two babies and Kyle is always getting into trouble or doing things that he isn't supposed to. He is just a bad kid—there is something wrong with him. I don't know why he can't just listen and do as he is told.
>
> Samantha goes on to describe that Kyle never helps with the younger children, washing the dishes, or cooking dinner. There is disdain and resentment in her voice when she says "I didn't sign up to be his mother, but I am the one who has to raise him and you'd think he would make it easier on me."
>
> Matthew reports that Samantha is "a good mother, but she gets stressed out really easily." He states that when he is home things are better, but that he has to take jobs when he is offered them and just can't be there to settle "arguments between Kyle and Samantha all the time." He reports that he and Samantha often argue about her treatment of Kyle, but that this just "makes things worse."

> When asked about what it is like at home, Kyle talks about getting yelled at "all the time." He mentions how Samantha sometimes gets really mad at his dad on the phone, but then yells at him and calls him bad names, such as worthless, bad, and a pain. Kyle says in a confused voice, "I try to be good, but she is always yelling at me. She never yells at Zoe and Nevaeh." Kyle describes one occasion when Samantha threw a shoe at the TV when he would not get up and help his sister, and another time when he knocked a can of soda onto the carpet and Samantha responded by calling him an "idiot" and then went on to talk about how she did not love him and would never be his mother. He also describes that when he is "bad" he has to stay in his room "all day and not bother her." Sometimes Samantha says that she can't wait for his "real mom" to get out of jail so that she can send him to go live with her.
>
> **Reflection Questions**
>
> 1. Which categories of harmful parent–child interaction might Samantha's treatment of Kyle fall into?
> 2. According to the FRAMEA framework, what might be the first course of intervention with this family?
> 3. As you read through the various intervention approaches, which programs might be the most appropriate for this family?

The FRAMEA approach provides a useful framework to help determine the best course of action in cases of emotional abuse. It is also important to note that when parents are receiving individual services prior to conjoint work with the child, the child may need to be concurrently receiving a child-focused intervention if the assessment indicated that he or she could benefit from therapeutic support. A few examples of child-focused interventions will be provided later in the chapter; however, we now turn our attention to parent-focused interventions that directly address the emotionally abusive behavior.

Parent-Focused Approaches

As is evident, work with families where emotional abuse is present often first involves individual, parent-focused work to address the underlying issues contributing to the emotionally abusive behavior and any barriers interfering with effective parenting. Parent-focused approaches attempt to develop parents' ability to meet the needs of all family members while also providing them with resources to ensure the safety and well-being of the family (DHHS, 2006). Strategies vary widely, but can include parent training, family preservation or in-home services, and interventions aimed at meeting the individual needs of parents, such as treatment for substance abuse, domestic violence, or depression. Often, referrals to services which can provide resources to reduce environmental stressors (e.g., affordable housing, employment, etc.) are included as part of these approaches. We now provide examples of two different parent-focused interventions—one is a parent training model while the other is a family preservation program.

Triple P—Positive Parenting Program®—Level 4 (Level 4 Triple P)

Within the FRAMEA framework, several categories of emotionally abusive behavior necessitate the need for parent training to address maladaptive, coercive, or developmentally inappropriate practices. Parent training is considered one of the least intensive interventions for emotional abuse and would be appropriate only in more mild cases. The Triple P—Positive Parenting Program® is one example of a parent training program that is specifically aimed at developing the skills and knowledge of parents while also enhancing their self-confidence. The entire Triple P system includes five levels, and each level is targeted at slightly different populations and areas of need (Mazzucchelli & Sanders, 2010). Level 4 Triple P is considered to be a moderate to high intensity program, and is often used with children who have behavioral issues, as well as with parents who have a lack of positive parenting skills, poor stress management, mild to moderate depression, anxiety, anger issues, partner conflict, and/or negative attributional thinking (Sanders, 2012).

Level 4 Triple P utilizes a cognitive-behavioral approach to teach parents strategies that promote social competence and self-regulation in children as well as decrease problem behaviors (Sanders, 2012). The program can be delivered individually to parents or in a group format, and can be offered in the home, online, or in community settings. Although training for facilitators is required, they do not need to be clinicians. The program emphasizes developmentally appropriate interventions for children and five core principles form the basis of the program: safe and engaging environment, positive learning environment, assertive discipline, realistic expectations, and parent self-care (Mazzucchelli & Sanders, 2010). Level 4 Triple P teaches an explicit self-regulatory framework to assist parents, which emphasizes self-efficacy, self-sufficiency, self-management, and problem-solving skills (Sanders & Mazzucchelli, 2013). As part of the program, parents develop and then practice a parenting plan that uses the new tools they have acquired. Parents also learn how to monitor their own and their children's behavior and then set measurable goals for change. Through a process of reflection and evaluation, parents work with their practitioner to further develop their plan and reach identified goals. The desired outcomes of the program are to:

- Increase parents' competence and confidence, as well as the use of positive parenting strategies
- Reduce the use of coercive and punitive methods of disciplining children
- Decrease child behavior problems (for families with difficult child behavior)
- Improve parenting partners' communication
- Reduce parenting stress associated with raising children.

(Mazzucchelli & Sanders, 2010)

Level 4 Triple P is rated a 1 (well supported by research evidence) by the CEBC in the areas of Parent Training Program and Disruptive Behavior Treatment (Child and Adolescent). Outcome studies found that Level 4 Triple P was able to decrease dysfunctional parenting practices, increase self-reported competence of parents, and decrease problem behaviors in children when compared to a comparison group and/or waitlist control group (De Graff, Speetjens, Smit, De Wolff, & Tavecchio, 2008; Sanders, Bor, & Morawska, 2007; Sanders, Markie-Dadds, Tully, & Bor, 2000).

In cases of low risk and mild emotional abuse, where the parent is motivated to change his or her parenting practices but lacks the knowledge and skills to do so, a program such as Level 4 Triple P may be a viable option. However, in cases where higher levels of risk exist, more intensive interventions are likely necessary.

Family Preservation and the Homebuilders® Program

The family preservation model was first popularized by Kinney and colleagues (Kinney, Madsen, Fleming, & Haapala, 1977) in the late 1970s, and many of the defining characteristics of that program can still be evidenced in current models. Family preservation programs today vary in their eligibility criteria, and in the specific program components, but generally involve the provision of intensive in-home services (Wells & Tracy, 1996). The aim of family preservation programs is to prevent out-of-home placements in families who have involvement with child welfare agencies with the secondary goals of resolving family crises and improving parenting skills (Child Welfare Information Gateway, 2014; Kinney, Haapala, & Booth, 1991; Wells & Tracy, 1996).

As Mather, Lager, and Harris (2007) note, family preservation services have been criticized by some who claim that evaluation and outcome studies have demonstrated mixed findings. In response to these criticisms, others have cited a lack of *treatment fidelity* and the use of the intervention with families who were not appropriate for the program as the reasons for the mixed findings, rather than the ineffectiveness of the model itself (Kirk, 2001).

While the term family preservation has been widely used to describe a variety of different policies, practices, and programs, Homebuilders® constitutes one type of family preservation program that has demonstrated positive outcomes in empirical studies. The Homebuilders® Program is rated as a 2 (supported by research evidence) by the CEBC in the areas of Interventions for Neglect (including emotional neglect), Post-Permanency Services, Reunification Programs, and Family Stabilization Programs. A study conducted by Kirk and Griffith (2004) found that within a sample of high-risk families involved with child welfare, those who received intensive family preservation services had reduced or delayed out-of-home placement rates even after controlling for risk factors such as prior placement and prior substantiations of abuse or neglect. Additionally, among high-risk families without a new substantiated report of abuse or neglect within 12 months of the start of services, children who received intensive family preservation services were 32% less likely than children in families who did not receive Homebuilders® to be removed from the home (Kirk & Griffith, 2004).

The program focuses on enhancing family relationships, teaching parenting skills, and addressing concrete needs. The stated goals of the program are to reduce child abuse and neglect; decrease family conflict; moderate child behavior problems; and teach families the skills they need to prevent placement or to successfully reunify with their children (Child Welfare Information Gateway, 2014). The program typically lasts four to six weeks, is facilitated by a master's level clinician, and utilizes a wide variety of activities to suit the individual needs of families. Essential components of the program as outlined by the Institute for Family Development (2013) include:

- **Engagement:** Use of a collaborative approach to engage and motivate families.
- **Assessment and Goal Setting:** Use of comprehensive and family-directed assessment that includes goal setting as well as ongoing safety and crisis planning.
- **Behavior Change:** Use of cognitive and behavioral practices and interventions to target maladaptive parenting practices.
- **Skills Development:** Teaching parents and children a wide variety of skills that they practice and receive feedback on.
- **Concrete Services:** Providing and/or helping the family access services that are directly related to achieving the family's goals, while encouraging self-sufficiency.
- **Community Coordination and Interactions:** Coordinating, collaborating, and advocating with other services and systems affecting the family, while teaching parents to advocate and access support for themselves.
- **Immediate Response to Referral:** Accepting referrals 24 hours a day, seven days a week.
- **Provided in the Natural Environment:** Providing services in the families' homes and community.
- **Caseload Size:** Carrying caseloads of two families at a time on average, but can be as high as five.

- **Flexibility and Responsiveness:** Services are individually tailored to each family with attention to strengths, needs, lifestyle, and culture.

The Homebuilders® program and Level 4 Triple P offer two examples of parent-focused interventions. While parent-focused work is often necessary in cases of emotional abuse, these approaches do not address how to repair the damage the abuse may have caused to the child. So, now we turn our attention to child-focused approaches.

Child-Focused Approaches

Being that children exist in the context of a family, child-centered interventions include, to varying degrees, the participation of a parent. It will ultimately be up to clinicians and/or child welfare agencies to determine whether and at which point parents are able to participate in the child's treatment in a productive manner. In situations where the child remains in the care of a parent who has been emotionally abusive, at some point the focus of the work will need to directly address parent–child interactions, although separate but concurrent individual work may need to occur first.

In cases of more severe emotional abuse, or in instances where emotional abuse co-occurred with other types of maltreatment, it may be that the child is in foster care, living with a relative, or has been adopted. While it may not be appropriate or even possible to include the abusive parent in these situations, it can still be valuable to include a supportive adult in the child's treatment. Studies have shown that recovery from trauma-related problems can be enhanced by the active participation of a caregiver in treatment (Deblinger, Lippman, & Steer, 1996; King et al., 2000). Children's ability to recover from traumatic experiences is contingent on their present environments, and parents can help to ensure that positive improvements continue after therapy has concluded. Additionally, inclusion of a parent can help to attain treatment goals concerning parent–child communication, trauma-informed parenting techniques, and application of adaptive coping skills (Cohen, Mannarino, & Deblinger, 2006).

Child Traumatic Stress and Emotional Abuse

Children who experience emotional abuse may develop a broad range of difficulties which are commonly referred to as *child traumatic stress* reactions, which the National Child Traumatic Stress Network (NCTSN) defines as reactions that develop after exposure to one or more traumas which persist after the traumatic event has ended. These reactions can include a variety of responses, such as emotional upset, depressive symptoms, anxiety, behavioral changes, difficulties with attention, academic problems, nightmares, physical symptoms such aches and pains, and relational difficulties. Although emotional abuse may not meet criteria for the definition of a trauma in the strictest sense of the word, exposure to emotional abuse can lead to child traumatic stress reactions because it occurs in the context of a caregiving relationship and is perpetrated by a parent who the child is dependent upon for safety, love, and survival (Glaser, 2002).

The term *complex trauma* is also utilized to refer to children's exposure to multiple traumatic events and stressors, including physical abuse, sexual abuse, emotional abuse, neglect, and witnessing family violence, which begin in childhood, occur repeatedly, and are perpetrated by an individual who is within the caregiving system (Cook et al., 2003; Courtois & Ford, 2009). Underpinning conceptualizations of complex trauma are the multitude of studies which have consistently found that child maltreatment is typically not a one-time event, and that children are often exposed to multiple forms and incidences of abuse. While emotional abuse alone would not result in complex trauma, it is important to mention the concept because of the high co-occurrence rates between emotional abuse and other forms of maltreatment.

Due to the absence of interventions which have been designed primarily for emotional abuse, the child-focused interventions that are presented in this chapter were initially developed for other forms of maltreatment, but focus more broadly on addressing the symptoms and behaviors associated with child traumatic stress reactions. These types of treatments are often referred to as *trauma-focused interventions*. The NCTSN conducted a review of existing empirically supported trauma-focused interventions and identified the common elements that cut across different treatments. These core components are:

- Comprehensive assessment, case conceptualization, and treatment planning
- Providing psychoeducation
- Addressing children and families' traumatic stress reactions and experiences
- Developing and processing a trauma narration
- Enhancing emotional regulation and anxiety management skills
- Facilitating adaptive coping and maintaining adaptive routines
- Teaching parenting skills and behavior management strategies
- Promoting adaptive developmental progression
- Addressing grief and loss
- Promoting safety skills
- Incorporating relapse prevention
- Evaluation of treatment response and effectiveness
- Engagement/addressing barriers to service-seeking.

(NCTSN, 2003)

Two empirically supported interventions for child traumatic stress, Trauma-Focused Cognitive Behavioral Therapy and Child Parent Psychotherapy, are provided as examples of trauma-focused interventions. Remember, however, that a one-size-fits-all approach to this work is never advised and the specific circumstances of each child and family will dictate the intervention that is best suited to address their needs.

Trauma-Focused Cognitive Behavioral Therapy (TF-CBT)

TF-CBT is a phase-based intervention for children aged three to 18 that typically lasts 12–20 sessions (Cohen, Mannarino, & Deblinger, 2006). TF-CBT was originally developed for children who suffered sexual abuse, but it has been applied to children who have experienced a wide range of traumas including emotional abuse (Cohen, Mannarino, Kliethermes, & Murray, 2012). The intervention utilizes cognitive-behavioral theory as its theoretical foundation, but it pulls from other theories such as family relations, empowerment, attachment, and psychobiology in order to provide a comprehensive approach to treatment.

The treatment addresses a wide range of problem domains found in children with child traumatic stress reactions including cognitive, relational and attachment, affective, family, traumatic behavior problems such as those associated with PTSD, and somatic problems (Cohen, Mannarino, & Deblinger, 2006). The following is a synopsis of each phase of treatment:

- **Psychoeducation:** Children and parents receive education throughout treatment regarding each of the phases, and on relevant topics such as child traumatic stress and child abuse.
- **Parenting Skills:** Parents learn and practice effective skills including specific praise, selective attention, and time out, as well as develop contingency reinforcement programs to target specific maladaptive behaviors of the child.
- **Relaxation Skills:** Children develop relaxation techniques and coping skills such as focused breathing and progressive muscle relaxation to manage distressing thoughts and feelings.
- **Affective Expression and Modulation:** Youth work on feelings identification and learn healthy ways to express emotions; they practice strategies such as thought stopping, positive imagery, and positive self-talk to combat negative or distressing thoughts and feelings; and develop problem-solving and social skills.
- **Cognitive Coping I:** Children cultivate an understanding of the relationship between thoughts, feelings, and behaviors and learn about unhelpful and/or inaccurate thoughts.
- **Trauma Narrative:** Youth develop a trauma narrative which describes the traumatic events.
- *In Vivo* **Mastery of Trauma Reminders:** Children identify trauma reminders and then through the process of gradual exposure work to achieve mastery of those trauma reminders.
- **Cognitive Coping and Processing II:** Clinicians assist children in reprocessing cognitive distortions and negative affective states connected to the traumatic exposure.
- **Conjoint Parent–Child Sessions:** The child and parent meet together with the clinician in order to review psychoeducational material; practice and develop new adaptive coping skills; facilitate open and productive communication; and in order for the child to present and discuss the trauma narrative with the parent.

- **Enhancing Future Safety and Development:** Youth engage in activities which promote healthy development and create safety plans for high-risk or potentially challenging situations.

(Cohen, Mannarino, & Deblinger, 2006)

It is important to note that TF-CBT was not designed to include offending parents, and is focused on reducing traumatic stress-related symptoms and behaviors in children. Thus, when applied to emotional abuse, great consideration will need to be taken when deciding whether or not a parent is appropriate to include in treatment. In cases where there is not a parent who is appropriate to partake, there may be other supportive adults in the child's life who can participate (e.g., grandparents, foster providers, etc.).

TF-CBT has led to improvements in symptoms of PTSD, depression, fear, anxiety, behavior problems, and social competence when compared with either other treatment modalities or waitlist control groups (Cohen & Mannarino, 1996, 1998; Cohen, Deblinger, Mannarino, & Steer, 2004; Deblinger et al., 1996; King et al., 2000). Additionally, when appropriate parents are included in treatment, the treatment has been effective in decreasing depressive symptoms and abuse-specific distress of non-offending parents (Cohen et al., 2004). TF-CBT has also shown a reduction of symptoms in samples of children with complex trauma (Cohen et al., 2012). The CEBC has given TF-CBT a rating of 1 (well supported by research evidence) in the areas of Trauma Treatment (Child and Adolescent) and Anxiety Treatment (Child and Adolescent).

Child Parent Psychotherapy (CPP)

Child Parent Psychotherapy (CPP) grew out of infant–parent psychotherapy and is an intervention for children from birth through age five who are experiencing behavioral, emotional, attachment, and/or mental health problems as a result of exposure to traumatic events (Lieberman & Van Horn, 2005). The intervention was originally developed for children and parents who had experienced domestic violence, but it has been applied to other forms of child maltreatment as well. CPP is based in attachment theory, but also integrates elements of psychodynamic, developmental trauma, social learning, and cognitive behavioral theories (Lieberman & Van Horn, 2008).

The primary goal of CPP is to support and strengthen the relationship between the child and parent, and this helps to restore the child's sense of safety, attachment, and appropriate affect, thereby improving his or her behavioral, affective, and social functioning (Lieberman & Van Horn, 2008). The intervention rests on the premise that due to young children's dependency on parents, the attachment system is the main organizer of their responses to danger and safety (Lieberman & Van Horn, 2005).

Young children have a developmentally appropriate expectation that parents will be reliable and protect them from danger, yet when those same individuals become the sources of danger, a child's sense of self and others becomes filled with fear, anger, mistrust, and hypervigilance (Lieberman & Van Horn, 2005). Further, young children are particularly sensitive to maltreatment not only due to their dependency on parents, but also because during this developmental stage they learn primarily from observing and imitating the behavior of those adults around them (Kagan, 1981). As a result of these factors, the developers contend that emotional, behavioral, and attachment problems are best addressed in the context of the child's relationship with the parent. So, although the primary focus of the intervention is on the health and well-being of the child, the intervention occurs mostly through conjoint sessions with the parent and child.

The nature of the trauma the child experienced in conjunction with his or her developmental level determine the structure of CPP sessions. The intervention uses a combination of behavior-based strategies, play, and verbal interpretations (Lieberman & Van Horn, 2005). Through these means, the intervention targets the parent and child's maladaptive representations of themselves and each other, as well as interactions that interfere with the child's functioning and development (Lieberman & Van Horn, 2005). With infants, for example, the child may be present in sessions with the parent, but given the child's limited capabilities, the sessions may focus on teaching the parent to effectively interpret and respond to the infant's needs, and on promoting healthy bonding with the child. With older children, treatment strategies often include play therapy in order to facilitate communication between the child and parent. In addition, when parents have their own trauma histories which interfere with their ability to effectively parent, the clinician helps the parent to process how this can affect perceptions of and interactions with the child (Lieberman & Van Horn, 2005). The clinician then guides the parent in developing new ways to interact with the child that are developmentally appropriate and promote secure attachment. Within this framework, the intervention focuses on the following key components:

- Focus on the **Parent–Child Relationship** as the primary target of the intervention.
- **Continuity of Daily Living**—encouraging a return to normal development, adaptive coping and engagement with present activities and future goals.
- **Safety**—increasing capacity to respond to threats and appropriately appraise situations.
- **Affect Regulation**—maintaining regular levels of affective arousal and reestablishing trust in bodily sensations.
- **Reciprocity in Relationships**—healing relational and interactional difficulties; facilitating secure and healthy attachment; changing maladaptive patterns of interaction.
- **Traumatic Events**—normalization of the traumatic response; encouraging differentiation between reliving and remembering; placing the traumatic events in perspective and developing a conjoint trauma narrative.

(Lieberman & Van Horn, 2005)

CPP is rated a 2 (supported by research evidence) by the CEBC in the areas of Domestic/Intimate Partner Violence, Services for Victims and their Children, Infant and Toddler Mental Health, and Trauma Treatment (Child and Adolescent). Through a series of studies, the intervention has been found to decrease child traumatic stress symptoms, decrease children's maladaptive maternal representations, decrease children's maladaptive representations of themselves, improve parent expectations, and decrease mental health symptoms of parents (Lieberman, Ghosh Ippen, & Van Horn, 2005, 2006; Toth, Maughan, Manly, Spagnola, & Cicchetti, 2002; Toth, Rogosch, Manly, & Cicchetti, 2006).

Case Example 16

Isabella is four years old and attends a preschool program for low-income families. In a recent parent–teacher conference the school suggested Isabella's mother, Carla, seek mental health support for Isabella. The school reports that Isabella is having difficulty calming down; easily becomes frustrated or upset with small tasks; has trouble concentrating; at times becomes hyperactive, but at other times appears withdrawn and depressed; and has difficulty getting along with other children, often hitting or biting when she does not get what she wants. Carla reports that she also sees similar behaviors at home, and states that she just "isn't sure what to do ... nothing seems to help." Carla goes on to say that although things are better now, the first three years of Isabella's life were difficult because "Carla's father—Freddy—is not a nice man. He used to hit me sometimes and we were always yelling at each other." Carla states that during this time she was "distracted, depressed and unhappy" and unable to give Isabella "the attention and love she needed." Carla was silent for a moment then said, "I stopped doing everything for a while, and didn't really talk to friends or family. I was really scared, didn't know what to do."

Carla has not been involved with Isabella's father for over a year, and says that she keeps "hoping that Isabella's behaviors will improve since he is gone and I am doing better, but I feel like nothing seems to calm her down. Sometimes she won't even let me comfort her." Carla also talks about feeling guilty for exposing Isabella to Freddy and so sometimes she just gives her "whatever she wants to try to make her happy."

Reflection Questions

1. Do you think Carla has inflicted emotional abuse on Isabella? According to the FRAMEA framework, what category might Carla's behaviors fall into? What might be the best intervention approach?
2. Do you think any of the treatments presented in this section are appropriate in this case? Why or why not? What other approaches might be necessary?

Child-focused interventions are appropriate in those instances where the child needs individualized attention and treatment for the effects of the emotional abuse, although as you can see they often include the involvement of a parent. We will now turn our attention to interventions whose primary focus is on improving child and parent interactions.

Child–Parent-Focused Approaches

Approaches which target both the child and parent seek to change negative aspects of the parent–child interactions while also enhancing parenting skills (Barlow & Schrader-MacMillan, 2009; DHHS, 2006). These approaches also include family interventions, where treatment is delivered to all members of the family and seeks to improve or change some aspect of the family's functioning. In a literature review on interventions for emotional abuse, Barlow and Schrader-McMillan (2009) note that despite the enormous contribution of family systems theory to understanding the dynamics of emotional abuse, there are not any effectiveness studies of family interventions where the primary focus is emotional abuse. However, two examples of child–parent-focused approaches with particular relevance to emotional abuse are provided.

Parent Child Interaction Therapy (PCIT)

PCIT is an empirically supported treatment originally developed to target maladaptive behaviors in children ages 2–12 while also increasing parenting skills. PCIT teaches parents play-therapy skills to enhance the parent–child relationship as well as problem-solving skills to develop strategies for managing problem behaviors (Eyberg & Boggs, 1989). Accordingly, PCIT uses a developmental approach, behavioral theory, and social learning theory as its foundation while also incorporating elements of attachment theory. The emphasis of the treatment is on changing negative parent–child interactional patterns and the goals of treatment are to improve the quality of the parent–child relationship; decrease child behavior problems and increase prosocial behaviors; increase parenting skills, including positive discipline; and decrease parenting stress (Hembree-Kigin & McNeil, 1995).

PCIT involves two components: a Child-Directed Intervention (CDI) and a Parent-Directed Intervention (PDI). During both components, the child and parent attend sessions together. Parents are taught and coached in the attainment of relationship building skills known as PRIDE skills: Praise, Reflection, Imitation, Description, and Enthusiasm (McNeil & Hembree-Kigin, 2010). Parents receive immediate feedback, coaching, and reinforcement of these skills through the use of a transmitter and receiver system (e.g., a bug in the parent's ear while the clinician observes and provides feedback from behind a one-way mirror). During the CDI component, parents learn how to follow the child's lead in play and how to use identified skills. During the PDI, parents are taught to use direct commands with their child, to follow through with these commands, and to use a time out procedure (McNeil & Hembree-Kigin, 2010). PCIT is mastery-based and progression to the next phase is contingent upon the mastery of skills in the current phase (McNeil & Hembree-Kigin, 2010).

PCIT has demonstrated effectiveness in decreasing child behavior problems, building parenting skills, and strengthening the relationship between the child and parent (Bell & Eyberg, 2002; Eisenstadt, Eyberg, McNeil, Newcomb, & Funderburk, 1993; Eyberg, Funderburk, Hembree-Kigin, McNeil, Querido, & Hood, 2001; Hood & Eyberg, 2003; McNeil & Hembree-Kigin, 2010). The CEBC gives PCIT a rating of 1 (well supported by research evidence) out of 5 in the areas of Parent Training Programs and Disruptive Behavior Treatment (Child and Adolescent).

As you can see, PCIT does not focus on the direct processing of any traumatic events, but rather on the relationship between the children and parent. Nevertheless, the intervention has shown effectiveness with children who have histories of child maltreatment. In cases where there has been mild to moderate emotional abuse which may have, at least in part, developed out of unreasonable developmental expectations and a lack of adequate skills, PCIT may provide parents with the opportunity to learn and develop more effective and supportive skills while also building the relationship with the child.

Combined Parent Child Cognitive Behavioral Approach

CPC-CBT is an empirically supported intervention for children and parents that can be offered to individual families or to groups of families. This treatment was developed for families who are at risk of physical abuse or where there have been instances of physical abuse; where coercive or inappropriate parenting practices are present; and/or where there exists substantial parent–child conflict (Runyon, Deblinger, & Schroeder, 2009).

Research has found this intervention is effective in reducing the use of physical punishment, lessening a parent's anger toward the child, improving consistency in parenting practices, and decreasing child traumatic stress symptoms and behavioral problems in children (Runyon et al., 2009; Runyon, Deblinger, & Steer, 2010). The CEBC gives this intervention a rating of 3 (promising research evidence) in the areas of Parent Training Programs, Prevention of Child Abuse and Neglect (Secondary) Programs, Trauma Treatment (Children and Adolescents), and Interventions for Abusive Behavior.

CPC-CBT utilizes an integrated parent–child cognitive-behavioral model and aims to empower parents to effectively parent their children in a non-coercive and supportive manner; improve parent–child relationships; assist children in healing from abusive experiences; and enhance the safety of family members (Runyon, Deblinger, Ryan, & Thakakar-Kolar, 2004). The intervention employs elements of cognitive behavioral therapy found to be effective in other trauma-focused work and consists of 16 structured sessions that are broken up into four components: Engagement and Psychoeducation; Effective Coping Skills Building; Family Safety Planning; and Abuse Clarification (Runyon et al., 2009). CPC-CBT includes individual sessions with the parent(s), individual sessions with the child(ren), and conjoint sessions with both the parent(s) and child(ren). The following is a synopsis of the topics addressed during different components:

Engagement and Psychoeducation
- Problem-solving barriers that hinder parents' commitment to intervention.
- Eliciting parents' goals and formulating mutually beneficial and agreed-upon goals.
- Psychoeducation about child maltreatment, child development, and age-appropriate expectations, emotions, and ways to manage feelings.
- Processing with parents the impact of their behaviors on their relationships.

Effective Coping Skills Building
- Parents and children develop adaptive coping skills, such as anger management skills.
- Parents practice non-violent and non-coercive conflict resolution, problem-solving, and child behavior management skills.
- The ABC model (antecedent, behavior, consequence) is applied to child–parent interactions.

Family Safety Planning
- Families develop a safety plan for escalating and high-risk situations.
- In conjoint sessions families practice implementation of the safety plan and parents practice the skills they have learned while clinicians coach the development of these skills through the use of corrective feedback and positive reinforcement.

Abuse Clarification
- The clinician works with the child to develop a "praise letter," in which he or she outlines observed changes in the parent's behaviors since involvement in the intervention.
- The child develops a trauma narrative regarding the traumatic parent–child interactions and processes thoughts and feelings related to those experiences.
- The parent writes a clarification letter in which he/she takes full responsibility for abusive behavior, alleviates any of the child's self-blame, and directly addresses any ongoing fears the child may have.

(Runyon et al., 2004)

Although not developed specifically for emotional abuse, CPC-CBT incorporates elements and practice strategies that may work well with families in which emotional abuse has occurred. The intervention addresses not only maladaptive parenting, but also provides an opportunity for the child and parent to process and clarify the abusive experiences and develop more adaptive skills in order to help prevent abuse from occurring in the future.

Case Example 17

Clarissa and Clarence have three children—Janice, age 14, Dante, age 11, and Marshall, age five. They live in an urban neighborhood where there are frequent incidences of violence. The family lacks stable housing and has moved frequently throughout the children's lives. Clarissa had regular involvement with child protective services as a child due to her mother's substance abuse and because she was sexually abused by her mother's boyfriend when she was an adolescent. The family has three prior CPS reports, all of which were unsubstantiated. The first report was for neglect due to a lack of adequate food in the house. In response, the family was provided with resources for the local food bank and social welfare programs. The second referral made was due to an allegation of sexual abuse regarding Janice and an uncle. This referral was also not substantiated, although the family no longer spends time with the uncle. The most recent referral was for physical abuse for an incident where Dante was reportedly "whopped" after his mother found out that he stole from a local convenience store.

The children all describe that sometimes they are "spanked" when they misbehave or are yelled at and told that they will never amount to anything. They also report that their mother does not let them "do anything, like play outside or go to the store" because she is always worried something bad is going to happen. Clarissa also appears "depressed" and often lacks the energy to engage with the children or respond to their emotional needs. The children describe her as "lying in bed most of the day, but getting mad at us when we want to do the same thing." "Sometimes," Janice explains, "when Mom is sad she wants me to stay home just to take care of her ... it's like she needs me to make her feel happy, but I want to have my own life. I'm 14 and I want to spend time with friends." Dante feels that he gets the brunt of his mother's anger and reports that she is "unpredictable—like sometimes she is all nice and doesn't care what I do, but other times I get in really big trouble for little things and have to do a million chores." He goes on to say that she always compares him to Janice and asks him why he can't be more like her. The children describe their father as "a drinker" and that he is "scary when he drinks sometimes—like he says really mean things and calls us horrible names, so we just know to stay away." At other times, however, when Clarence is not drinking, the children describe him as "a good Dad, he works hard and tries to make Mom and everyone happy."

Reflection Questions

1. What are the risk factors present in this family? What protective factors can you identify?
2. What intervention approaches are needed in addressing this family's needs?

School-Based Approaches to Intervention

Given that we know a collaborative approach to intervention can contribute to positive outcomes, involvement of schools becomes not only preferable, but necessary. The adage that it takes a village to raise a child is particularly pertinent in cases of emotional abuse. Clinicians, caseworkers, and others involved with these children and families should make efforts to coordinate services with teachers and school counselors. They are a valuable source of information given that they spend so much time with these children and often have important insights regarding their functioning. Additionally, many children who suffer emotional abuse will experience academic and/or social difficulties; collaboration with school personnel can help to establish school-based supports to encourage school success.

There are programs in many schools which seek to enhance protective factors for youth. Examples of such programs include mentoring programs, after-school programs, and social skills groups. School systems are also increasingly implementing interventions that are specifically geared toward children adversely affected by trauma. In fact, several trauma-focused interventions are being adapted for delivery in school systems in order to meet the needs of children who are unable to access services outside of the school setting. One such intervention, Cognitive Behavioral Intervention for Trauma in Schools (CBITS), was developed for the school setting.

Cognitive Behavioral Intervention for Trauma in Schools (CBITS)

CBITS is a cognitive-behavioral, skills-based group intervention for children who have experienced a wide range of traumas, and is aimed at relieving symptoms of child traumatic stress, depression, and anxiety. The program consists of 10 group sessions, one to three individual sessions with the child depending on level of need, two parent education sessions, and one teacher-education session. CBITS focuses on teaching the following cognitive behavioral techniques:

- Psychoeducation about reactions to trauma
- Relaxation training
- Cognitive restructuring

- Gradual exposure to trauma reminders
- Development of a trauma narrative.

(Schultz, Barnes-Proby, Chandra, Jaycox, Maher, & Pecora, 2010)

CBITS has been given a rating of 3 (promising research evidence) by the CEBC in the areas of Trauma Treatment (Child and Adolescent) and Anxiety Treatment (Child and Adolescent). In randomized controlled trials, children who received the intervention had a significantly higher reduction in symptoms of child traumatic stress and depression compared to those on a waitlist at a three-month follow up (Stein et al., 2003).

Prevention of Emotional Abuse

Many of the programs funded by the federal and state governments are intervention approaches aimed toward providing services to families in crisis where maltreatment has already occurred. As a publication on prevention efforts produced by the United States Department of Health and Human Services' Office of Child Abuse and Neglect (OCAN) points out:

> only a small percentage of all resources specifically earmarked for child maltreatment in the United States is actually devoted to prevention. Furthermore, investment in prevention can be highly vulnerable during economic downturns, when legislatures search for line items to trim from overburdened State and Federal budgets.
>
> (2003, p. 2)

While intervention programs are invariably necessary, prevention efforts are also crucial in adequately addressing the problem. As Mary Richmond, an early pioneer of social work, commented, "The good social worker ... doesn't go on helping people out of a ditch. Pretty soon she begins to find out what ought to be done to get rid of the ditch" (in Abbott, 1919, p. 313, as cited in Morales & Sheafor, 2004).

Despite the challenges, prevention and early intervention monies and policies have been incorporated into many federal programs, and national advocacy organizations continue to support and develop prevention efforts (Mather et al., 2007). Prevention strategies include universal, selective, and targeted efforts. Universal interventions take the broadest approach and target the general population, while selective preventive programs target individuals or sub-populations who have identified risk factors. Targeted interventions focus on high-risk families where abuse has not occurred, but where there are concerning behaviors and/or signs suggesting that without intervention it is likely to occur (Mikton & Butchart, 2009).

Universal Prevention Approaches

Universal prevention efforts seek to raise awareness of the general population, service providers, and decision-makers regarding emotional abuse and its associated consequences. These can be viewed as macro-level approaches to intervention and might include:

- Public service announcements and media campaigns that raise awareness about the scope of the problem.
- Education campaigns that promote positive parenting, such as hospitals and medical offices distributing information on child development and effective parenting practices.
- Parent education and training programs offered to the general public.
- School-based child abuse prevention curriculums.

Evaluation of general population based approaches to prevention can be difficult, and there do not appear to be any studies on the effectiveness of programs that specifically target emotional abuse. However, public awareness and education campaigns directed at other public health concerns have demonstrated positive outcomes, such as anti-smoking initiatives and efforts to curtail drinking and driving.

Selective Prevention Approaches

Selective prevention programs target risk factors that are prominent among high-risk groups. Risk factors can include child factors, such as behavior problems or developmental disabilities; parent factors, such as the presence of mental health problems or substance misuse; and environmental factors, such as poverty, the presence of community violence, or a lack of adequate resources (DHHS OCAN, 2003). Accordingly, selective prevention efforts target specific risk factors and also seek to enhance related protective factors.

There is a scarcity of literature regarding selective prevention programs aimed specifically at emotional abuse; however, there are a number of programs directed at preventing child maltreatment. Two of these approaches, parent training programs and home visiting programs, have shown promise in preventing child maltreatment (see Mikton & Butchart, 2009). The Triple P—Positive Parenting Program® that was previously described can be viewed as a selective prevention program when it is targeted toward families where abuse has not occurred but where there are general risk factors present. One example of a home visiting program, the Nurse–Family Partnership, is also outlined here.

Nurse–Family Partnership

The Nurse–Family Partnership (NFP), is a prenatal and infancy home visitation program that aims to improve the health, well-being, and self-sufficiency in parents and their children (Dawley, Loch, & Bindrich, 2007). NFP is a selective prevention program because it targets first-time low-income mothers, a group at a higher risk of child maltreatment when compared to the general population. Nurses follow a detailed program that provides education and support to parents on a range of topics including nutrition, parenting, creating safe households, identifying symptoms of illness or pregnancy complications, effective communication with service providers, and educational and career opportunities (Dawley et al., 2007). Nurses also assist in parent–child interactions and teach skills such as how to appropriately attune and respond to the needs of the child.

NFP has been found to be effective in reducing a range of risk factors and in enhancing several protective factors. Notably, in one long-term study mothers who received the NFP program from pregnancy until the child's second year of life had considerably fewer cases of substantiated abuse or neglect over a 15-year period when compared to the control group (Olds et al., 1997). Additionally, findings also indicated that when compared to the control group, mothers who received NFP services reported fewer parenting beliefs that are associated with child maltreatment, such as a lack of empathy, belief in physical punishment, and unrealistic expectations (Olds et al., 1997; Olds, Henderson, & Kitzman, 1994). The CEBC has also given NFP a rating of 1 (well supported by research evidence) in the areas of Home Visiting Programs for Child Well-Being, Home Visiting Programs for Prevention of Child Abuse and Neglect, Teen Pregnancy Services, and Prevention of Child Abuse and Neglect Programs.

Targeted Prevention Approaches

Targeted prevention approaches focus on delivering services to families who have been identified as high risk, but whose behaviors have not crossed the threshold of what is considered abuse. For example, CPS may investigate a referral regarding emotional abuse and not find that abuse was occurring, but identify several risk factors or signs that abuse is likely to occur in the absence of intervention. This family may then be referred to a targeted prevention program in an effort to prevent maltreatment. PCIT and the Triple P—Positive Parenting Program® can both be used as targeted preventive measures with families. One other program, Trauma-Adapted Family Connections, is also provided as an example of a targeted approach.

Trauma-Adapted Family Connections (TA-FC)

Family Connections (FC) is a program developed by the University of Maryland that targets low-income families with at least one child who is at risk of abuse or neglect. Understanding that community violence and intergenerational trauma often impact the lives of the families FC targeted, TA-FC was created with trauma-informed modifications. The goals of the intervention are to decrease risk factors for child maltreatment, increase protective factors, increase the safety of children in the home, and decrease maladaptive behaviors of children in families. The intervention is grounded in an ecological systems approach, and includes elements of trauma theory, Bowen Family Therapy, cognitive-behavioral strategies, and attachment theory (Collins et al., 2011).

Outcomes studies found that families who completed the treatment showed reductions in several risk factors, including a decrease in parents' depressive symptoms, parenting stress, and children's trauma symptoms, as well as an increase in parents' psychological functioning (Collins et al., 2011; DePanfilis & Dubowitz, 2005). An increase in protective factors has also been demonstrated, including improvements in a parent's sense of competence, sense of community, and perceived access to family resources (Collins et al., 2011; DePanfilis & Dubowitz, 2005). The CEBC rates the intervention a 3 (promising research evidence) in the areas of Casework Practice, Interventions for Neglect, and Prevention of Child Abuse and Neglect.

The treatment typically lasts six months and emphasizes engagement strategies with the family and encourages collaboration, while also providing resources to meet basic needs, a service plan, advocacy on behalf of the family's needs and rights, and referrals to other community agencies (Collins et al., 2011). Following a comprehensive family assessment, intervention strategies include individual, family, and group modalities which seek to promote family cohesion and improve relationships. Services are typically delivered on a weekly basis in the home, although community settings can also be utilized. The treatment includes three phases:

Phase One: Engagement, assessment, enhancing and building emotional and physical safety, developing a service plan
Phase Two: Family psychoeducation, emotion identification and affect regulation, building family cohesion and communication-strengthening
Phase Three: Family shared meaning of traumas, case closure and endings.
(Collins et al., 2011)

Trauma-Informed Care

Despite the strong research base which draws the link between social and economic injustice and child maltreatment, prevention and intervention efforts continue to be directed toward individuals and families, rather than focused on resolving the structural problems and inequalities in society which contribute to social and economic difficulties in the first place. It is crucial to retain an ecological perspective in confronting emotional abuse and remember that in order to deliver effective interventions certain environmental contexts which promote and support practice are necessary. These social network factors, such as adequate funding, appropriate policies, supportive values, and organizational support, provide the framework within which effective intervention and prevention can occur. In the absence of these entities, practitioners and local agencies lack the necessary tools to deliver high quality services. In an effort to emphasize the importance of these social network factors, this chapter concludes with discussion of one initiative that seeks to change the structure and culture of social service agencies in a way that will inevitably make them more responsive and sensitive to the needs of the individuals and families they serve.

Given the astonishing prevalence of emotional abuse and child maltreatment in general, not to mention other forms of trauma that children experience during childhood, social service agencies will undoubtedly work with individuals whose lives have been negatively impacted by trauma, regardless of their specific area of focus. In fact, studies have demonstrated that trauma survivors are the majority of clients in human service systems including health and mental health centers, substance abuse facilities, detention centers, and social welfare agencies (Finkelhor, 1986; Najavits, Weiss, & Shaw, 1997). Since providers outside the realm of child welfare often have no way of knowing whether or not clients have experienced trauma, best practice demands reliance on procedures and policies most likely to promote growth and least likely to be re-traumatizing (Elliot, Bjelajac, Fallot, Markoff, & Reed, 2005).

Consequently, there has been a growing push for agencies to adopt a systems-focused framework that has been termed trauma-informed care (TIC). Although not designed to treat the effects of traumatization, TIC fosters a common language and supports an environment that minimizes the likelihood of re-traumatization (Butler, Critelli, & Rinfrette, 2011). According to Harris and Fallot (2001), TIC involves the establishment of a culture that emphasizes five key values:

1. ensuring physical and emotional **safety**;
2. maximizing **trustworthiness** through task clarity, consistency, and interpersonal boundaries;

3. maximizing consumer **choice** and control;
4. maximizing **collaboration** and sharing power; and
5. prioritizing **empowerment** and skills building.

In addition, Carol Muskett (2014), in a review of the literature on TIC in inpatient mental health settings, found that there are three key principles of TIC: clients need to feel connected, valued, informed, and hopeful of recovery; the connection between childhood trauma and adult psychopathology needs to be understood by all employees; and staff need to work in mindful and empowering ways with individuals, families, social support networks, and other social service agencies to promote and protect the autonomy of each individual.

Elliot et al. (2005) developed 10 principles that define trauma-informed care to help guide policy-makers and social service agencies who strive to adopt better practices. They argue that when organizations are trauma-informed, services will be more accessible and more effective for survivors of traumatic events. Trauma-informed services:

1. Recognize the impact of violence and victimization on development and coping strategies.
2. Identify recovery from trauma as a primary goal.
3. Employ an empowerment model.
4. Strive to maximize an individual's choices and control over her recovery.
5. Are based in a relational collaboration.
6. Create an atmosphere that is respectful of a survivor's need for safety, respect, and acceptance.
7. Emphasize strengths, highlighting adaptations over symptoms and resilience over pathology.
8. Aim to minimize the possibilities of revictimization.
9. Strive to be culturally competent and to understand each individual in the context of his or her life experiences and cultural background.
10. Solicit consumer input and involve consumers in designing and evaluating services.

The task of creating more trauma-informed systems of care may at first seem daunting to agencies who have not previously fully considered the role or impact of trauma in the lives of their consumers. As Harris and Fallot (2001) note, "The shift in philosophy amounts to nothing less than a paradigm shift within service delivery systems" (p. 21). However, given the current state of knowledge regarding the profound impact trauma has on individuals, families, and communities, as well as the tremendous prevalence of adverse childhood experiences, the only ethical choice is to shift programs and practices to reflect this knowledge. Harris and Fallot (2001) offer the following requirements for creating TIC:

- Administrative commitment to change.
- Universal screening of consumers for trauma.
- Training and Education for all staff on issues related to trauma.
- Review hiring practices and hire individuals with a commitment to TIC, and include training and education on trauma for new hires.
- Review policies and procedures and revise as necessary to reflect core values of TIC.

It is our obligation, as policy-makers, legislators, and practitioners who choose to work in the social service industry, and most importantly as individuals concerned with human rights, to consider the impact agency policies and procedures have on consumers. Although difficult, we must reflect on the ways in which the very structures and agencies that were designed to help and provide services to individuals and families in need may also be sources of oppression or re-traumatization. And, with this knowledge, we must facilitate changes.

Key Chapter Takeaways

- A comprehensive assessment must be conducted in order to determine the appropriate level and modes of intervention.
- A framework for intervention is needed which utilizes an ecological systems and developmental perspective, is child-centered, trauma-informed, strengths-based, and culturally competent.
- Evidence-based practice is a process-oriented decision-making approach that requires the interchange between client values,

practitioner expertise, and applicable research that is reliant upon reflection and critical thinking on the part of the clinician.
- Common factors of effective interventions include client factors, practitioner factors, relationship factors, practice factors, change factors, and social network factors.
- Interventions for emotional abuse are multifaceted and interdisciplinary, and can include parent-focused, child-focused, and parent–child-focused approaches. These approaches are often mutually reinforcing and there exists a certain degree of overlap between them given the relational context of the problem.
- Parent-focused interventions are services directed at the parent that aim to change some aspect of the parent's well-being, address environmental factors impacting their ability to parent, and/or correct the abusive behavior. These can include parent training programs, family preservation services, individual therapy for the parent, and the provision of resources to meet basic needs and decrease environmental stressors.
- Child-focused approaches focus on healing the effects of the abuse on the child. These typically involve trauma-focused interventions with an appropriate parent to varying degrees.
- Parent–child-focused interventions are relationship approaches that typically involve therapeutic work with the child and parent or the entire family. These approaches seek to improve parent–child interactions and parenting skills, and in some cases also strive to clarify and process past abusive experiences.
- Universal prevention efforts seek to raise awareness of the general population, service providers, and decision-makers regarding emotional abuse and its associated consequences.
- Targeted prevention programs (also called early intervention) are aimed at families who have risk factors which increase the likelihood that abuse or neglect may occur.
- Trauma-informed care involves the establishment of an agency culture that emphasizes safety, trustworthiness, choice, collaboration, and empowerment.

Glossary

Affect Regulation: Also called emotion regulation, this is the ability of an individual to initiate, inhibit, or modulate their emotional state in an environment. Affect regulation is a process that involves subjective experiences (feelings), cognitive processes, and emotion-related physiological responses.

Child Traumatic Stress: The term used to describe reactions that develop in children after exposure to one or more traumas, and which persist after the traumatic event has ended. These reactions can include a variety of responses, such as emotional upset, depressive symptoms, anxiety, behavioral changes, difficulties with attention, academic problems, nightmares, physical symptoms such aches and pains, and relational difficulties.

Multidisciplinary: The involvement of several different disciplines (e.g., social worker, psychologist, medical professional, etc.) and/or agencies in the delivery of intervention services for emotional abuse.

Multimodal: The use of several different intervention approaches and/or methods in treating or preventing emotional abuse.

Trauma-Focused Interventions: Empirically supported interventions that target child traumatic stress reactions and focus on repairing the direct and indirect consequences of traumatic exposure while also enhancing resiliency.

Trauma-Informed: A perspective that considers and infuses knowledge of trauma and its adverse consequences when conceptualizing clients' problems, strengths, and possible solutions, and acting in collaboration with all those involved to support recovery and resiliency.

Treatment Fidelity: A term used to describe the degree to which an intervention is implemented and delivered in a manner that is accurate and consistent with the original model.

Class Discussion Questions

1. Why is it so important to have a multidisciplinary response to emotional abuse? Why do you think it is often necessary to include many different types of interventions for these families?
2. How might you utilize a strengths-based perspective when developing a treatment plan for a child or parent? What activities or interventions might you suggest in an effort to enhance protective factors?
3. What are some of the considerations that need to be taken into account when determining the best intervention approach? What factors would you contemplate when deciding whether or not to include an abusive parent in a child's treatment?
4. What are the benefits of parent–child-focused approaches? When might they be appropriate and when might they be contra-indicated?
5. What prevention efforts have you observed in your community concerning emotional abuse? Do you think they work? Why or why not?
6. What are the difficulties in implementing trauma-informed care in organizations? What are the benefits of this approach?

APPENDIX A
ADDITIONAL INSTRUMENTS FOR ASSESSING ABUSE/NEGLECT

Childhood Experience of Care and Abuse (Centre for Abuse and Trauma Studies, Middlesex University, London) has both training for interviewing and a questionnaire (CECA.Q) that is available from its website. This is what the website says about the instrument:

> A brief self-report version has been validated against the interview. This assesses loss of parents, neglect, antipathy from main carers and physical and sexual abuse. Support in childhood is also included. The measure shows acceptable sensitivity and specificity against the interview measure, and published cut-off scores are available. The CECA.Q has been translated into a number of languages (e.g. Italian, German, Spanish, Portuguese, Chinese) and has been used in Europe, USA, Canada, South America and the Far East. The measure is significantly associated with both the Parental Bonding Instrument and the Childhood Trauma Questionnaire3, but has wider coverage of maltreatment, shows a dose-response effect in relation to lifetime clinical depression and has improved prediction of disorder.
>
> (www.cecainterview.com/)

Comprehensive Child Maltreatment Scale (CCMS)

The CCMS is a self-report measure assessing the experience of various maltreating acts during childhood.... Participants report how frequently their primary maternal figure, primary paternal figure, and another adult or older adolescent performed each of the listed acts on a Likert-type scale ranging from 0 (never) to 4 (very frequently). The current study utilized three scales of the CCMS: physical abuse, psychological abuse, and neglect.

(Allen, 2011, p. 2097)

The original article on this instrument is found in Higgins and McCabe (2003).

Early Trauma Inventory Self-Report-Short Form (ETISR-SF)

The ETISR-SF is a 27-item questionnaire used for the assessment of physical, emotional, and sexual abuse, and a general traumatic experience that may have occurred before age 18.

(Jeon et al., 2009, p. 212)

The original article concerning this instrument is Bremner et al. (2000).

The Psychological Treatment Measure (PMM). A five-item measure of exposure to parental behaviors that meets the definition of psychological maltreatment was developed by Baker and Festinger (2011). The instrument was based on the definition of psychological maltreatment endorsed by the American Professional Society on the Abuse of Children. One item represents each of the areas of spurning, terrorizing, isolating, exploiting/corrupting, and denying emotional responsiveness. The measure was previously validated against four already established measures of psychological maltreatment with statistically significant correlations indicating good validity (Baker & Festinger, 2011). Those four measures drew from: the Childhood Trauma Questionnaire (CTQ)—Emotional Abuse subscale, and the CTQ—Emotional Neglect Subscale, the emotional abuse subscale of the Childhood Abuse and Trauma Scale, the Family Environment

Questionnaire psychological abuse subscale, the Family Environment Questionnaire psychological abuse subscale, and the Conflict Tactics Scale—Parent–Child version psychological aggression subscale.

Each of the five items in the PMM is rated separately for mother/stepfather and father/stepmother on a five-point scale from never (score of 0) to very often (score of 4). Total scores could range from 0 (score of 0 on all five items) to 40 (score of 4 on all five items for both parents). The item description presented to the participants was taken directly from the APSAC Handbook (Binggeli, Hart, & Brassard, 2001) for: (1) spurning, (2) terrorizing, (3) isolating, (4) exploited/corrupted, (5) and denying emotional responsiveness (Baker & Festinger, 2011).

World Health Organization Composite International Diagnostic Interview (WHO CIDI)

> The WHO CIDI is a fully structured diagnostic instrument for the assessment of mental disorders. It must be administered by trained lay interviewers: diagnoses are based on the definitions and criteria of the Diagnostic and Statistical Manual of Mental Disorders, Fourth Edition (DSM-IV) and the International Classification of Disease (ICD) 10-symptom criteria. This analysis uses reports of specific trauma events only and not the full diagnosis of posttraumatic stress disorder (PTSD). The WHO CIDI section of PTSD collects comprehensive data on lifetime trauma exposure, including information on 30 specific types of trauma and age of first exposure to each qualifying trauma and assesses for the presence and severity of PTSD symptoms for each reported exposure.
>
> (Porche et al., 2011, p. 986)

It is available as a computer-assisted interview as well as a paper-and-pencil instrument. Short forms of the instrument are also available (see Kessler et al., 2002, 2003, 2004; Kessler & Üstün, 2004).

Lifetime Experiences Questionnaire (LEQ)

The Lifetime Experiences Questionnaire (LEQ) is an 82-item measure containing items that inquire about various forms of childhood emotional abuse and neglect, physical abuse and neglect, and sexual abuse experiences that occurred prior to age 15. For example, participants responded to questions such as, "Did anyone humiliate or demean you in the presence of other people?", "Were you ever beaten up?" Participants were asked then to report how often each situation occurred prior to age 15, from "never" to "more than 20 times," and also reported who perpetrated the action. Continuous variables for each type of child abuse (emotional abuse/neglect, physical abuse/neglect, and sexual abuse) were created by averaging the participants' frequency ratings across the items designed to measure each type of abuse. The 11 items assessing emotional neglect referred exclusively to neglect by the parent or caregiver. Forms of emotional neglect assessed included ignoring, isolating, lack of praise or affection, parentification, and psychological unavailability. The 27 items assessing emotional abuse assessed such experiences across the extended family. Forms of emotional abuse assessed included belittling, ridiculing, spurning, humiliating, rejecting, extorting, and terrorizing.

(Wright et al., 2009, p. 62)

See also Gibb et al. (2001) and Gibb, Alloy, and Abramson (2003).

Parental Attachment Questionnaire (PAQ)

A 55-item measure intended to assess perceptions of parental availability and support using a 5-point Likert scale. A total score captures their overall view of their personal attachment to their parents, using dimensions that capture the nature of the relationship on three subscales: (1) Affective Quality of Attachment, (2) Parental Fostering of Autonomy, and (3) Parental Support. Higher PAQ scores indicate greater sense of attachment to parents.

(Rodriguez & Tucker, 2011, p. 249)

Original article on the PAQ was developed by Kenny (1987).

Trauma Symptom Checklist for Children (TSCC)

Developed by John Briere, the TSCC is used to evaluate acute and posttraumatic symptomatology in children aged eight to 16 and requires approximately 15 to 20 minutes. The manual, test booklets, and profile forms must be purchased from www4.parinc.com/Products/Product.aspx?ProductID=TSCC.

Trauma Antecedents Questionnaire

> ...was used to measure exposure to physical abuse, sexual abuse, emotional abuse, emotional neglect and witnessing domestic violence. Although the questionnaire consists of 42 items that assess a range of adverse and adaptive experiences, only 10 items assessing these 5 domains of maltreatment were included in the current analyses.
>
> (Rosenkranz et al., 2012, p. 441)

Assessment instrumentation software must be purchased from the Trauma Center at the Justice Resource Institute: www.traumacenter.org/products/instruments.php.

APPENDIX B
RESOURCES

Adults Surviving Child Abuse (www.asca.org.au).
American Psychological Association. Guidelines for Psychological Evaluation in Child Protection Matters (www.apa.org/practice/guidelines/child-protection.pdf).
The American Society on the Abuse of Children (www.apsac.org/). This organization has an annual colloquium with workshops and training institutes, publications, practice guidelines, and study guides.
Australian Childhood Foundation. *Heart Felt: A Collection of Children's Experiences and Stories of Abuse, Recovery and Hope*. Pictures drawn by abused Australian children can be seen in file:///C:/Users/David.David-PC/Downloads/heartfelt%20small.pdf.
Baker, A.J.L. (2009). Adult recall of childhood psychological maltreatment: Definitional strategies and challenges. *Children and Youth Services Review*, 31, 703–714. Note: This article contains a review of 15 different measures of adult retrospective recall of abuse/neglect.
California Evidence Based Clearinghouse for Child Welfare (www.cebc4cw.org/).
Child Welfare Information Gateway (www.childwelfare.gov). A service of the Children's Bureau, Administration for Children and Families, U.S. Department of Health Services.
Kisiel, C., Conradi, L., Fehrenbach, T., Torgersen, E., & Briggs, E.C. (2014). Assessing the effects of trauma in children and adolescents in practice settings. *Child and Adolescent Clinics of North America*, 23, 223–242. This article identifies a number of child and adolescent trauma-focused assessment tools and discusses considerations in the assessment process.
Levis, D.J. (2012). A review of childhood abuse questionnaires and suggested treatment approaches (http://cdn.intechopen.com/pdfs/33654.pdf). This chapter reviews and discusses a number of instruments that can be used to assess child maltreatment.
National Child Traumatic Stress Network (www.nctsn.org).
National Resource Center for Family-Centered Practice at The University of Iowa (http://clas.uiowa.edu/nrcfcp/).

National Resources Center for In-Home Services at The University of Iowa (www.uiowa.edu/nrcihs/home-services).

National Society for Prevention of Cruelty to Children (www.nspcc.org.uk).

Rape, Abuse & Incest National Network (National Sexual Assault Hotline) (www.rainn.org).

Strand, V.C., Pasquale, L.E., & Sarmiento, T.L. (2005) (Children and Families Institute for Research, Support, and Training at Fordham University) *Child and adolescent trauma measures: A review* (https://ncwwi.org/files/Evidence_Based_and_Trauma-Informed_Practice/Child-and-Adolescent-Trauma-Measures_A-Review-with-Measures.pdf). This collection contains measures of exposure to trauma, symptoms of trauma, and distress indices.

Substance Abuse and Mental Health Services Administration's (SAMHSA) National Registry for Evidence-Based Programs and Practices (www.nrepp.samhsa.gov/).

Tonmyr, L., Draca, J., Crain, J., & MacMillan, H.L. (2011). Measurement of emotional/psychological child maltreatment: A review. *Child Abuse & Neglect*, 35, 767–782. This article reports an extensive review of measures of emotional child abuse that have been tested for reliability and validity.

APPENDIX C
BIOPSYCHOSOCIAL AND TRAUMA-INFORMED CLINICAL ASSESSMENT OF CHILDREN

Clinical assessments of children who have experienced emotional abuse follow the same theoretical framework that was outlined at the beginning of Chapter 5. The accepted standard of care in clinical practice is to conduct a comprehensive assessment prior to making any decisions regarding treatment. In fact, the information collected during the assessment process informs the decision-making process and will help to indicate the interventions that are necessary. This is considered good practice in all clinical work, but it becomes particularly important when working with children who have experienced emotional abuse given the myriad of direct and indirect consequences of abuse.

Clinicians should carefully observe children and their caregivers throughout all assessment interviews. Initial history-taking and assessment can guide clinicians in choosing standardized assessment instruments. Critically, clinicians should also make use of information obtained from teachers, other therapists, physicians, protective services workers, and extant court or criminal records. To provide effective care, clinicians will not restrict assessment to the first few visits but will continue to assess throughout the plan of care.

The Presenting Problem and Referral Source
Children who have experienced emotional abuse may be referred to intervention services from a variety of sources, such as caregivers, teachers,

juvenile or family court, child protective services, and medical professionals. The clinical assessment needs to explore not only the reason for the referral—often called the presenting problem—but also examine other factors which could be contributing to the child's problem behaviors.

A thorough clinical assessment is particularly important because those adults interacting with the child may have mislabeled or misunderstood the child's symptoms and behaviors. For example, while an adolescent may be referred by a school counselor for self-injurious behaviors such as cutting and a decline in school performance, the underlying cause of these symptoms and behaviors may be the emotional abuse he or she is suffering at home. Likewise, the juvenile courts may refer an adolescent for therapy after being charged with underage drinking and assault for fighting with a peer, when the youth's aggression and substance use stem from exposure to emotional abuse. A comprehensive assessment that considers multiple factors and the interactions between the various systems is the best way to uncover underlying causes of behaviors and symptoms.

Similarly, it is also crucial to consider what type of work the child or family is seeking. Is a mother bringing her child to therapy because of behavioral issues that she is unaware are being caused by maladaptive or harsh parenting practices? Is a father seeking services as a result of a mandate by child protective services? Is the caregiver looking for family therapy, or individual therapy for the child? Clinicians need to consider what type of therapy is being requested, and whether or not the request is appropriate given the nature of the issues. An important part of the therapeutic process is collaborating with the client and caregiver (when involved) in order to reach agreement regarding the intervention method and to develop mutually agreed upon treatment goals.

Observations

Clinicians observe clients throughout the assessment process, either through formal or informal means. In a formal observation, the child may be directed to conduct an activity, or the child and parent may be instructed to interact together while the clinician utilizes some form of standardized criteria by which to assess functioning or interactions. The data obtained provides valuable information that often cannot be garnered through other means. More informal observations also occur, whereby the clinician notices the client and/or caregiver's reactions, behavior, affect, and demeanor throughout the assessment process.

Standardized Measures

Clinicians choose standardized assessment measures based on the information they obtain during clinical interviews. These measures are completed as part of the initial evaluation, but also at regular intervals to track progress and inform clinical decision-making. Table A3.1 provides a list of some commonly utilized measures. Notice that some of these

Table A3.1 Standardized assessment measures

Measure	Format
Achenbach Child Behavior Checklist (CBCL; Achenbach & Rescorla, 2000, 2001)	Caregiver report on children ages 1.5–5 or 6–18 (two versions)
Alabama Parenting Questionnaire–Child Report (APQ; Frick, 1991)	Youth self-report for ages 6–18
Alabama Parenting Questionnaire–Parent Self-Report (APQ; Frick, 1991)	Caregiver self-report (for caregivers with children ages 6–18)
Child Abuse Potential Inventory (CAPI; Milner, 1990)	Caregiver self-report
Children's Depression Inventory (CDI-II; Kovacs, 1985)	Youth self-report for ages 7–17
Parent–Child Conflict Tactics Scales (CTSPA; Straus et al., 1998)	Caregiver self-report
Parental Stress Index (PSI; Abidin, 1995)	Caregiver self-report (for caregivers with children 0–12)
Strengths and Differences Questionnaire (SDQ; Goodman, 1997) Youth Version	Youth self-report for ages 11–16
Trauma Symptom Checklist for Children—Adolescent Version (TSCC-A; Briere, 1996)	Youth self-report for ages 8–16
Trauma Symptom Checklist for Young Children (TSCYC; Briere, 2005)	Caregiver report on children ages 3–12
UCLA Post-Traumatic Stress Reaction Index (UCLA PTSD-RI; Pynoos, Rodriguez, Steinberg, Stuber, & Frederick, 1998)	Youth self-report for ages 7+

measures are focused on gaging the child's functioning, while others are targeted at assessing the caregiver's view of the child and/or his or her own attitudes and beliefs about parenting.

Clinical Interviews

Clinical interviews are conducted with the child and caregiver separately. Clinicians generally utilize intake forms to gather information about the presenting problem, but also to obtain information pertaining to the client's history, current and past symptoms and behaviors, and various other psychosocial factors. In cases where the child is in the custody of child protective services and/or in an out-of-home placement, these interviews can occur with foster providers, caseworkers, and others who may have regular interaction with the child. More information about the data gathered during these interviews is outlined below.

Collaboration with Collateral Sources

Given the nature of these cases, children are often understandably reticent to engage during the assessment process. Caregivers also vary in their willingness and ability to participate in treatment, and sometimes have skewed perceptions of their child's behavior. Consequently, information from collateral professionals can provide important information and clinicians will often consult with other individuals who regularly work with the child in order to hear their concerns and observations. It is not uncommon for various adults in the child's life to express different—even seemingly conflicting—views of the child's behavior. Collecting information from a variety of sources provides a more complete picture of the child's functioning.

Information Collected and Considerations

Table A3.2 applies the ecological systems framework to the assessment process and provides a summary of areas that need to be considered within each level of a child's ecosystem. The list is by no means exhaustive, and will need to be tailored to each child's needs and circumstances.

As mentioned previously, in cases where mild to moderate emotional abuse is the only form of maltreatment identified child

Table A3.2 Ecological framework for assessment

Ecosystem	Areas to consider
Individual	Current and past cognitive, emotional, and behavioral development; medical history; symptoms and behaviors; problem solving skills; intelligence; communication and language; temperament; social skills and interpersonal relationship skills; attitudes and beliefs about self, world, and self in relation to world; religious or spiritual beliefs and activities; attachment; coping skills; and strengths; history of traumatic exposure or loss; history of child welfare involvement and any placement disruptions; substance use; and any legal involvement
Family	General family history; interfamilial interaction; family values, beliefs and authority levels; religion and spirituality; affective style; emotional support; parenting behaviors and discipline; economic resources; extended family relationships; strengths; how stress is managed; vulnerabilities; substance use and mental health of members; history of family trauma and/or loss; legal history
Community	Community resources; social supports; community safety and violence; involvement in community activities
Culture	Cultural values, belief systems, ethnicity, societal norms of U.S. culture and, if applicable, culture of origin; ethnic/cultural identification; sex and gender roles; kinship styles; language; food; and customs
Environmental-structural	Impact of social, economic, and political structural forces in social environment; consideration of the educational, medical, welfare, religious, mental health, etc. systems including child welfare involvement
Historical	Historical roots and heritage; issues relating to historical oppression and discrimination and how these may impact child and/or family; intergenerational trauma

protective services are often not involved. And, children who have experienced emotional abuse but no other forms of child maltreatment typically remain in the home where the abuse occurred. Consequently, while the child is the primary client, it is vital to also assess the child within a family context. Clinicians also assess the caregiver's attitudes, beliefs, and parenting practices, including how they view the current issues, their level of motivation to change, and willingness to engage in the process. This information will assist clinicians in determining whether conjoint sessions (e.g., sessions with the child and caregiver together) are appropriate initially, or if the caregiver will need more extensive individual therapeutic support prior to sessions which include the child. Depending on the information gathered, it also may be necessary for clinicians to refer the caregiver to other services, such as substance abuse treatment or support for ongoing mental health issues.

A conceptual framework geared specifically toward recognizing, assessing, and intervening in emotional abuse has been developed in the United Kingdom by Danya Glaser and colleagues (Glaser et al., 2001; Glaser, 2002, 2011) and is termed FRAMEA. The FRAMEA approach begins with gathering information during the assessment process and then organizing the data obtained into tiers of concern specific to emotional abuse. The tiers of concern are outlined in Table A3.3.

Table A3.3 FRAMEA tiers of concern in cases of emotional abuse

Tier	Factor	Examples of factor elements
Tier 0	Social and environmental	Poverty, homelessness, social isolation, lack of employment, community safety, access to resources
Tier 1	Caregiver risk	Mental health issues, domestic violence, substantial parental conflict, significant child trauma history
Tier 2	Caregiver–child interactions	Caregiver's emotional availability, responsiveness and ability meet emotional needs; extent and severity of harmful interactions, including consideration of discipline practices; expectations of the child in a developmental context; ability to recognize psychological boundary between caregiver and child; socialization of the child (see five criteria outlined below)
Tier 3	Child's functioning	Cognitive, emotional, and behavioral development in different settings (e.g., at home, with peers, at school), symptoms and concerning behaviors, sense of self

Source: Adapted from Glaser et al. (2012).

FRAMEA also breaks down caregiver–child interactions into five different categories to reflect the various forms of harmful interactions as well as the rights of the child that have been violated. These categories are:

1. **Emotional unavailability, unresponsiveness and neglect:** Violation of the child's basic need and right to have her/his existence acknowledged.
2. **Interacting with the child with hostility, blame, denigration, rejection or scapegoating, based on the belief that the child deserves this due to basic negative attributions to the child:** Violation of child's basic need and right to be valued and loved for what s/he is.
3. **Developmentally inappropriate or inconsistent interactions with the child. These include expectations beyond or below the child's developmental capacity; harsh and inconsistent discipline; and exposure to confusing or traumatic events and interactions, in particular domestic violence:** Violation of the child's basic need and right to be considered at their particular age/developmental stage.
4. **Failure to recognize or acknowledge the child's individuality and the psychological boundary between the parent and the child. There is an inability to distinguish between the child's reality and the adult's belief & wishes; the child is used for the fulfilment of the parents' needs as a virtual extension of the parent:** Violation of the child's basic need and right to be recognized or acknowledged as a unique individual with their own feelings and perceptions.
5. **Failure to promote the child's socialization within the child's context, by either active mis-socialization or corruption; by isolating the child or by failing to provide adequate stimulation and opportunities for learning:** Violation of the child's basic need and right to be able to function progressively outside the family.

(Glaser, 2011)

Given the substantial body of research which suggests emotional abuse often co-occurs with other types of child maltreatment and trauma, assessments also explore whether there have been other forms of traumatic exposure. This involves asking the client about other forms of child maltreatment as well as other events which are potentially traumatic, such as forced displacement, natural disasters, community violence, or death of a loved one. As children often do not initially label their experiences as abusive, it is helpful to include questions that do not directly ask whether they have been a victim of a particular type of abuse, but rather ask whether they have experienced those behaviors which would constitute different forms of abuse. For example, instead of asking a child whether or not they have been emotionally abused, clinicians ask about what happens when the child misbehaves, things they like and do not like about family members, what a typical day looks like at home, and the child's thoughts and feelings about family members.

Clinicians also assess the ways in which the child has adapted to or attempted to cope with traumatic experiences. This is achieved by examining the child's functioning in his or her different microsystems (e.g., school, family, peer relationships, etc.) as well as through exploration of how the abuse may have impacted the different areas of the child's life, his or her cognitions, beliefs about self and others, and so forth. Remember that there are direct and indirect consequences of maltreatment, and during this process clinicians begin to make connections between symptoms and behaviors which may have been indirectly caused by the abuse (e.g., substance misuse problems stemming from an attempt to avoid thoughts and feelings about the abuse). As Harris and Fallot (2001) note:

> An individual constructs a sense of self, a sense of others, and a belief about the world after trauma and abuse have occurred that incorporates and is in many cases based on the horrific event or events. That meaning system then informs other life choices and guides the development of particular coping strategies. The impact of trauma is thus felt throughout an individual's life in areas of functioning that may seem quite removed

from the abuse, as well as in areas that are more obviously connected to the trauma.

(p. 12)

In instances where a child discloses emotional abuse or exposure to any potentially traumatic events, additional information is asked about the specific circumstances of those events, including the duration, frequency, severity, and other important contextual factors. It is crucial to ask questions about whether the incidents have previously been disclosed, the responses of family members or professionals, and questions which will help assess whether there are any current safety or risk issues (e.g., suicidal ideation, self-injurious behaviors, etc.) that need to be addressed immediately.

Because some of these events may not have been previously disclosed and also because these cases often involve child protective services or criminal and family court, it is vital that assessments be conducted in a forensically sound manner (Kuehnle & Connell, 2010). The forensic process, which often includes interviews with the child and others involved, is the means by which investigators gather evidence regarding allegations. It is important for clinicians to be knowledgeable of this process and to be clinically rigorous in their assessment, but also be cognizant not to interfere with any investigative process. Consequently, questions need to be asked in a non-leading manner and any statements the child makes need to be documented. As mandated reporters, clinicians are legally obligated to report any disclosures of abuse or neglect that have not been previously reported whether statements are made during the assessment or treatment phase. Jurisdictions have different investigative protocols and clinicians working with children need to be knowledgeable of the process in their communities in order to ensure that they are supporting the child without compromising the integrity of the child's statements or the investigative process.

Intake Report and Recommendations

It becomes the task of the clinician to consider the validity of different sources of information and to utilize the information to help paint a picture of the child's current functioning, adaptations—both positive and negative—to the emotional abuse, strengths, and areas of need. Essentially, the clinician uses a trauma lens and attempts to put all the pieces together to conceptualize the case (often called case conceptualization), and this will then inform treatment planning. Notably, it is also necessary to remember that the assessment is a "snapshot" of the child and the pieces of the puzzle are ever changing in the dynamic world of the child.

After all the relevant information is collected and synthesized, an intake report is typically produced which provides a summary of the assessment data and makes recommendations for treatment. A typical intake report might include the following information:

- demographic information pertaining to the child, including custody information;
- presenting problems and symptoms;
- risk assessment;
- psychosocial history, including maltreatment and trauma exposure;
- client presentation;
- current emotional/psychological functioning and coping patterns;
- academic functioning;
- relational functioning and attachment;
- parenting behaviors;
- treatment history;
- standardized assessment instrument results;
- client strengths;
- family strengths;
- diagnosis;
- treatment recommendations.

BIBLIOGRAPHY

Abbott, E. (1919). *The social caseworker and the enforcement of industrial legislation.* Chicago: Rogers and Hall.

Abidin, R.R. (1995). *Parenting Stress Index (PSI).* Odessa, FL: Psychological Assessment Resources.

Achenbach, T.M. (2001). *Manual for the ASEBA school-age: Forms & profiles.* Burlington: University of Vermont Research Center for Children, Youth & Families.

Achenbach, T.M., & Rescorla, L.A. (2000). *Manual for the ASEBA preschool forms & profiles.* Burlington: University of Vermont, Research Center for Children, Youth & Families.

Aikens, N.L., & Barbarin, O. (2008). Socioeconomic differences in reading trajectories: The contribution of family, neighborhood, and school contexts. *Journal of Educational Psychology*, 100 (2), 235–251.

Allen, B. (2011). Childhood psychological abuse and adult aggression: The mediating role of self-capacities. *Journal of Interpersonal Violence*, 26 (10), 2093–2110.

Allison, K.C., Grilo, C.M., Masheb, R.M., & Stunkard, A.J. (2007). High self-reported rates of neglect and emotional abuse, by persons with binge eating disorder and night eating syndrome. *Behaviour Research and Therapy*, 45 (12), 2874–2883.

American Professional Society on the Abuse of Children (APSAC) (1995). *Guidelines for the psychosocial evaluation of suspected psychological maltreatment in children and adolescents.* Chicago: APSAC.

Ammerman, R.T., Hersen, M., van Hasselt, V.B., Lubetsky, M., & Sieck, W.R. (1994). Maltreatment in psychiatrically hospitalized children and adolescents with developmental disabilities: Prevalence and correlates. *Journal of the American Academy of Child and Adolescent Psychiatry*, 33 (4), 567–576.

Anda, R.F., Butchart, A., Felitti, V.J., & Brown, D.W. (2010). Building a framework for global surveillance of the public health implications of Adverse Childhood Experiences. *American Journal of Preventive Medicine*, 39 (1), 93–98.

Anderson, R., Ambrosino, R., Valentine, D., & Lauderdale, M. (1983). Child deaths attributed to abuse and neglect: An empirical study. *Children and Youth Services Review*, 5 (1), 75–89.

Appleton, J.V. (2012). Perspectives of neglect. *Child Abuse Review*, 21, 77–80.

Ascione, F.R. (1998). Battered women's reports of their partners' and their children's cruelty to animals. *Journal of Emotional Abuse*, 1 (1), 119–133.

Baker, A.J.L. (2009). Adult recall of childhood psychological maltreatment: Definitional strategies and challenges. *Children and Youth Services Review*, 31, 703–714.

Baker, A.J.L., & Festinger, T. (2011). Emotional abuse and emotional neglect subscales of the CTQ: Associations with each other, other measures of psychological maltreatment, and demographic variables. *Children and Youth Services Review*, 33, 2297–2302.

Baker, A.J.L., & Maiorino, E. (2010). Assessments of emotional abuse and neglect with the CTQ: Issues and estimates. *Children and Youth Services Review*, 32, 740–748.

Bandura, A. (1963). *Social learning and personality development*. New York: Holt, Rinehart & Winston.

Bandura, A. (1976). *Social learning theory*. Englewood Cliffs: Prentice-Hall.

Barker, J., & Hodes, D. (2007). *The child in mind: A child protection handbook*. London: Routledge.

Barlow, J., & Schrader-MacMillan, A. (2009). *Safeguarding children from emotional abuse – what works?* (Research Brief DCSF-RBX-09-09). London: Department for Children, Schools and Families. Retrieved from www.cscb-new.co.uk/downloads/reports_research/Safeguarding%20Children%20from%20emotional%20abuse.pdf.

Bartlett, J.D., & Easterbrooks, M.A. (2012). Links between physical abuse in childhood and child neglect among adolescent mothers. *Children and Youth Services Review*, 34, 2164–2169.

Bartlett, J.D., Raskin, M., Kotake, C., Nearing, K.D., & Easterbrooks, M.A. (2014). An ecological analysis of infant neglect by adolescent mothers. *Child Abuse & Neglect*, 38, 723–734.

Bell, S., & Eyberg, S.M. (2002). Parent-child interaction therapy. In L. Vandecreek, S. Knapp, & T.L. Jackson (Eds.). *Innovations in clinical practice: A source book* (Vol. 20; pp. 57–74). Sarasota: Professional Resource Press.

Belsky, J. (1980). Child maltreatment: An ecological integration. *American Psychologist*, 35 (4), 320–335.

Belsky, J. (1993). Etiology of child maltreatment: A developmental-ecological analysis. *Psychological Bulletin*, 114 (3), 314–334.

Berlin, L.J., Appleyard, K., & Dodge, K.A. (2011). Intergenerational continuity in child maltreatment: Mediating mechanisms and implications for prevention. *Child Development*, 82 (1), 162–176.

Bernstein, D.P., Ahluvalia, T., Pogge, D., & Handelsman, L. (1997). Validity of the Childhood Trauma Questionnaire in an adolescent psychiatric population. *Journal of the American Academy of Child and Adolescent Psychiatry*, 36 (3), 340–348.

Bernstein, D.P., Fink, L., Handelsman, L., Foote, J., Lovejoy, M., Wenzel, K., et al. (1994). Initial reliability and validity of a new retrospective measure of child abuse and neglect. *American Journal of Psychiatry*, 151 (8), 1132–1136.

Beveridge, J. (1994). Analysis of Colorado child maltreatment fatalities. *Colorado's Children*, 13 (2), 3–6.

Binggeli, N.J., Hart, S.N., & Brassard, M.R. (2001). Psychological maltreatment of children. *The APSAC study guides*. Thousand Oaks: Sage Publications.
Bowlby, J. (1969). *Attachment and loss*. Vol. 1. *Attachment*. New York: Basic Books.
Bowlby, J. (1973). *Attachment and loss*. Vol. 2. *Separation*. New York: Basic Books.
Bowlby, J. (1979). *The making and breaking of affectional bonds*. New York: Tavistock.
Bowlby, J. (1980). *Attachment and loss*. Vol. 3. *Loss*. New York: Basic Books.
Bowlby, J. (1982). Attachment and loss: Retrospect and prospect. *American Journal of Orthopsychiatry*, 52, 664–678.
Bowlby, J. (1988). Developmental psychiatry comes of age. *American Journal of Psychiatry*, 145, 1–10.
Brassard, M.R., & Hart, S. (2000). How do I determine whether a child has been psychologically maltreated? In Howard Dubowitz and Diane DePanfilis (Eds.). *Handbook for child protection practice* (pp. 215–220). Thousand Oaks: Sage Publications.
Bremner, J.D., Bolus, R., & Mayer, E.A. (2007). Psychometric properties of the Early Trauma Inventory—Self-Report. *Journal of Nervous and Mental Disease*, 195 (3), 211–218.
Bremner, J.D., Vermetten, E., & Mazure, C.M. (2000). Development and preliminary psychometric properties of an instrument for the measurement of childhood trauma: The Early Trauma Inventory. *Depression & Anxiety*, 12, 1–12.
Briere, J. (1992). *Child Abuse Trauma: Theory and Treatment of the Lasting Effects*. Newbury Park: Sage Publications.
Briere, J. (1996). *Trauma Symptom Checklist for Children* (TSCC). Odessa, FL: Psychological Assessment Resources, Inc.
Briere, J. (2005). *Trauma Symptom Checklist for Young Children* (TSCYC). Odessa, FL: Psychological Assessment Resources.
Briere, J., & Runtz, M. (1988). Multivariate correlates of childhood psychological and physical maltreatment among university women. *Child Abuse & Neglect: The International Journal*, 12, 331–341.
Briere, J., & Runtz, M. (1990). Differential adult symptomatology associated with three types of child abuse histories. *Child Abuse & Neglect: The International Journal*, 14, 357–364.
Bronfenbrenner, U. (1979). *The ecology of human development: Experiment by nature and design*. Cambridge, MA: Harvard University Press.
Brown, K.D., & Herbert, M. (1997). *Preventing family violence*. Chichester: Wiley.
Butler, L.D., Critelli, F.M., & Rinfrette, E.S. (2011). Trauma-informed care and mental health. *Directions in Psychiatry*, 31, 197–209.
Cameron, M., & Keenan, E.K. (2010). The common factors model: Implications for transtheoretical clinical social work practice. *Social Work*, 55 (1), 63–73.
Chamberland, C., Fallon, B., Black, T., & Trocmé, N. (2011). Emotional maltreatment in Canada: Prevalence, reporting, and child welfare responses (CIS2). *Child Abuse & Neglect*, 35, 841–864.
Chamberland, C., Fallon, B., Black, T., Trocme, N., & Chabot, M. (2012). Correlates of substantiated emotional maltreatment in the second Canadian incidence study. *Journal of Family Violence*, 27, 201–213.
Child Welfare Information Gateway (2006). *Child neglect: A guide for prevention, assessment and intervention*. Washington, DC: U.S. Department of Health and Human Services, Children's Bureau.

Child Welfare Information Gateway (2013). *What is child abuse and neglect? Recognizing the signs and symptoms*. Washington, DC: U.S. Department of Health and Human Services, Children's Bureau.

Child Welfare Information Gateway (2014). *In-home services in child welfare*. Washington, DC: U.S. Department of Health and Human Services, Children's Bureau.

Chorpita, B.F., Daleiden, E., & Weisz, J.R. (2005). Identifying and selecting the common elements of evidence based interventions: A distillation and matching model. *Mental Health Services*, 7, 5–20.

Cicchetti, D., Rogosch, F., & Toth, S. (2006). Fostering secure attachment in infants in maltreating families through preventative interventions. *Development and Psychopathology*, 18, 623–649.

Claussen, A., & Crittenden, P. (1991). Physical and psychological maltreatment: Relations among types of maltreatment. *Child Abuse & Neglect*, 15, 5–18.

Cohen, J.A., & Mannarino, A.P. (1996). A treatment outcome study for sexually abused preschool children: Initial findings. *Journal of the American Academy of Child and Adolescent Psychiatry*, 30, 42–50.

Cohen, J.A., & Mannarino, A.P. (1998). Factors that mediate treatment outcome of sexually abused preschool children: Six- and 12-month follow-up. *Journal of the American Academy of Child and Adolescent Psychiatry*, 37, 44–51.

Cohen, J.A., Mannarino, A.P., & Deblinger, E. (2006). *Treating trauma and traumatic grief in children and adolescents*. New York: The Guilford Press.

Cohen, J.A., Deblinger, E., Mannarino, A.P., & de Arellano, M.A. (2001). The importance of culture in treating abused and neglected children: An empirical review. *Child Maltreatment*, 6 (2), 148–157.

Cohen, J.A., Deblinger, E., Mannarino, A.P., & Steer, R.A. (2004). A multisite, randomized controlled trial for children with sexual abuse-related PTSD symptoms. *Journal of the American Academy of Child and Adolescent Psychiatry*, 43 (4), 393–402.

Cohen, J.A., Mannarino, A.P., Kliethermes, M., & Murray, L.K. (2012). Trauma-focused CBT for youth with complex trauma. *Child Abuse & Neglect*, 36, 528–541.

Cohen, J.A., Mannarino, A.P., Murray, L.K., & Igelman, R. (2006). Psychosocial interventions for maltreated and violence exposed children. *Journal of Social Issues*, 62 (4), 737–766.

Collins, K.S., Strieder, F., DePanfilis, D., Tabor, M., Freeman, P., Linde, L., et al. (2011). Trauma Adapted Family Connections (TA-FC): Reducing developmental and complex trauma symptomatology to prevent child abuse and neglect. *Child Welfare*, 90, 29–47.

Cook, A., Blaustein, M., Spinazzola, J., van der Kolk, B., & the Complex Trauma Task Force (2003). *Complex trauma in children and adolescents: White paper from the National Child Traumatic Stress Network Complex Trauma Task Force*. Los Angeles and Durham, NC: National Center for Child Traumatic Stress. Retrieved from www.NCTSNet.org/nctsn_assets/pdfs_materials/Complex-Trauma_All.pdf.

Corcoran, K., & Fischer, J. (2013). *Measures for clinical practice and research: A sourcebook*. New York: Oxford University Press.

Courtois, C.A., & Ford, J.D. (Eds.) (2009). *Treating complex traumatic stress disorders*. New York: Guilford.

Covitz, J. (1986). *Emotional child abuse: The family curse*. Boston: Sigo Press.

Crawford, E., & Wright, O. (2007). The impact of childhood psychological maltreatment on interpersonal schemas and subsequent experiences of relationship aggression. *Journal of Emotional Abuse*, 7, 93–116.

Crittenden, P.M., Claussen, A.H., & Sugarman, D.B. (1994). Physical and psychological maltreatment in middle childhood and adolescents. *Development and Psychopathology*, 6, 145–164.

Crosson-Tower, C. (2009). *Exploring child welfare: A practice perspective*. Boston: Pearson Education.

Dawley, K., Loch, J., & Bindrich, I. (2007). The nurse-family partnership. *American Journal of Nursing*, 107 (11), 60–67.

De Graff, I., Speetjens, P., Smit, F., De Wolff, M., & Tavecchio, L. (2008). Effectiveness of the Triple P Positive Parenting Program on parenting: A meta-analysis. *Family Relations*, 57, 553–566.

Deblinger, E., Lippmann, J., & Steer, R.A. (1996). Treating sexually abused children suffering posttraumatic stress symptoms: Initial treatment outcome findings. *Child Maltreatment*, 1, 310–321.

DePanfilis, D., & Dubowitz, H. (2005). Family Connections: A program for preventing child neglect. *Child Maltreatment*, 10 (2), 108–123.

Dixon, L.O., Browne, K., & Hamilton-Giachritsis, C. (2005). Risk factors of parents as children: A mediational analysis of the intergenerational continuity of child maltreatment (Part I). *Journal of Child Psychology and Psychiatry*, 46 (1), 47–57.

Dong, M., Giles, W.H., Felitti, V.J., Dube, S., Williams, J.E., Chapman, D.P., et al. (2004). Insights into causal pathways for ischemic heart disease: Adverse childhood experiences study. *Circulation*, 110, 1761–1766.

Douglas, E.M. (2013). Child welfare workers who experience the death of a child client. *Administration in Social Work*, 37, 59–72.

Drisko, J.W. (2004). Common factors in psychotherapy outcome: Meta-analytic findings and their implications for practice and research. *Families in Society*, 85 (1), 81–90.

Dube, S.R., Felitti, V.J., Dong, M., Chapman, D.P., Giles, W.H., & Anda, R.F. (2003). Childhood abuse, neglect, and household dysfunction and the risk of illicit drug use: The Adverse Childhood Experiences Study. *Pediatrics*, 111 (3), 564–572.

Dubowitz, H., Newton, R.R., Litrownik, A.J., Lewis, T., Briggs, E.C., Thompson, R., et al. (2005). Examination of a conceptual model of child neglect. *Child Maltreatment*, 10 (2), 173–189.

Duke, N.N., Pettingell, S.L., McMorris, B.J., & Borowsky, I.W. (2010). Adolescent violence perpetration: Associations with multiple types of adverse childhood experiences. *Pediatrics*, 125 (4), e778–e786.

Dvir, Y, Ford, J.D., Hill, M., & Frazier, J.A. (2014). Childhood maltreatment, emotional dysregulation, and psychiatric comorbidities. *Harvard Review of Psychiatry*, 22 (3), 149–161.

Edwards, V.J., Holden, G.W., Felitti, V.J., & Anda, R.F. (2003). Relationship between multiple forms of childhood mistreatment and adult mental health in community respondents: Results from the Adverse Childhood Experiences study. *American Journal of Psychiatry*, 160 (8), 1453–1460.

Eisenstadt, T.H., Eyberg, S., McNeil, C.B., Newcomb, K., & Funderburk, B. (1993). Parent-child interaction therapy with behavior problem children: Relative effectiveness of two stages and overall treatment outcome. *Journal of Clinical Child Psychology*, 22, 42–51.

Elliot, D.E., Bjelajac, P., Fallot, R.D., Markoff, L.S., & Reed, B.G. (2005). Trauma-informed or trauma-denied: Principles and implementation of trauma-informed services. *Journal of Community Psychology*, 33 (4), 461–477.

Else, L., Wonderlich, S.A., Beatty, W.W., Christie, D.W., & Staton, R.D. (1993). Personality characteristics of men who physically abuse women. *Hospital and Community Psychiatry*, 44 (1), 54–58.

Enns, M.W., Cox, B.J., Afifi, T.O., De Graaf, R., Ten Have, M., & Sareen, J. (2006). Childhood adversities and risk for suicidal ideation and attempts: A longitudinal population-based study. *Psychological Medicine*, 36, 1769–1778.

Etter, D.J., & Rickert, V.I. (2013). The complex etiology and lasting consequences of child maltreatment. *Journal of Adolescent Health*, 53, S39–S41.

Eyberg, S.M., & Boggs, S.R. (1989). Parent training for oppositional-defiant preschoolers. In C.E. Schaeffer & J.M. Briesmeister (Eds.), *Handbook of parent training: Parents as co-therapists for children's behavior problems* (pp. 105–132). New York: Wiley.

Eyberg, S.M., Funderburk, B.W., Hembree-Kigin, T.L., McNeil, C.B., Querido, J.G., & Hood, K. (2001). Parent-child interaction therapy with behavior problem children: One and two year maintenance of treatment effects in the family. *Child and Family Behavior Therapy*, 23, 1–20.

Fallon, B., Trocme, N., Fluke, J., MacLaurin, B., Tonmyr, L., & Yuan, Y.-Y. (2010). Methodological challenges in measuring child maltreatment. *Child Abuse & Neglect*, 70–79.

Feindler, E.L., Rathus, J.H., & Silver, L.B. (2003). *Assessment of family violence: A handbook for researchers and practitioners*. Washington, DC: American Psychological Association.

Felitti, V.J., Anda, R.F., Nordenberg, D., Williamson, D.F., Spitz, A.M., Edwards, V., et al. (1998). Relationship of childhood abuse and household dysfunction to many of the leading causes of death in adults. *American Journal of Preventive Medicine*, 14 (4), 245–258.

Ferguson, K., & Dacey, C. (1997). Anxiety, depression and dissociation in women health care providers reporting a history of childhood psychological abuse. *Child Abuse & Neglect*, 21, 941–952.

Fink, L.A., Bernstein, D., Handelsman, L., Foote, J., & Lovejoy, M. (1995). Initial reliability and validity of the childhood trauma interview: A new multidimensional measure of childhood interpersonal trauma. *American Journal of Psychiatry*, 152 (9), 1329–1335.

Finkelhor, D., Ormrod, R.K., & Turner, H.A. (2009). Lifetime assessment of polyvictimization in a national sample of children and youth. *Child Abuse & Neglect*, 33, 403–411.

Finkelhor, D., Ormrod, R., Turner, H., & Hamby, S.L. (2005). The victimization of children and youth: A comprehensive, national survey. *Child Maltreatment*, 10 (1), 5–25.

Finkelhor, D., Turner, H., Ormrod, R., & Hamby, S.L. (2009). Violence, abuse, and crime exposure in a national sample of children and youth. *Pediatrics*, 124 (5), 1411–1423.

Finkelhor, D., Vanderminden, J., Turner, H., Hamby, S., & Shattuck, A. (2014). Child maltreatment rates assessed in a national household survey of caregivers and youth. *Child Abuse & Neglect*, 38, 1421–1435.

Finkelhor, F. (1986). *A sourcebook on child sexual abuse and neglect*. Beverly Hills: Sage.
Frick, P.J. (1991). *The Alabama Parenting Questionnaire (APQ)*. Unpublished rating scales. The University of Alabama.
George, C., Kaplan, N., & Main, M. (1985). The Adult Attachment Interview. Unpublished manuscript, University of California at Berkeley.
Gibb, B.E., Alloy, L.B., & Abramson, L.Y. (2003). Global reports of childhood maltreatment versus recall of specific maltreatment experiences: Relationships with dysfunctional attitudes and depressive symptoms. *Cognition and Emotion*, 17 (6), 903–915.
Gibb, B.E., Alloy, L.B., Abramson, L.Y., Rose, D.T., Whitehouse, W.G., Donovan, P., et al. (2001). History of childhood maltreatment, depressogenic cognitive style, and episodes of depression in adulthood. *Cognitive Therapy and Research*, 25, 425–446.
Gilbert, R., Widom, C.S., Browne, K., Fergusson, D., Webb, E., & Janson, S. (2009). Burden and consequences of child maltreatment in high-income countries. *Lancet*, 373, 68–81.
Glaser, D. (2002). Emotional abuse and neglect (psychological maltreatment): A conceptual framework. *Child Abuse & Neglect*, 26, 697–714.
Glaser, D. (2011). How to deal with emotional abuse and neglect: Further development of a conceptual framework (FRAMEA). *Child Abuse & Neglect*, 35, 866–875.
Glaser, D., Prior, V., & Lynch, M. (2001). *Emotional abuse and emotional neglect: Antecedents, operational definitions and consequences*. York: British Association for the Study and Prevention of Child Abuse and Neglect.
Glaser, D., Prior, V., Auty, K., & Tilki, S. (2012). *Does training in a systemic approach to emotional abuse improve the quality of children's services?* (Research brief DFE-RB196). London: Department for Children, Schools, and Families. Retrieved from www.gov.uk/government/uploads/system/uploads/attachment_data/file/181602/DFE-RB196.pdf.
Goldman, D., Oroszi, G., & Ducci, F. (2005). The genetics of addictions: Uncovering the genes. *Nature Reviews Genetics*, 6, 521–532.
Goodman, R. (1997). The Strengths and Difficulties Questionnaire: A research note. *Journal of Child Psychology and Psychiatry*, 38 (5), 581–586.
Gray, J.A.M. (2001). The origin of evidence-based practice. In A. Edwards & G. Elwyn (Eds.). *Evidence-informed client choice* (pp. 19–33). New York: Oxford University Press.
Green, J.G., McLaughlin, K.A., Berglund, P.A., Gruber, M.J., Sampson, N.A., Zaslavsky, A.M., et al. (2010). Childhood adversities and adult psychiatric disorders in the National Comorbidity Survey Replication I: Associations with first onset of DSM-IV Disorders. *Archives of General Psychiatry*, 67 (2), 113–123.
Grencavage, L.M., & Norcross, J.C. (1990). Where are all the commonalities among the therapeutic common factors? *Professional Psychology: Research and Practice*, 21, 372–378.
Groleau, P., Steiger, H., Bruce, K., Israel, M., Sycz, L., Badawi, G., et al. (2012). Childhood emotional abuse and eating symptoms in bulimic disorders: An examination of possible mediating variables. *International Journal of Eating Disorders*, 45 (3), 326–332.
Guirguis, W.R. (1979). Physical indicators of emotional abuse in children. *British Medical Journal*, 2, 1290.

Harris, M., & Fallot, R.D. (Eds.) (2001). *Using trauma theory to design service systems.* San Francisco: Jossey-Bass.

Hart, S.N., Brassard, M.R., Binggeli, N.J., & Davidson, H.A. (2002). Psychological maltreatment. In J.B. Myers, L. Berliner, J. Briere, C.T. Hendrix, C. Jenny, & T.A. Reid (Eds.). *The APSAC handbook on child maltreatment* (2nd edn; pp. 79–104). Thousand Oaks: Sage Publications.

Hart, S.N., Brassard, M.R., Davidson, H.A., Rivelis, E., Diaz, V., & Binggeli, N.J. (2010). Psychological maltreatment. In John E.B. Myers (Ed.). *The APSAC handbook on child maltreatment* (pp. 125–144). Thousand Oaks: Sage Publications.

Hembree-Kigin, T.L., & McNeil, C.B. (1995). *Parent–child interaction therapy.* New York: Plenum Press.

Hemmingsson, E., Johansson, K., & Reynisdottir, S. (2014). Effects of childhood abuse on adult obesity: A systematic review and meta-analysis. *Obesity Reviews*, 15, 882–893.

Hibbard, R., Barlow, J., MacMillan, H. & Committee on Child Abuse and Neglect and American Academy of Child and Adolescent Psychiatry, Child Maltreatment and Violence Committee (2012). Psychological maltreatment. *Pediatrics*, 130, 372–378.

Higgins, D.J., & McCabe, M.P. (2003). Maltreatment and family dysfunction in childhood and the subsequent adjustment of children and adults. *Journal of Family Violence*, 18 (2), 107–120.

Hoglund, W.L.G., Lalonde, C.E., & Leadbeater, B.J. (2008). Social-cognitive competence, peer rejection and neglect, and behavioral and emotional problems in middle childhood. *Social Development*, 17 (3), 528–553.

Hood, K., & Eyberg, S. (2003). Outcomes of parent-child interaction therapy: Mothers' reports of maintenance three to six years after treatment. *Journal of Clinical Child and Adolescent Psychology*, 32, 412–429.

Hornor, G. (2014). Child neglect: Assessment and intervention. *Journal of Pediatric Health Care*, 28 (2), 186–192.

Horvath, A.O., & Bedi, R.P. (2002). The alliance. In *Psychotherapy relationships that work: Therapist contributions and responsiveness to patients* (pp. 37–70). New York: Oxford University Press.

Horwath, J. (2007). *Child neglect: Identification & assessment.* New York: Palgrave Macmillan.

Hovens, J.G.F.M., Giltay, E.J., Wiersma, J.E., Spinhoven, P., Penninx, B.W.J.H., & Zitman, F.G. (2012). Impact of childhood life events and trauma on the course of depressive and anxiety disorders. *Acta Psychiatrica Scandinavica*, 126, 198–207.

Hughes, J., & Chau, S. (2013). Making complex decisions: Child protection workers' practicers and interventions with families experiencing intimate partner violence. *Children and Youth Services Review*, 35, 611–617.

Institute for Family Development (2013). Homebuilders® Program. Retrieved from www.institutefamily.org/programs_IFPS.asp.

Iwaniec, D. (1997). An overview of emotional maltreatment and failure-to-thrive. *Child Abuse Review*, 6, 370–388.

Iwaniec, D., & Herbert, M. (1999). Multidimensional approach to helping emotionally abused and neglected children and abusive parents. *Children & Society*, 13, 365–379.

Jaffee, S.R., Bowes, L., Ouellet-Morin, I., Fisher, H.I., Moffitt, T.E., Merrick, M.T., et al. (2013). Safe, stable, nurturing relationships break the intergenerational cycle of abuse: A prospective nationally representative cohort in the United Kingdom. *Journal of Adolescent Health*, 53, S4–S10.

Jeon, H.J., Roh, M.S., Kim, K.H., Lee, J.R., Lee, D., Yoon, S.C., et al. (2009). Early trauma and lifetime suicidal behavior in a nationwide sample of Korean medical students. *Journal of Affective Disorders*, 119, 210–214.

Jewkes, R.K., Dunkle, K., Nduna, M., Jama, N., & Puren, A. (2010). Associations between childhood adversity and depression, substance abuse and HIV and HSV2 incident infections in rural South African youth. *Child Abuse & Neglect*, 34, 833–841.

Kagan, J. (1981). *The second year of life*. Cambridge, MA: Harvard University Press.

Kairys, S.W., Johnson, C.F. & the Committee on Child Abuse & Neglect (2002). The psychological maltreatment of children—technical report. *Pediatrics*, 109 (4), April, 3 pages electronic.

Kantor, G.K., Holt, M.K., Mebert, C.J., Straus, M.A. Drach, K.M., Ricci, R., et al. (2004). Development and preliminary psychometric properties of the multidimensional neglectful behavior scale child report. *Child Maltreatment*, 9 (5), 409–428.

Kaplan, S.J., Pelcovitz, D., & Labruna, V. (1999). Child and adolescent abuse and neglect research: A review of the past 10 years. Part I: Physical and emotional abuse and neglect. *Journal of the American Academy of Child and Adolescent Psychiatry*, 38 (10), 1214–1222.

Kaufman, J., & Zigler, E. (1987). Do abused children become abusive parents? *American Journal of Orthopsychiatry*, 57 (2), 186–192.

Kaufman-Kantor, G., Holt, M.K., Mebert, C.J., Straus, M.A., Drach, K.M., Ricci, R., et al. (2004). Development and preliminary psychometric properties of the multidimensional neglectful behavior scale—child report. *Child Maltreatment*, 9 (5), 409–428.

Kelly-Irving, M., Lepage, B., Dedieu, D., Lacey, R., Cable, N., Bartley, M., et al. (2013). Childhood adversity as a risk for cancer: Findings from the 1958 British birth cohort study. *BMC Public Health*, 13, 767.

Kempe, C.H., & Helfer, R.E. (1968). *The battered child*. Chicago: University of Chicago Press.

Kempe, C.H., Silverman, F.N., Steele, B.F., Droegemuller, W., & Silver, H.K. (1962). The battered child syndrome. *JAMA*, 181 (1), 17–24.

Kenny, M. (1987). The extent and function of parental attachment among first-year college students. *Journal of Youth and Adolescence*, 16 (1), 17–27.

Kent, A., & Waller, G. (1998). The impact of childhood emotional abuse: An extension of the child abuse and trauma scale. *Child Abuse & Neglect*, 22 (5), 393–399.

Kerr, D.C.R., Capaldi, D.M., Pears, K.C., & Owen, L.D. (2009). A prospective three generational study of fathers' constructive parenting: Influences from family of origin, adolescent adjustment, and offspring temperament. *Developmental Psychology*, 45, 1257–1275.

Kessler, R.C., & Ustün, T.B. (2004). The World Mental Health (WMH) Survey Initiative version of the World Health Organization (WHO) Composite International Diagnostic Interview (CIDI). *International Journal of Methods in Psychiatric Research*, 13 (2), 93–121.

Kessler, R.C., Andrews, G., Colpe, L.J., Hiripi, E., Mroczek, D.K., Normand, S.-L.T., et al. (2002). Short screening scales to monitor population prevalences and trends in nonspecific psychological distress. *Psychological Medicine*, 32 (6), 959–976.

Kessler, R.C., Barker, P.R., Colpe, L.J., Epstein, J.F., Gfroerer, J.C., Hiripi, E., et al. (2003). Screening for serious mental illness in the general population. *Archives of General Psychiatry*, 60 (2), 184–189.

Kessler, R.C., Abelson, J., Demler, O., Escobar, J.I., Gibbon, M., Guyer, M.E., et al. (2004). Clinical calibration of DSM-IV diagnoses in the World Mental Health (WMH) version of the World Health Organization (WHO) Composite International Diagnostic Interview (WMH-CIDI). *International Journal of Methods in Psychiatric Research*, 13 (2), 122–139.

Kim, J. (2009). Type-specific intergenerational transmission of neglectful and physically abusive parenting behaviors among young parents. *Children and Youth Services Review*, 31, 761–767.

King, N.J., Tonge, B.J., Mullen, P., Myerson, N., Heyne, D., Rollings, S., et al. (2000). Treating sexually abused children with posttraumatic stress symptoms: A randomized clinical trial. *Journal of the American Academy of Child and Adolescent Psychiatry*, 39, 1347–1355.

Kinney, J., Haapala, D., & Booth, C. (1991). *Keeping families together: The Homebuilders Model*. New York: Aldine de Gruyter.

Kinney, J., Madsen, B., Fleming, T., & Haapala, D.A. (1977). Homesbuilders: Keeping families together. *Journal of Consulting and Clinical Psychology*, 45, 667–673.

Kirisci, L., Dunn, M.G., Mezzich, A.C., & Tarter, R.I. (2001). Impact of parental substance use disorder and child neglect severity on substance use involvement in male offspring. *Prevention Science*, 2 (4), 241–255.

Kirk, R. (2001). *A critique of the evaluation of family preservation and reunification programs: Interim report*. National Family Preservation Network.

Kirk, R., & Griffith, D.P. (2004). Intensive family preservation services: Demonstrating placement prevention using event history analysis. *Social Work Research*, 28 (1), 5–16.

Korbin, J.E. (2002). Culture and child maltreatment: Cultural competence and beyond. *Child Abuse and Neglect*, 26 (6), 637–634.

Kovacs, M. (1985). The Children's Depression Inventory (CDI). *Psychopharmacology Bulletin*, 21, 995–998.

Kuehnle, K., & Connell, M. (2010). Child sexual abuse suspicions: Treatment considerations during investigation. *Journal of Child Sexual Abuse*, 19, 554–571.

Lambert, M.J., & Ogles, B.M. (2004). The efficacy and effectiveness of psychotherapy integration. In J.C. Norcross & M.C. Goldfried (Eds.). *Handbook of psychotherapy integration* (pp. 94–129). New York: Oxford University Press.

Lee, S.J., Sobeck, J.L., Djelaj, V., & Agius, E. (2013). When practice and policy collide: Child welfare workers' perceptions of investigation processes. *Children and Youth Services Review*, 35, 634–641.

Leeson, F., & Nixon, R.D.V. (2010). Therapy for child psychological maltreatment. *Clinical Psychologist*, 14 (2), 30–38.

Leifer, M., Kilbane, T., Jacobsen, T., & Grossman, G. (2004). A three generational study of transmission of risk for sexual abuse. *Journal of Clinical Child and Adolescent Psychology*, 33 (4), 662–672.

Leventhal, J.M., & Krugman, R.D. (2012). The battered-child syndrome 50 years later: Much accomplished, much left to do. *JAMA*, 308 (1), 35–36.

Lieberman, A.F., & Van Horn, P. (2005). *Don't hit my mommy: A manual for child-parent psychotherapy with young witnesses of family violence.* Washington, DC: Zero to Three.

Lieberman, A.F., & Van Horn, P. (2008). *Psychotherapy with infants and young children: Repairing the effects of stress and trauma on early attachment.* New York: The Guilford Press.

Lieberman, A.F., Ghosh Ippen, C., & Van Horn, P. (2006). Child-parent psychotherapy: 6-month follow-up of a randomized controlled trial. *Journal of the American Academy of Child and Adolescent Psychiatry*, 45 (8), 913–918.

Lieberman, A.F., Van Horn, P., & Ghosh Ippen, C. (2005). Toward evidence-based treatment: Child-parent psychotherapy with preschoolers exposed to marital violence. *Journal of the American Academy of Child and Adolescent Psychiatry*, 44 (12), 1241–1448.

Liu, R.T., Alloy, L.B., Abramson, L.Y., Iacoviello, B.M., & Whitehouse, W.G. (2009). Emotional maltreatment and depression: Prospective prediction of depressive episodes. *Depression and Anxiety*, 26, 174–181.

Lounds, J.J., Borkowski, J.G., & Whitman, T.L. (2004). Reliability and validity of the Mother-Child Neglect Scale. *Child Maltreatment*, 9 (4), 371–381.

McCloskey, L.A., & Bailey, J.A. (2000). The intergenerational transmission of risk for child sexual abuse. *Journal of Interpersonal Violence*, 15 (10), 1019–1035.

McCracken, S.G., & Marsh, J.C. (2008). Practitioner expertise in evidence-based practice decision making. *Research on Social Work Practice*, 18, 301–310.

McLaughlin, K.A., Green, J.G., Grukber M.J., Sampson, N.A., Zaslavsky, A.M., & Kessler, R.C. (2012). Childhood adversities and first onset of psychiatric disorders in a national sample of US adolescents. *Archives of General Psychiatry*, 69 (11), 1151–1160.

McNeil, C.B., & Hembree-Kigin, T.L. (2010). *Parent-child interaction therapy* (2nd edn). New York: Springer.

McWey, L.M., Pazdera, A.L., Vennum, A., & Wojciak, A.S. (2013). Intergenerational patterns of maltreatment in families at risk for foster care. *Journal of Marital & Family Therapy*, 39 (2), 133–147.

Maguire-Jack, K., & Font, S.A. (2014). Predicting recurrent maltreatment among high-risk families: Applying the Decision-Making Ecology Framework. *Children and Youth Services Review*, 43, 29–39.

Main, M., & Goldwyn, R. (1998). Adult attachment scoring and classification system. Unpublished manuscript, University of California at Berkeley.

Mather, J., Lager, P.B., & Harris, N.J. (2007). *Child welfare: Policies and best practices* (2nd edn). Belmont: Brooks/Cole.

Marshall, N.A. (2012). A clinician's guide to recognizing and reporting parental psychological maltreatment of children. *Professional Psychology: Research and Practice*, 43 (2), 73–79.

May-Chahal, C., & Cawson, P. (2005). Measuring child maltreatment in the United Kingdom: A study of the prevalence of child abuse and neglect. *Child Abuse & Neglect*, 29, 969–984.

Mazzucchelli, T.G., & Sanders, M.R. (2010). Facilitating practitioner flexibility within evidence based practice: Lessons from a system of parenting support. *Clinical Psychology: Science and Practice*, 17, 238–252.

Mennen, F.E., Kim, K., Sang, J., & Trickett, P.K. (2010). Child neglect: Definition and identification of youth's experiences in official reports of maltreatment. *Child Abuse & Neglect*, 34, 647–658.

Messman-Moore, T.L., & Coates, A.A. (2007). The impact of childhood psychological abuse on adult interpersonal conflict: The role of early maladaptive schemas and patterns of interpersonal behavior. *Journal of Emotional Abuse*, 7, 75–92.

Mikton, C., & Butchart, A. (2009). Child maltreatment prevention: A systematic review of reviews. *Bulletin of the World Health Organization*, 87, 353–361.

Miller, E.A., Green, A.E., Fettes, D.L., & Aarons, G.A. (2011). Prevalence of maltreatment among youths in public sectors of care. *Child Maltreatment*, 16 (3), 196–204.

Mills, R., Scott, J., Alati, R., O'Callaghan, M., Najman, J.M., & Strathearn, L. (2013). Child maltreatment and adolescent mental health problems in a large birth cohort. *Child Abuse & Neglect*, 37, 292–302.

Milner, J.S. (1990). *An interpretative manual for the child abuse potential inventory*. Psytec Incorporated.

Milner, J.S., Thomsen, C.J., Crouch, J.L., Rabenhorst, M.M., Martens, P.M., Dyslin, C.W., et al. (2010). Do trauma symptoms mediate the relationship between childhood physical abuse and adult child abuse risk? *Child Abuse & Neglect*, 34 (5), 332–344.

Morales, A.T., & Sheafor, B.N. (2004). *Social work: A profession of many faces*. New York: Pearson Education.

Morton, P.M., Mustillo, S.A., & Ferraro, K.F. (2014). Does childhood misfortune raise the risk of acute myocardial infarction in adulthood? *Social Science & Medicine*, 104, 133–141.

Muskett, C. (2014). Trauma-informed care in inpatient mental health settings: A review of the literature. *International Journal of Mental Health Nursing*, 23, 51–59.

Najavits, L.M., Weiss, R.D., & Shaw, S.R. (1997). The link between substance abuse and post-traumatic stress disorder in women: A research review. *The American Journal on the Addictions*, 6, 273–283.

National Child Traumatic Stress Network (NCTSN) (n.d.). *National child traumatic stress network empirically supported treatments and promising practices*. Retrieved from http://nctsn.org/resources/topics/treatments-that-work/promising-practices.

National Child Traumatic Stress Network (NCTSN) (2003). What is child traumatic stress? Retrieved from www.nctsnet.org/sites/default/files/assets/pdfs/what_is_child_traumatic_stress_0.pdf.

Naughton, A.M., Maguire, S.A., Mann, M.K., Tempest, V., Gracias, S., & Kemp, A.M. (2013). Emotional, behavioral, and developmental features indicative of neglect or emotional abuse in preschool children: A systematic review. *JAMA Pediatrics*, 167 (8), 769–775.

Norman, R.E., Byambaa, M., De, R., Butchart, A., Scott, J., & Vos, T. (2012). The long-term health consequences of child physical abuse, emotional abuse, and neglect: A systematic review and meta-analysis. *PLoS Med*, 9 (11): e1001349.

Norcross, J.C. (2001). Purposes, processes, and products of the task force on empirically supported therapy relationships. *Psychotherapy: Theory, Research, Practice, Training*, 38, 345–356.

O'Hagan, K. (1995). Emotional and psychological abuse: Problems of definition. *Child Abuse & Neglect*, 19, 449–461.

Okin, R.L. (2014). *Silent voices: People with mental disorders on the streets*. Mill Valley: Golden Pine Press.

Olds, D.L., Henderson, C.R., & Kitzman, H. (1994). Does prenatal and infancy nurse home visitation have enduring effects on qualities of parental caregiving and child health at 25 to 50 months of life? *Pediatrics*, 93, 89–98.

Olds, D.L., Eckenrode, J., Henderson, C.R., Kitzman, H., Powers, J., Cole, R., et al. (1997). Long-term effects of home visitation on maternal life course and child abuse and neglect: Fifteen-year follow-up of a randomized trial. *Journal of the American Medical Association*, 278 (8), 637–643.

Orlinsky, D.E., Rønnestad, M.H., & Willutzki, U. (2004). Fifty years of psychotherapy process-outcome research: Continuity and change. In M.J. Lambert (Ed.), *Bergin and Garfield's handbook of psychotherapy and behavior change* (5th edn; pp. 307–389). New York: John Wiley and Sons.

Orsi, R., Drury, I.J., & Mackert, M.J. (2014). Reliable and valid: A procedure for establishing item-level interrater reliability for child maltreatment risk and safety assessments. *Children and Youth Services Review*, 43, 58–66.

Pears, K.C., & Capaldi, D.M. (2001). Intergenerational transmission of abuse: A two-generational prospective study of an at-risk sample. *Child Abuse & Neglect*, 25, 1439–1461.

Perepletchikova, F., & Kaufman, J. (2010). Emotional and behavioral sequelae of childhood maltreatment. *Current Opinion in Pediatrics*, 22, 610–615.

Perez, C.M., & Widom, C.S. (1994). Childhood victimization and long-term intellectual and academic outcomes. *Child Abuse & Neglect*, 18 (8), 617–633.

Piescher, K., Colburn, G., LaLiberte, T., & Hong, S. (2014). Child protective services and the achievement gap. *Children and Youth Services Review*, 47, 408–415.

Pitzner, J.K., & Drummond, P.D. (1997). The reliability and validity of empirically scaled measures of psychological/verbal control and physical/sexual abuse. Relationship between current negative mood and a history of abuse independent of other negative life events. *Journal of Psychosomatic Research*, 43 (2), 125–142.

Porche, M.V., Fortuna, L.R., Lin, J., & Alegria, M. (2011). Childhood trauma and psychiatric disorders as correlates of school dropout in a national sample of young adults. *Child Development*, 82 (6), 982–998.

Portwood, S.G. (2006). Self-report approaches. In Margaret M. Feerick, John F. Knutson, Penelope K. Trickett, & Sally M. Flanzer (Eds.). *Child abuse and neglect: Definitions, classifications, and a framework for research* (pp. 233–253). London: Paul H. Brookes Publishing Co.

Pynoos, R., Rodriguez, N., Steinberg, A., Stuber, M., & Frederick, C. (1998). *The UCLA PTSD reaction index for DSM IV (revision 1)*. Los Angeles: UCLA Trauma Psychiatry Program.

Ramiro, L.S., Madrid, B.J., & Brown, D.W. (2010). Adverse childhood experiences (ACE) and health-risk behaviors among adults in a developing country setting. *Child Abuse & Neglect*, 34, 842–855.

Reinert, D., & Edwards, C.E. (2009). Childhood physical and verbal mistreatment, psychological symptoms, and substance use: Sex differences and the moderating role of attachment. *Journal of Family Violence*, 24, 589–596.

Renner, L.M., & Slack, K.S. (2006). Intimate partner violence and child maltreatment: Understanding intra- and intergenerational connections. *Child Abuse & Neglect*, 30, 599–617.

Riggs, S.A. (2010). Childhood emotional abuse and the attachment system across the life cycle: What theory and research tell us. *Journal of Aggression, Maltreatment & Trauma*, 19, 5–51.

Ritchie, K., Jaussent, I., Stewart, R., Dupuy, A.M., Courtet, P., Ancelin, M.L., et al. (2009). Association of adverse childhood environment and 5-HTTLPR Genotype with late-life depression. *Journal of Clinical Psychiatry*, 70 (9), 1281–1288.

Rodriguez, C.M., & Tucker, M.A. (2011). Behind the cycle of violence, beyond abuse history: A brief report on the association of parental attachment to physical abuse potential. *Violence and Victims*, 26 (1), 246–256.

Rogers, C.R. (1957). The necessary and sufficient conditions of therapeutic personality change. *Journal of Consulting Psychology*, 21, 95–103.

Rohner, R., & Khaleque, A. (2005). *Handbook for the study of parental acceptance and rejection, revised*. Storrs: The University of Connecticut, Center for the Study of Parental Acceptance and Rejection.

Rorty, M., Yager, J., & Rossotto, E. (1994). Childhood sexual, physical, and psychological abuse in bulimia nervosa. *American Journal of Psychiatry*, 151, 1122–1126.

Rosenkranz, S.E., Muller, R.T., & Henderson, J.L. (2012). Psychological maltreatment in relation to substance use problem severity among youth. *Child Abuse & Neglect*, 36, 438–448.

Royse, D. (1994). *How do I know it's abuse? Identifying and countering emotional maltreatment from friends and family members*. Springfield, IL: Charles C Thomas.

Royse, D., Rompf, B.L., & Dhooper, S.S. (1991). Childhood trauma and adult life satisfaction in a random adult sample. *Psychological Reports*, 69, 1227–1231.

Runyon, M.K., Deblinger, E., & Schroeder, C.M. (2009). Pilot evaluation of outcomes of combined parent-child cognitive-behavioral group therapy for families at-risk for child physical abuse. *Cognitive and Behavioral Practice*, 16, 101–118.

Runyon, M.K., Deblinger, E., & Steer, R. (2010). Group cognitive behavioral treatment for parents and children at-risk for physical abuse: An initial study. *Child & Family Behavior Therapy*, 32, 196–218.

Runyon, M.K., Deblinger, E., Ryan, E.E., & Thakkar-Kolar, R. (2004). An overview of child physical abuse: Developing an integrated parent-child cognitive-behavioral treatment approach. *Trauma, Violence, and Abuse*, 5 (1), 65–85.

Sackett, D.L., Straus, S.E., Richardson, W.S., Rosenberd, W., & Haynes, R.B. (2000). *Evidenced-based medicine: How to practice and teach EMB* (2nd edn). New York: Churchill Livingstone.

Saleeby, D. (1996). The strengths perspective in social work practice: Extensions and cautions. *Social Work*, 41 (3), 296–305.

Sanders, B., & Becker-Lausen, E. (1995). The measurement of psychological maltreatment: Early data on the Child Abuse and Trauma Scale. *Child Abuse & Neglect*, 19 (3), 315–323.

Sanders, M.R. (2012). Development, evaluation, and multinational dissemination of the Triple P-Positive Parenting Program. *Annual Review of Clinical Psychology*, 8, 345–379.

Sanders, M.R., & Mazzucchelli, T.G. (2013). The promotion of self-regulation through parenting interventions. *Clinical Child and Family Psychological Review*, 16, 1–17.

Sanders, M.R., Bor, W., & Morawska, A. (2007). Maintenance of treatment gains: A comparison of Enhanced, Standard, and Self-directed Triple P – Positive Parenting Program. *Journal of Abnormal Child Psychology*, 35, 983–998.

Sanders, M.R., Markie-Dadds, C., Tully, L.A., & Bor, W. (2000). The Triple P-Positive Parent Program: A comparison of enhanced, standard and, behavioral family intervention for parents of children with early onset conduct problems. *Journal of Consulting and Clinical Psychology*, 68 (4), 624–640.

Schechter, D.S. (2012). The developmental neuroscience of emotional neglect, its consequences, and the psychosocial interventions that can reverse them. *American Journal of Psychiatry*, 169 (5), 452–454.

Schofield, T.J., Lee, R.D., & Merrick, M.T. (2013). Safe, stable, nurturing relationships as a moderator of intergenerational continuity of child maltreatment: A meta-analysis. *Journal of Adolescent Health*, 53, S32–S38.

Schultz, D., Barnes-Proby, D., Chandra, A., Jaycox, L.H., Maher, E., & Pecora, P. (2010). *Toolkit for adapting Cognitive Behavioral Intervention for Trauma in Schools (CBITS) or Supporting Students Exposed to Trauma (SSET) for implementation with youth in foster care*. TR722. Santa Monica: RAND Corporation.

Schwandt, M.L., Heilig, M., Hommer, D.W., George, D.T., & Ramchandani, V.A. (2013). Childhood trauma exposure and alcohol dependence severity in adulthood: Mediation by emotional abuse severity and neuroticism. *Alcoholism: Clinical and Experimental Research*, 37 (6), 984–992.

Sedlak, A.J., Mettenburg, J., Basena, M., Petta, I., McPherson, K., Greene, A., et al. (2010). Fourth National Incidence Study of Child Abuse and Neglect (NIS-4): Report to Congress. Washington, DC: U.S. Department of Health and Human Services, Administration for Children and Families.

Shlonsky, A., & Gibbs, L. (2004). Will the real evidence-based practice please stand up: Teaching the process of evidence-based practice to the helping professions. *Brief Treatment and Crisis Intervention*, 4, 137–153.

Simmel, C., & Shpiegel, S. (2013). Describing the context and nature of emotional maltreatment reports in children. *Children and Youth Services Review*, 35, 626–633.

Simonic, B., Mandelj, T.R., & Novsak, R. (2013). Religious-related abuse in the family. *Journal of Family Violence*, 28, 339–349.

Slack, K.S., Berger, L.M., DuMont, K., Yang, M.-Y, Kim, B., Ehrhard-Dietzel, S., et al. (2011). Risk and protective factors for child neglect during early childhood: A cross-study comparison. *Children and Youth Services Review*, 33, 1354–1363.

Solomon, D., Morgan, B., Asberg, K., & McCord, D. (2014). Treatment implications based on measures of child abuse potential and parent mental health: Are we missing an intervention opportunity? *Children and Youth Services Review*, 43, 153–159.

Spertus, I.L., Yehuda, R., Wong, C.M., Halligan, S., & Seremetis, S.V. (2003). Childhood emotional abuse and neglect as predictors of psychological and physical symptoms in women presenting to a primary care practice. *Child Abuse & Neglect*, 27, 1247–1258.

Stein, B.D., Jaycox, L.H., Kataoka, S.H., Wong, M., Tu, W., Elliott, M.N., et al. (2003). A mental health intervention for schoolchildren exposed to violence: A randomized controlled trial. *JAMA: Journal of the American Medical Association*, 290(5), 603–611.

Stith, S.M., Liu, T., Davies, C., Boykin, I.L., Alder, M.C., Harris, J.M., et al. (2009). Risk factors in child maltreatment: A meta-analytic review of the literature. *Aggression and Violent Behavior*, 14, 13–29.

Stoltenborgh, M., Bakermans-Kranenburg, M.J., & van IJzendoorn, M.H. (2013). The neglect of child neglect: A meta-analytic review of the prevalence of neglect. *Social Psychiatry and Psychiatric Epidemiology*, 48, 345–355.

Straus, M.A., & Douglas, E.M. (2004). A short form of the revised Conflict Tactics Scales, and typologies for severity and mutuality. *Violence and Victims*, 19 (5), 507–520.

Straus, M.A., & Field, C.J. (2003). Psychological aggression by American parents: National data on prevalence, chronicity, and severity. *Journal of Marriage and Family*, 65, 795–808.

Straus, M.A., Hamby, S.L., Boney-McCoy, S., & Sugarman, D.B. (1996). The revised Conflict Tactics Scales (CTS2): Development and preliminary psychometric data. *Journal of Family Issues*, 17 (3), 283–316.

Straus, M.A., Hamby, S.L., Finkelhor, D., Moore, D., & Runyan, D.K. (1998). Identification of children maltreatment with the Parent-Child Conflict Tactics Scales: Development and psychometric properties data for a national sample of American parents. *Child Abuse & Neglect*, 22, 249–270.

Strine, T.W., Dube, S.R., Edwards, V.J., Prehn, A.W., Rasmussen, S., Wagenfeld, M., et al. (2012). Associations between adverse childhood experiences, psychological distress, and adult alcohol problems. *American Journal of Health Behavior*, 36 (3), 408–423.

Sue, D.W., & Sue, D. (1999). *Counseling the culturally different: Theory and practice.* New York: Wiley and Sons.

Thompson, R., Proctor, L.J., English, D.J., Dubowitz, H., Narasimhan, S., & Everson, M.D. (2012). Suicidal ideation in adolescence: Examining the role of recent adverse experiences. *Journal of Adolescence*, 35, 175–186.

Thornberry, T.P., Knight, K.E., & Lovegrove, P.J. (2012). Does maltreatment beget maltreatment? A systematic review of the intergenerational literature. *Trauma, Violence, & Abuse*, 13 (3), 135–152.

Thyer, B.A., & Pignotti, M. (2011). Evidence based practices do not exist. *Clinical Social Work Journal*, 39, 328–333.

Timko, C., Sutkowi, A., Pavao, J., & Kimerling, R. (2008). Women's childhood and adult adverse experiences, mental health, and binge drinking: The California Women's Health Survey. *Substance Abuse Treatment, Prevention, and Policy*, 3, 15. Retrieved from www.substanceabusepolicy.com/content/3/1/15.

Tonmyr, L., Draca, J., Crain, J., & MacMillan, H.L. (2011). Measurement of emotional/psychological child maltreatment: A review. *Child Abuse & Neglect*, 767–872.

Toth, S.L., Rogosch, F.A., Manly, J.T., & Cicchetti, D. (2006). The efficacy of toddler-parent psychotherapy to reorganize attachment in the young offspring of mothers with major depressive disorder: A randomized preventive trial. *Journal of Consulting and Clinical Psychology*, 74 (6), 1006–1016.

Toth, S.L., Maughan, A., Manly, J.T., Spagnola, M., & Cicchetti, D. (2002). The relative efficacy of two interventions in altering maltreated preschool children's representational models: Implications for attachment theory. *Development and Psychopathology*, 14, 877–908.

United States Department of Health and Human Services (DHHS) (2001). *Mental health: culture, race, and ethnicity—a supplement to mental health: A report of the Surgeon General.* Washington, DC: US Department of Health and Human Services.

United States Department of Health and Human Services (DHHS) (2006). *Child neglect: A guide for prevention, assessment, and intervention.* Washington, DC: United States Department of Health and Human Services.

United States Department of Health and Human Services, Office of Child Abuse and Neglect (DHHS OCAN) (2003). *Emerging practices in the prevention of child abuse and neglect.* Washington, DC: US Department of Health and Human Services.

Wekerle, C. (2011). Emotionally maltreated: The under-current of impairment? *Child Abuse & Neglect*, 35, 899–903.

Wekerle, C., Leung, E., Wall, A.-M., MacMillan, H., Boyle, M., Trocme, N., et al. (2009). The contributions of childhood emotional abuse to teen dating violence among child protective services-involved youth. *Child Abuse & Neglect*, 33, 45–58.

Welch, G.L., & Bonner, B.L. (2013). Fatal child neglect: Characteristics, causation, and strategies for prevention. *Child Abuse & Neglect*, 37, 745–752.

Wells, K., & Tracy, E. (1996). Reorienting intensive family preservation services in relation to public child welfare practice. *Child Welfare*, 75 (6), 667–692.

Wolfe, D.A., & McIsaac, C. (2011). Distinguishing between poor/dysfunctioning parenting and child emotional maltreatment. *Child Abuse & Neglect*, 35, 802–813.

World Health Organization (1999). *Report of the consultation on child abuse prevention.* Geneva: World Health Organization.

Wright, M.O., Crawford, E., & Del Castillo, D. (2009). Childhood emotional maltreatment and later psychological distress among college students: The mediating role of maladaptive schemas. *Child Abuse & Neglect*, 33, 59–68.

Young, R., Lennie, S., & Minnis, H. (2011). Children's perceptions of parental neglect, control, and psychopathology. *Journal of Child Psychology and Psychiatry*, 52 (8), 889–897.

Young, S.Y.N., Hansen, C.J., Gibson, R.L., & Ryan, M.A.K. (2006). Risky alcohol use, age at onset of drinking, and adverse childhood experiences in young men entering the U.S. Marine Corps. *Archives of Pediatric and Adolescent Medicine*, 160, 1207–1214.

Ystrom, E., Kendler, K.S., & Reichborn-Kjennerud, T. (2014). Early age of alcohol initiation is not the cause of alcohol use disorders in adulthood, but is a major indicator of genetic risk: A population-based twin study. *Addiction*, 109, 1824–1832.

Zajac, K., & Kobak, R. (2009). Caregiver unresolved loss and abuse and child behavior problems: Intergenerational effects in a high-risk sample. *Development and Psychopathology*, 21, 173–187.

INDEX

AAI *see* age of alcohol initiation
abandonment 103
ABC model 160
abuse 9–11, 20, 24, 37, 43, 45–6, 49–51, 64, 71, 75–6, 86–7, 92, 95, 99, 102, 104–14, 122, 126–7, 132, 134, 136–7, 139–40, 143, 146–7, 151, 153–7, 165, 169, 170, 172–3; caregiver 35; child *see* child abuse; cycle of 47, 53, 60–1; drug abuse 39, 81; emotional *see* emotional abuse; physical 2, 7, 23, 31, 39–42, 44, 48, 55–6, 58–9, 61–3, 66, 68, 70, 73–4, 77, 80, 82–3, 85, 89, 98, 101, 120, 124, 130–1, 150, 158, 161; psychological 5, 12, 69, 72–3, 78, 80, 88, 118, 125; religious 38; sexual 4, 7, 14, 23, 28–9, 32, 38, 55–6, 58, 62, 66, 68, 70, 72, 74, 77, 80, 84, 89, 91, 98, 101, 103, 119, 120–1, 124, 130–1, 150–1, 161; substance 7, 38, 54, 67, 68, 80, 103, 135, 141, 145, 161, 168; threshold of 139; types of 101; verbal 21, 70, 124
abusive environment 5
academic: achievement 86; outcomes 83–4

ACE *see* adverse childhood experiences
adolescent mother 49–50, 52
Adult Attachment Interview 46
adverse childhood experiences (ACE) 66, 75–6, 78, 80–3, 89, 91, 170
advocacy campaigns 129; organizations 164
affect regulation 155, 167, 172
affective expression and modulation 152
after-school programs 162
aftercare plan 98, 115
age of alcohol initiation (AAI) 75, 76
aggression 7, 38, 47, 59, 63, 88–9, 95, 110–11, 124
agoraphobia 73
alcohol 47; dependence 32, 75; disorder 77; misuse 35; problems 75, 104; treatment 28; use disorder (AUD) 75–6, 90
alcoholic 19, 65, 75, 81, 90
American Academy of Pediatrics Committee on Child Abuse and Neglect 6, 8
American Professional Society on the Abuse of Children (APSAC) 6, 64, 106–9, 122, 127

American Psychiatric Association 98
Angie/Andy child rating scale 119–20
antisocial behavior 9, 54, 108
anxiety: disorder 67–9, 73; management 151; social 21; treatment 153, 163
Apgar score 51, 62
APSAC *see* American Professional Society on the Abuse of Children
assault: physical 25, 27, 74, 124; sexual 74; witness 27
assessment 1, 30, 32, 36, 43, 62, 73, 85, 95–6, 98, 101, 103–15, 118–21, 123, 126–7, 138, 144, 148, 151, 167, 170; emotional abuse 94, 110; framework 100; instrument 116, 122, 124–5, 128; procedure 94, 112, 139–40; tools 99, 117, 122
attachment: disorganized pattern of 47; styles 49; theory 46–7, 49, 60, 153, 157, 166
AUD *see* alcohol use disorder

behavior: abusive 6, 8, 30, 60, 138, 142, 144–5, 159, 160, 171; antisocial 9, 54, 108; caregiver 35, 101; change 148; deviant 108; disruptive 146, 158; externalizing 40–2, 63, 71; extremes 110; internalizing 40, 63, 71; maladaptive 152, 157, 166; management 151, 160; problems 153, 165; sexualized 68; suicidal 70
biological theory 57, 157
biological/genetic theory 60
biopsychosocial clinical assessment 140
boundaries 13, 19, 95, 100, 168
Bowen Family Therapy 166
Briere's Trauma Symptom Checklist for Children (TSCC) 119
BSD *see* bulimia-spectrum disorder
bulimia nervosa 80
bulimia-spectrum disorder (BSD) 79
bullying 11, 25, 27, 30, 89

CADRI *see* Conflict in Adolescent Data Relationships Inventory
California Evidence-Based Clearinghouse on Child Welfare (CEBC) 135, 146–7, 153, 155, 158–9, 163, 166–7
cancer 43, 80–2, 93
cancer risk 80, 83
CANIS-R *see* Child Abuse and Neglect Interview Schedule – Revised
CAPI *see* Child Abuse Potential Inventory
cardiovascular disease 80
caregiver abuse and neglect behaviors 35
caregiver behaviors/issues 101
caregiver grandmothers 49
caregiver-child relationship 109
casework practice 167
CATS *see* Child Abuse and Trauma Scale
CATS-EA *see* Child Abuse and Trauma Scale – Emotional Abuse
CBITS *see* Cognitive Behavioral Intervention for Trauma in Schools
CDI *see* Child-Directed Intervention
CEBC *see* California Evidence-Based Clearinghouse on Child Welfare
child abuse 1, 4, 7–8, 13, 15, 22–3, 27, 29, 32–3, 36, 38–9, 41–2, 44, 48, 52, 56–7, 59–63, 67, 69–70, 79–80, 83, 90, 94, 98, 100–1, 115–16, 121, 148, 152, 159, 163, 166–7; battered 1, 2; investigators 96; prevention 6, 14, 159, 164, 166–7
Child Abuse and Neglect Interview Schedule – Revised (CANIS-R) 118
Child Abuse and Trauma Scale (CATS) 121
Child Abuse and Trauma Scale – Emotional Abuse (CATS-EA) 121–2, 127–8
Child Abuse Potential Inventory (CAPI) 48, 56
child neglect 7, 13, 15–16, 26–7, 39–42, 44, 62, 94, 117

Child Neglect Scale 117
Child Parent Psychotherapy (CPP) 151, 153–5
child protection 4, 7, 14, 17–18, 29, 31–2, 34, 36, 42, 44, 46, 49, 71–2, 85–7, 94, 96, 101, 114–16, 123, 135; agency 32, 71–2, 101; authorities 14, 17, 34, 49, 86, 96, 115; investigators 94; workers 18, 36, 42, 94, 135
Child Protective Services (CPS) 23, 26, 31–2, 73, 85, 86, 98, 100–4, 106–8, 112–17, 122, 125, 139–40, 161, 166
child welfare 28, 96, 107, 116–17, 135, 137, 139, 147–8, 168; agency 114, 147, 149; information gateway 8, 15; intervention 107, 139; programs 135; work 116
child-centered 96, 170; approach 132, 173; interactions 97; interventions 144, 149
Child-Directed Intervention (CDI) 157–8
child-focused 130, 141; approaches 138, 149, 171; interventions 138, 144, 150, 156, 171
childhood adversity 66–7, 79, 82: misfortune 83; mistreatment 49, 60; victimization 83
Childhood Experiences Questionnaire 125
Childhood Maltreatment Interview Schedule (CMIS) 118
Childhood Trauma Questionnaire (CTQ) 28, 56, 73, 77, 88, 120–1, 123
child's developmental needs 100, 142
chronic bronchitis/emphysema 80
chronicity 73, 109, 133
CMIS *see* Childhood Maltreatment Interview Schedule
CN *see* child neglect
coercive: disciplinary methods 97; family processes 61; parenting 140

cognitive behavioral: approach 145, 158; intervention 162; model 159; strategies 166; techniques 162; theory 151, 154; therapy 151, 159
Cognitive Behavioral Intervention for Trauma in Schools (CBITS) 162–3
Cognitive Coping I 152
Cognitive Coping and Processing II 152
cognitive restructuring 162
Cognitive Style Questionnaire 71
Combined Parent Child Cognitive Behavioral Approach (CPC-CBT) 158–60
commitment to change 170
community 15, 17, 24–5, 27, 29, 31, 33–4, 36, 44, 49, 50, 62, 73, 78, 97, 120, 132, 134, 145, 148, 165–7, 173; resources 115
community-based: interventions 139; programs 130; providers 140; responses 129; services 100–2, 139
confinement 108–9
conflict 40–2, 47, 49, 51, 87, 123–4, 142, 145, 148, 158, 160; resolution 160
Conflict in Adolescent Data Relationships Inventory (CADRI) 87–8
Conflict Tactics Scale (CTS) 123–4
Conflict Tactics Scale: Parent Child Version (CTSPC) 124
conflicted relationships 49
control group 80, 84, 87, 92, 146, 153, 166
coping: skills 137, 149, 152, 159, 160; strategies 169
CP *see* child protection
CPA (child physical abuse) 39–40
CPC-CBT *see* Combined Parent Child Cognitive Behavioral Approach
CPP *see* Child-Parent Psychotherapy
CPS *see* Child Protective Services
cruelty 5, 68, 70
CTQ *see* Child Trauma Questionnaire

INDEX

CTS *see* Conflict Tactics Scale
CTSPC *see* Conflict Tactics Scale: Parent Child Version
cultural: competent 132, 134, 169, 170; disparities 134; diverse 134; variables 132

decision-making 116, 135, 140, 170
delinquency 55, 89, 111
denying emotional responsiveness 8–9, 109, 112
dependency 96–7, 114, 132, 154
depression 3, 7, 20, 39, 41–2, 50, 54, 60, 63, 68–74, 78–83, 104, 111, 139, 145, 150, 153, 156, 161–3, 167, 172; late-life 70–1
development 8–9, 14, 50, 56, 71, 76, 97, 99, 100, 110, 112, 132–5, 139, 142–3, 148, 153–5, 159–60, 163–4, 169
developmental disabilities 165; perspective 132–3, 170
developmentally inappropriate or inconsistent interactions 12
discipline 17, 48–9, 64, 96–7, 124, 126, 141, 146, 157; nonviolent 124
disorder: adolescent 67; anxiety 67–9, 73; bulimia-spectrum 79; childhood-onset 67; disruptive behavior 67; dysthymic 72; eating 68–9, 79–80; major depressive 72; mental 44, 67, 69, 74, 94; mood 67; oppositional and conduct 68; panic 72; personality 68, 111; post-traumatic stress (PTSD) 68, 73–4, 76, 118–19, 152–3; substance use 67–8, 90
dissociative symptoms 111
divorce 6, 66, 73
dose–response relationship 69, 74, 76, 79, 80, 91–3
drinking behavior 70, 77
drug 3, 16, 19, 47, 72, 104; abuse 81; addiction 65, 90; illegal 103; illicit 76, 78; problems 76; use 26, 38, 55, 67, 70, 76, 82, 89, 92; treatment 28

Dynamic Developmental Systems Approach 61
Dysfunctional: Disciplinary Style 48, 64; home 89, 90; parenting 94–5, 146

EA *see* emotional abuse
Early Intervention Services 114
Early Trauma Inventory (ETI) 117, 124
ecological model 49; perspective 132, 168; theory 49, 60
education: achievement 36, 83; environment 81; level 92; needs 9; neglect 15–16, 23–4, 104
effect size 40–2, 62
emergency protective order 106, 114
emotional abuse 1–2, 4–12, 14–15, 20, 22–34, 44, 65, 70, 74, 93–4, 98, 107, 116–17, 119, 120, 123, 127–9, 131, 133, 141, 149, 162; categories of 12, 107, 127, 141; prevention 133, 163
empathy 48, 50, 51, 136, 166
empowerment 134, 151, 169, 171
endangerment standard 23, 31, 36–7
engagement 137, 148, 151, 155, 159, 167
environment 33, 49, 63, 73, 86, 91, 108, 130, 148, 168; characteristics 50, 100; factors 58, 75–6, 112, 136, 138, 165, 171; neglect 103; risk factors 56, 141; stressors 145
ETI *see* Early Trauma Inventory
etiology 38, 43, 63; of child abuse 57; of child maltreatment 54
evidence-based: intervention 135, 172; practice 135, 170
exploitation 7, 9, 14, 58, 108, 112, 122

failure: to act 7, 14; to thrive 15; to report 115
family: assessment 167; characteristics 36, 63, 100; cohesion 40–2, 167; conflict 40–2, 148; connections 166; development 148; factors 40;

family *continued*
    functioning 67; income 71, 90; interventions 157; relations 58, 148, 151; size 37–8, 40, 42; structure 37
family preservation: and the Homebuilders® Program 147; model 147; program 145, 147; services 147–8, 171
Family Stabilization Programs 147
Family Support Services 139
Family Systems Theory 157
fear 4, 6, 9, 19, 39, 47, 63, 97, 106, 108, 110, 112–13, 122, 160
Federal: and State Child Protection Laws 7; Child Abuse Prevention 6; legislation 6
financial: circumstances 42; resources 52
food inadequacy 15–16
Food Stamps 37
foster care 49, 100, 113, 149; foster mother 19; providers 153
Fourth National Incidence Study of Child Abuse and Neglect Report to Congress (NIS-4) 23, 36, 38, 115
FRAMEA 140, 142, 144–5, 156

gender 28, 37, 40–1, 56–7, 71–2, 79, 81, 89, 92
Generalized Anxiety Disorder *see* disorder, anxiety
genetic inheritance 57, 75
goals, measurable 146
guilt 39, 54, 156

harassment 70, 93, 96, 107
harm: psychological 4, 96; risk of 32, 100, 103–4, 106, 114; self-harm 68, 89; standard 23, 36
healthy: attachment 155; bonding 154; parenting 52, 96–7
heart disease 80–1, 83, 92
hepatitis/jaundice 80
heritability 75, 92

high risk: families 130, 147, 164; groups 48, 164; mothers 48; situations 160
HIV prevention intervention 78
HMO 25, 92
home conditions 98; environment 60, 87, 89, 94, 108, 121
home literacy environment 86
home visiting programs 49, 139, 165, 166; for child well-being 166; for prevention of child abuse and neglect 166
Homebuilders® Program 147–9
hopelessness 71
hostility 10, 12, 47, 54, 87, 111, 124, 141
humiliation 9, 19, 21–2, 70, 107
hygiene/inadequate clothes 16
hyper-reactivity 39, 40–2
hypervigilance 154

impact of adverse childhood experiences 78
impulse control, poor 68
in-home services 145, 147
inadequacy, feelings of 79
incarceration 66, 143
incidence rates 37, 129
infant 15–16, 18–19, 46–7, 51–2, 95, 154; avoidant attachment 47, 110–11; neglect 51
insults, verbal 30
intellectual: development 133; functioning 83–4
intergenerational transmission: of abuse 57, 59–60; hypothesis 53; maltreatment 53–4, 59; model 60; neglect 59; rate 59; theory 52, 61; trauma 166
internal consistency 117–19, 121, 127
internalizing 41, 71, 111; behavior 40, 63, 71
interpersonal: boundaries 168; conflict 47; problems 88; relationships 142; trauma 68; violence 106, 123
investigative CPS worker 114
investigative process 98

INDEX

IPV *see* violence, intimate partner
ischemic heart disease *see* heart disease
isolation 6, 8–9, 13, 38, 49, 51, 59, 85, 108, 112, 139

lack of: affection 16; awareness 49; emotional responsiveness 122; empathy 166; food 104, 161; housing 161; hygiene 17, 26; love 4, 6, 8, 11, 19, 96, 109; nurturance 16; parenting skills 145; positive care 50; resources 17, 143, 165; sensitivity 10; shelter 16; social support 59
learned helplessness 58
life satisfaction 90
lifetime prevalence of emotional abuse or neglect 27
loneliness 19, 22, 51, 63
low self-esteem 21, 47, 110–11
low socio-economic: households 37; status 36, 87
low-income 50, 51, 156, 165–6

macro-level approaches to intervention 164
major depressive disorder 72
maladaptive behaviors 152, 157, 166; family functioning 67; parenting 140, 148, 160; patterns of interaction 155; practices 145
malnourished 18, 104
maltreatment: adolescent 68; caregivers 88; categorization of 120; child 32, 36, 41, 56, 61, 68, 86, 89, 90, 115, 134; cycle of 54, 59–60; duration and severity 133; emotional 4–5, 7, 13, 25, 28, 68, 71, 79, 95, 112, 131; environment 88; experience of 118; extent of 28; physical 56; psychological 5–9, 29, 107, 110–11, 120, 122–3; sexual 124; youth 88
mental cruelty 5, 70
mental health: association to child maltreatment 67, 90; issues 32; needs 139; neglect 9, 104; problems 60; services 28, 51, 156, 168–9; symptoms 155
mental illness 35, 38, 60, 66, 76–7, 80
mentoring programs 162
meta analysis 27, 33, 39, 41–2, 44, 69, 78–9
Minimization/Denial Scale 120
Minnesota Comprehensive Assessment II Tests 85
MNBS *see* Multidimensional Neglectful Behavior Scale
mother 46, 49–52, 95, 108, 126, 143; low-risk 48
Mother-Child Neglect Scale 117
Multidimensional Neglectful Behavior Scale (MNBS) 117, 119
multimodal response 138, 172
multiple victimization 31

National Child Abuse and Neglect Data System (NCANDS) 29
National Child Traumatic Stress Network (NCTSN) 135, 150–1
National Institute of Mental Health (NIMH) 85
National Longitudinal Study of Adolescent Health 61
National Suicide Prevention Life Line 106
NCANDS *see* National Child Abuse and Neglect Data System
NCTSN *see* National Child Traumatic Stress Network
negative attributions 12, 141
Negative Life Events Questionnaire 124
neglect: child 6–8, 13–16, 27, 32, 34, 39, 41–2, 44, 90, 100–1, 116, 148; clothing 104; criminal 15; dental 16; educational 9, 16, 23–4, 104; emotional 120; environmental 103; evidence of 100, 102; food 104; hygiene 104; infant 51;

neglect *continued*
  intergenerational transmission of 59; interventions for 147, 167; medical 9, 15–16, 29, 104; mental health 9, 104; physical 17–18, 23–4, 56, 66, 77–8, 80, 120; psychological 78; related to substance abuse 103; safety 16; supervisory 103; types of 101
neuroticism 77
NFP *see* nurse-family partnership
nightmares 110, 150, 172
NIS-4 *see* Fourth National Incidence Study of Child Abuse and Neglect Report to Congress
nurse–family partnership 165
nutrition 14, 16, 165

obesity 15, 78–81, 83, 93, 105
observable injuries 101
OCAN *see* Office of Child Abuse and Neglect
odds ratio 79, 81, 92
Office of Child Abuse and Neglect (OCAN) 163, 165
OHP *see* out-of-home placement
omission 13–14, 33, 36, 101, 114, 122, 128, 130
out-of-home placement (OHP) 85–6, 147
overweight 2, 10, 79, 80; see also obesity

Parent Child Interaction Therapy (PCIT) 157–8, 166
parent partner conflict 145
parent self-care 146
parent self-esteem 41
parent training program 145–6, 171
parent–child: centered 173; communication 149; focused 130, 138, 141, 171; interaction 39, 86, 138, 144, 149, 157, 160, 165; relationship 39, 42, 155, 157, 159
Parent-Directed Intervention (PDI) 157–8

parent-focused: approaches 144, 171; interventions 138, 144–5, 149, 171
parental: attitudes 70, 138; psychopathology 38; substance abuse 7, 67
Parental Acceptance/Rejection Questionnaire (PARQ) 124
parenting: approaches 142; attitudes 50; behaviors 39, 61–2, 95; beliefs 166; capacity 100; coercive 140; constructive 61; inconsistent 8–9; poor 4, 34, 49, 52, 59, 95–6, 127; problematic 50; scale 126; skills 4, 139, 145, 147, 151, 157, 158, 171; strategies 146; style 51, 97; suboptimal 4, 139; techniques 96, 149; unreliable 8–9
parents' involvement with the school 86
PARQ *see* Parental Acceptance/Rejection Questionnaire
PCIT *see* Parent Child Interaction Therapy
PDI *see* Parent Directed Intervention
perpetrator 6, 8, 37–9, 49, 51, 59, 63, 98, 106, 114, 137
Person-in-Environment framework 132
physical: altercations 106; health impact 78; illness 91; maltreatment 56; wound 11
physical-emotional abuse 88
PM *see* maltreatment, psychological
policies 7, 8, 115, 129, 130, 134, 138, 147, 164, 168, 170
poly-victimization 31–2
population: general 85–6, 164–5, 171; studies 23, 38
pornography 16, 101
post-permanency services 147
practitioner factors 136, 171
prejudice/racist values 51
preschool 110, 111, 156
prevalence of: child abuse 22, 33; child maltreatment 24, 168; child neglect 22, 33; emotional abuse 25, 27, 30, 32, 34,

INDEX

168; emotional neglect 27; suicidal behavior 70
prevention: efforts 131–2, 163–5, 171; plan 114; programs 130, 166
PRIDE skills 157
psychoeducation 137, 142, 151–2, 159, 162, 167
psychological: abuse 5, 12, 25, 69, 72–3, 78, 80, 88, 125; aggression 95, 124; battering 5; boundary 13, 142; capacity 7; control method 97; distress 75; functioning 167; harm 4, 96; maltreatment 5–9, 29, 107, 110–11, 120, 122–3; needs 13, 97; neglect 78; outcomes 72; problems 118; violence 123
Psychological Abuse Subscale 118
Psychological Aggression Scale 95
Psychological/Verbal Abuse Scale 124
psychometric: information 117, 121, 127; properties 121
psychopathology 38–9, 41–2, 169
psychosocial: adversity 82; factors 83; functioning 130
psychosocial-evaluation 110
psychotherapy 60, 136, 151, 153
PTSD *see* disorder, post-traumatic stress; Revised Civilian Mississippi Scale for 73
punish 9, 101, 106

Qualified Mental Health Professional (QMHP) 103, 112
Quick Test IQ 84

rape 19, 68, 85, 101, 105
re-traumatization 168, 170
rejection 4, 8–9, 12, 46–7, 96–7, 111, 124
relational dynamics 131, 138
relationship: experiences 88; factors 137, 171; to child
resilience 64, 67, 133–4, 169, 172
reunification programs 147

revictimization 68, 169
risk and risk factors: abuse 37, 41, 99–100, 166; alcohol abuse 75, 77–8; anxiety disorders 69; cancer 82–3; delinquency 55; depressive disorders 69, 71; disease 80; drug abuse 78; emotional abuse 36; foster care 49; harm 7, 14, 23, 32, 36, 100, 103–6, 112; infant neglect 51; injury 101, 114; maltreatment 42, 63, 73, 115, 165–6; reoccurrence 115; psychiatric disorders 67; self-harm 68; sexual abuse 55; sexual harm 103; suicide attempts 89, 111

sadomasochism 19
safety 16, 30, 97–100, 103, 114, 132, 140, 145, 148, 150–1, 153–5, 159, 166–9, 171
SAMSHA *see* Substance Abuse and Mental Health Services Administration
school-based abuse prevention 164; approaches to intervention 162; supports 162
selective prevention: approaches 164; efforts 165; programs 164–5
self-efficacy 47, 146
self-esteem 8, 21, 39, 41–2, 47, 62, 79, 110, 111
self-mutilation 89
self-regulating affective states 76
self-regulation 145
Self-regulatory Framework 146
self-report instruments 119, 126
Self-Report Questionnaire 119
self-sufficiency 146, 148
self-worth 91
sexual: abuse 7, 14, 58, 66, 89; assaults 74; behaviors 82; harm 103; maltreatment 69, 124; relationships 58
sexual offender registry 103
shame 9, 22, 39, 54
significant others 47, 60
significant person 8, 49, 125
sleep problems 110

SLT *see* Social Learning Theory
social: adaptation 13; class 84; competence 40, 42, 145, 153; influence 61; isolation 59, 139; network factors 137, 168, 171; phobia 73; relationships 90; relationships within the home 86
Social Learning Theory (SLT) 58, 62, 88, 157
Social Welfare Programs 161
socialization 6, 61, 142–3
socio-demographic: factors 72, 92; variables 71
somatic problems 152
somatization 74
spanking 95, 113, 161
special needs 50, 96
standardized tests 86
State Child Protection Laws 7
State Child Welfare Intervention 107
strengths-based: approach 133–4; perspective 133, 173
stress management 145
Structured Interview Guides 116; Instruments 117; Schedules 116, 118
Substance Abuse and Mental Health Services Administration (SAMSHA) 135
substance misuse 32, 35, 165, 141
substance use 67–8, 75, 77, 90, 103, 111; disorders 67–8, 90
suicidal: behavior 70; ideation 72–3, 78, 89, 92; statement 106; thoughts 63, 72
suicide 70, 89, 92–3; attempt 67, 81, 89, 104, 111; ideation 72, 92; plan 70
supervision 13, 16, 18, 33, 99, 101, 103, 119, 136
Symptom Checklist-90r 73
systematic literature review 63, 69
systematic review 69, 110
Systems-Focused Framework 168

TA-FC *see* Trauma-Adapted Family Connections

TANF *see* Temporary Assistance for Needy Families
Targeted Prevention: approaches 166; program 130, 166
Temporary Assistance for Needy Families 37, 55, 89
TF-CBT *see* Trauma Focused-Cognitive Behavioral Therapy
The Experience Project 19
Theory 35, 44, 50, 53, 57, 63, 136, 154; Attachment 46–7, 49, 60, 153, 157, 166; Biological 57, 60; Cognitive-Behavioral 151; Ecological 49, 60; Family Systems 157; Genetic 60; Intergeneration Transmission 52, 61; Person-Centered 136; Social Learning 58, 62, 88, 157; Trauma 133, 166
therapeutic alliance 136–7; interventions 139: relationships 136; support 144
THQ *see* Trauma History Questionnaire
TIC *see* Trauma Informed Care
threat 9, 16, 30, 95, 97, 108, 155
Threshold Needed for Intervention 139
transgender 20, 105
Trauma 32, 49, 70, 77, 90, 150–1, 162, 167, 169: complex 150, 153; developmental 154; general 124; intergenerational 68; interpersonal 68; histories 155; narrative 151–2, 155, 160, 163; survivors 168; symptoms 167; theory 133, 166; treatment 153, 155, 159, 163
Trauma History Questionnaire (THQ) 73
trauma scores 74
trauma symptom checklist for children 119
Trauma-Adapted Family Connections (TA-FC) 166
Trauma-Focused Cognitive Behavioral Therapy (TF-CBT) 151, 153; interventions 150–1, 162, 171
Trauma-Informed: Care (TIC) 167–71;

lens 133; parenting techniques 149; services 169
trauma-related problems 149
traumatic: behavior problems 152; childhood history 52; events 13, 91, 118, 150, 152–3, 155, 158, 169; experiences 76, 90, 131, 149; response
treatment: approaches 130, 135; fidelity 147, 172; programs 33, 77, 87, 130, 131
The Triple P—Positive Parenting Program® 145, 146, 149, 165–6
TSCC *see* Briere's Trauma Symptom Checklist for Children

unhealthy: conditions 26; for a child 17; interactions 142
universal: interventions 164; prevention approaches 164; prevention efforts 164

victim 36, 51, 87–8, 98
victimization 25, 27, 30–2, 47, 59, 83, 88, 169; intimate partner 47
violence 4, 24, 27, 40, 49, 58, 87, 161, 165–6; against child 9; community 120, 165–6; dating 88–9; domestic 7–9, 13, 25, 30, 32, 38, 61, 66–7, 85, 87, 106–8, 123, 131, 141–2, 145, 153; domestic orders 106; domestic partner 54; family violence 67, 89, 118, 120, 139, 150; impact of 169; interpersonal 90, 106, 123; intimate partner 8–9, 16, 32, 51, 58, 155; perpetration 88; physical 87, 89, 123; psychological 123; witness 7–9, 25, 30, 66, 85, 150

Wide Range Achievement Test-Revised (WRAT-R) 84
witness: assault 27; community violence 120; domestic violence 7, 25, 30, 66, 85; family violence 89, 120, 150; interpersonal violence 90; intimate partner violence 8, 9; maternal battering 25; murder 25, 74; physical abuse 89; physical violence 85, 89; sexual activity 101; violence 30
women, battered 55, 58
World Health Organization 13
WRAT-R *see* Wide Range Achievement Test-Revised

Taylor & Francis eBooks

Helping you to choose the right eBooks for your Library

Add Routledge titles to your library's digital collection today. Taylor and Francis ebooks contains over 50,000 titles in the Humanities, Social Sciences, Behavioural Sciences, Built Environment and Law.

Choose from a range of subject packages or create your own!

Benefits for you
- Free MARC records
- COUNTER-compliant usage statistics
- Flexible purchase and pricing options
- All titles DRM-free.

Benefits for your user
- Off-site, anytime access via Athens or referring URL
- Print or copy pages or chapters
- Full content search
- Bookmark, highlight and annotate text
- Access to thousands of pages of quality research at the click of a button.

REQUEST YOUR FREE INSTITUTIONAL TRIAL TODAY

Free Trials Available
We offer free trials to qualifying academic, corporate and government customers.

eCollections – Choose from over 30 subject eCollections, including:

Archaeology	Language Learning
Architecture	Law
Asian Studies	Literature
Business & Management	Media & Communication
Classical Studies	Middle East Studies
Construction	Music
Creative & Media Arts	Philosophy
Criminology & Criminal Justice	Planning
Economics	Politics
Education	Psychology & Mental Health
Energy	Religion
Engineering	Security
English Language & Linguistics	Social Work
Environment & Sustainability	Sociology
Geography	Sport
Health Studies	Theatre & Performance
History	Tourism, Hospitality & Events

For more information, pricing enquiries or to order a free trial, please contact your local sales team: www.tandfebooks.com/page/sales

Routledge Taylor & Francis Group | The home of Routledge books

www.tandfebooks.com